THE INQUISITION

Nihil obstat

EDUARDUS MAHONEY, S.T.D.
Censor deputatus.

Imprimatur

EDM. CAN. SURMONT
Vic. Gen.

Westmonasterii, die 24° Junii, 1926.

ST. THOMAS AQUINAS.

THE INQUISITION

FROM ITS ESTABLISHMENT
TO THE GREAT SCHISM

AN INTRODUCTORY STUDY

By A. L. MAYCOCK, M.A.

WITH AN INTRODUCTION BY
FATHER RONALD KNOX

J. & J. HARPER EDITIONS

HARPER & ROW, PUBLISHERS

NEW YORK AND EVANSTON

THE INQUISITION, by A. L. Maycock.

FIRST J. & J. HARPER EDITION 1969
Printed on long-life, acid-free paper, with reinforced bindings

LIBRARY OF CONGRESS CATALOG CARD NUMBER: 75-81866

DEDICATED

TO

O. S.

PREFATORY NOTE

THE present study of the mediæval Inquisition makes no pretence either to exhaustiveness or to originality. Indeed, it may be said to take the form rather of a study than of a history—a study of the particular problem of mediæval heresy and of the means taken to combat it. Mediæval heresy possessed a dual nature; and therein lies its chief interest and significance. Membership of an heretical sect was both a crime in the eyes of the State and a sin in the eyes of the Church. Consequently there grew up, on the one hand, a great mass of secular legislation which prescribed death as the legal punishment for heresy; and, on the other hand, an ecclesiastical tribunal—the Inquisition—whose function was to determine what was heresy and who was heretical. The coercive power belonged to the former; and the legal punishment could only be enforced when the latter sanctioned it.

Further, we have to recognize a corresponding duality in the Inquisitorial office itself. Primarily it was a penitential, and not a penal tribunal. Its purpose was not to punish but to reconcile. Imprisonment, for instance, was theoretically a penance rather than a punishment. Yet in case of obstinate refusal to abjure and to seek reconciliation with the Church, the Inquisitor had no alternative but to withdraw the protection of the Church from the impenitent sinner by handing him over to the secular arm to be punished as a criminal. Clearly a wide field of thought is opened up by such considerations as these. The present study is an attempt to view the Inquisition in the light of its own times, to comprehend the forces which led up to its establishment, to discuss one or two points concerning its methods and procedure, and to review, in the broadest outline, the scope of its activities during the first century and a half of its existence.

We are so accustomed to using the words Church and State as representing wholly different entities that we find, at first, considerable difficulty in apprehending the mediæval position. Church and State were merely different aspects of a single society—the Christian commonwealth.

" Mankind is one ' mystical body ' ; . . . it is an all-embracing corporation which constitutes that Universal Realm, spiritual and temporal, which may be called the Universal Church or, with equal propriety, the Commonwealth of the human race. . . . If Mankind be only one and if there can be but one State that comprises all Mankind, that State can be no other than the Church that God Himself has founded." *

This conception is fairly accurately summarized by the statement that, in the Middle Ages, Baptism was an essential element in true citizenship. Thus excommunication implied a virtual loss of citizenship and of all civic privileges. Dr. Figgis finds in Philip II's remark—that he would rather not reign at all than reign over heretics—a perfect expression of the mediæval principle by one who still believed in it.

Whilst, therefore, we must guard against the oft-repeated assertion that the Inquisition was a purely criminal tribunal which became swamped in political intrigue and subserved to political ends, we must recognize the intimate connection between the secular and ecclesiastical aspects of heresy. The interests of Church and State were identical. A full appreciation of the significance of this point is essential to the proper understanding of our subject. Indeed the reader may consider that, in the present study, a disproportionate amount of space has been devoted to its emphasis ; and that, as a consequence, many other important matters have been treated too summarily. The author can only reply by

* Gierke, *Political Theories of the Middle Age* (trans. F. W. Maitland), pp. 10, 11.

pointing in apologetic fashion to his sub-title. He makes no claim to have written an historical text-book on the mediæval Inquisition. Rather he has sought to bring forward one or two points to which, as it seems to him, insufficient attention has hitherto been paid. The Inquisition is one of the most interesting phenomena in history. He has attempted to make it not only interesting, but intelligible.

The first four chapters are expanded from two essays which appeared in *The Nineteenth Century and After*, August and September 1925. To the Editor of that review the author owes his thanks for permission to reprint them in the present form.

A. L. M.

June 1926

INTRODUCTION

A HEARTY British tradition, instilled into us not so much by the history books as by the swashbuckling novels of our boyhood, has taught us to fear and to hate the name of the Inquisition. We imagined, missing the mark by three centuries, that this institution had come into being as a counterblast to the heroic Protestantism of Luther; we imagined the word itself to be a polite euphemism for the use of rack and thumbscrew; and our picture of those who served on it was derived, probably, from that Grand Inquisitor in *The Gondoliers*, who explains that the old nurse is in the torture-chamber, but considerately adds, " She's all right; she has all the illustrated papers." Recently, non-Catholic authors like Mr. Turberville and Mr. Nickerson have attempted to give the general reading public a juster idea of this dreaded tribunal; of its history, its scope, the situation which evoked it. It is beginning to dawn on that public that the Inquisition, so far from being a counterblow to the Reformation, was already a little antiquated, a little past its prime (you might almost call it a revival), when it had to meet the unique conditions of the sixteenth century. It is well that a Catholic author in England should have attempted, as Mr. Maycock here attempts, to correct our old, exaggerated notions by an impartial survey of its early activities.

A Catholic author is not in a position to write of the Inquisition as if it were all past history. It still exists. It employs, to-day, only spiritual weapons, and functions only as the organ of a spiritual body; it is no more an interference with the liberty of the subject than the Court of Arches. To the Catholic author, then, it is an institution which has evolved, not an isolated phenomenon belonging to one particular historical period. He must distinguish its essential from its transient characteristics, its unconscious presuppositions from its conscious aims. He must see it in its context.

The dislike which is registered by the average English citizen upon the mention of the word " Inquisition " is a complex of several moral sentiments, which may be disentangled as follows :—

(1) It is wrong for a Church to have any fixed body of doctrine, departure from which is branded as heresy, and becomes a ground for exclusion from its membership.

(2) It is still more wrong to reinforce this spiritual penalty of exclusion from membership by any kind of secular penalties, fines, imprisonment, etc.

(3) Especially is it wrong to suppose that doctrinal error is a sufficiently severe offence to merit the death penalty.

(4) It is wrong for any tribunal, whether its terms of reference are spiritual or secular, to inflict torture on a human being.

If this analysis be accepted, it will be seen at once that the objections raised are on very different levels. The proposition marked (1) is a proposition which no Catholic in any age of the Church could possibly admit in any sense. The proposition marked (4) is one which, I suppose, most Catholics, like most non-Catholics, would admit nowadays. It is not true that the method of torture is nowhere used to-day in civilized communities; there is the Third Degree. But it is the general view of the modern world that physical tortures, at any rate, should not be used for the purpose of extracting evidence. The propositions marked (2) and (3) are more debatable; they cannot be dismissed in a phrase.

The historical perspective of the four propositions is interesting. No. 1, which is only a journalist's dream and is nowhere operative in fact, is an invention of the century in which we live. No. 2 was grudgingly recognized at the beginning of last century, when Catholics won emancipation—with what difficulty, the Gordon riots are sufficient proof. No. 3 became current in the eighteenth century, when juries refused to convict under the penal laws, and witch trials were abolished (in 1736). No. 4 was admitted in the seventeenth century—to be precise, in 1640. In the spacious times of Queen Bess, from which our inherited prejudice against the Inquisition dates, all four propositions were unheard of amongst the general public, whether Catholic or Protestant.

It is impossible to think ourselves back behind so many years of history. The brain attempts it, but the nerves revolt, and imagination refuses its office. Almost equally impossible do we find it, in England at any rate, to read ourselves back into the atmosphere of a Catholic State. We are so accustomed (in spite of inherited Erastianism) to think of the Church as a mere corporation within the state, with a purely contractual existence much as is enjoyed by a cricket club or an Ancient Order of Buffaloes, that we cannot properly conceive of a State which gives corporate recognition to a revealed religion, which takes it for granted that there are Three Persons in one Godhead as it takes it for granted that two and two makes four. We do not realize how intimately, in such a community, the interests of religion are bound up with those of public morality and of social order; how natural (and, we may add, how just) is the suspicion that a secret sect which attacks the truths of revealed theology attacks also the moral presuppositions of the whole community.

This consideration applies particularly to the mediæval heresies, which the Inquisition was primarily designed to combat. When every possible allowance has been made for the popular tendency to tar all suspicious persons with the same brush, calling all heretics " Manicheans " as it calls all Socialists " Bolshevists," it remains clear that some at least of the mediæval heretics discouraged the natural use of marriage, and such movements as those of Amauri and Doucin boldly attacked the foundations of sexual morality. Wyclif's doctrine that dominion is founded in grace, which is thoroughly typical of the whole Manichean philosophy, attacks no less clearly the foundations of social order ; it means that if your landlord is in a state of mortal sin you are under no obligation to pay the rent. There are sure indications that Manicheism was the parent of the Anabaptist movement in the sixteenth century ; the Anabaptists, as we know, were cheerfully persecuted by Luther, and were burned in Protestant England, with Thomas Cranmer conducting the interrogation.

The mediæval Inquisitors, then, were combating a social, not merely a theological danger. Nor is it matter for wonder if they failed to discriminate, as a modern tribunal would perhaps try to discriminate, between those who held practical and those who held merely speculative doctrines. The head and chief of the offence, in their eyes, was that defiance of spiritual authority of which their other doctrines were merely the corollaries. The idea of liberty of conscience did not present itself to them any more than to Calvin ; heresy, since it affected the soul, was a crime more dangerous than murder ; Church interests were even more important than State interests, and if the rack could be justified by the one, why not by the other ? This sounds nonsense, of course, to those Protestants (and they are numerous) who think in the back of their minds that the religious truths they hold are not really certain, only probable opinions. But the faith which is strong enough to make martyrs is strong enough to make persecutors.

There is, however, a practical supplementary question which most Protestants will be anxious to raise. Granted that we can condone the behaviour of the Inquisitors in the past, considering the circumstances of their time, what would the attitude of the Catholic Church be towards persecution if it were, nowadays, in a position to persecute? If Italy, under its present *régime*, should become fanatically religious, would the freethinker have no worse fate to fear than castor oil? Or (since charity begins at home) what if England became preponderantly Catholic, say by a four-fifths majority? Would the Catholic Church, this "bloody and treacherous corporation," as Dean Inge playfully calls it, observe any principles of religious toleration? Or do Catholics only admit the principles of religious toleration when they are themselves the sufferers? Would a Catholic England revive Smithfield, as surely as a Protestant England would not revive Tyburn?

As I have already indicated, the danger that the Catholic Church would, if it gained ascendancy, employ torture again in judicial interrogations is no greater than the danger that Mr. Baldwin should employ such methods against the Communists. Nor do I conceive that in practice the death penalty could ever be revived. It is a matter of feeling rather than of doctrine, for in the abstract a culpable apostasy which threatens to propagate apostasy is a sin worse than murder. But in such matters we are not ruled by abstract logic. Turn up an old issue of the *Gentleman's Magazine*, and see how month after month, in the days of Dr. Johnson, boys of sixteen (say) would be condemned to death for stealing a horse. We are not less conscious than our great-grandfathers of the guilt of horse-stealing, yet the thing reads like a nightmare. Are we to suppose that because Cardinal Merry del Val is not less conscious than Torquemada of the guilt of heresy, his attitude towards the death-penalty must be the same? It is such a pity Dean Inge does not understand that Catholics are real people.

It may be objected that Proposition No. 2 (among those given above) is the real nerve of the controversy. Does the Catholic Church repudiate the idea of inflicting civil loss *of any kind* upon those who are guilty of merely spiritual offences? I say, merely spiritual; it would be better to say, merely speculative. It is easy to imagine even a Protestant Government, did any exist, taking coercive measures against such movements as that in favour of birth-control. But, granted that no moral or social effects were even anticipated, could the teaching of false doctrine be made an offence punishable by law?

A clear distinction must here be drawn between heresy as such and apostasy from the faith. *Melior est conditio possidentis* ; there is no general agreement that a Catholic power is justified in coercing a heretical minority which has already established itself long since; although such persons are technically, if baptized, subject to the authority of the Church. In order to construct a picture of the conditions in which persecution might be revived, you must imagine a country to be first of all wholly converted to the Faith, as England was in the Middle Ages; you must then suppose that some fresh heretical tendency grows up, and is condemned. Given those conditions, it is possible that some European country of the future might banish innovators in religion as they were banished from France under Louis XIV. I do not say that this would certainly be done; I do not say that it would be politic. I only say that it seems to me a quite reasonable attitude for a Catholic country to take up.

The Catholic religion is a formative element, the chief formative element, in the common life of the country. Its rulers believe that loss of belief is not normally possible without some fault of obstinacy or pride; that such loss is therefore (on the human side) morally culpable, and is accordingly a possible matter for legislation; that it is a kind of spiritual suicide, against which, no less than against attempted self-murder, the law should provide deterrents. They would certainly prohibit public attacks on religion; conceivably they would deport the agitators from their soil.

I must apologize to Mr. Maycock for rambling on like this; have I not suffered often enough myself from the Chairman who gets up to introduce the lecturer, and then cannot sit down? Let me stand no more between him and his public.

R. A. KNOX.

CONTENTS

	PAGE
PREFATORY NOTE	vii
INTRODUCTION	xi

CHAPTER I
THE SPIRIT OF THE MIDDLE AGES . . I

CHAPTER II
THE RISE OF THE HERESIES

The Gathering of the Clouds	26
The Waldenses	32
The Albigensian Heresy	37
Spread of the Heresy in the North	43
Reasons for the Spread of the Heresy . . .	47

CHAPTER III
LANGUEDOC AND THE CRUSADE

The Roman Tradition in Languedoc . . .	54
Contact with the Eastern Empire	55
Moslem Influences	56
The Troubadours	59
The Social Significance of Mediæval Heresy . .	63
The Albigensian Heresy in Languedoc . . .	67
Pope Innocent III	73
The Papal Mission	74
The Crusade and the Albigensian War . . .	77

CHAPTER IV
THE ESTABLISHMENT OF THE INQUISITION

St. Dominic and the Inquisition	82
The Return of Roman Law	86

	PAGE
Development of Anti-heretical Legislation	88
Frederick II and the Heretics	90
Dominicans and Franciscans	92
Summary	95
The Nature of Mediæval Heresy	97
The Task of the Inquisition	99
The Capital Penalty	102

CHAPTER V

THE INQUISITION IN ACTION (I)

The *Accusatio*	106
The *Denunciatio*	111
The *Inquisitio*	114
The Keeping of the Records	122
The Notaries	123
The Position of the Inquisitor	124
Rules concerning Appointment and Deposition	126
General Integrity of the Inquisitors	129
The *Periti* or *Viri Boni*	131

CHAPTER VI

THE INQUISITION IN ACTION (II)

The Thought and the Act	135
Suspicion of Heresy	138
Jews and Infidels	140
Fautors	141
Sorcerers	142
Other Heretical Offences	143
Denunciation of Heretics to the Inquisitor	145
Witnesses	147
False Witnesses	147
The Summons	148
Suppression of the Names of Witnesses	149
The Trial	151
The Interrogations	154

CONTENTS

	PAGE
Antecedent Imprisonment	156
The Use of Torture	157
The Instruments of Torture	162

CHAPTER VII
THE MAJOR PENALTIES

The *Sermo Generalis* or *Auto-da-fé*	166
Bernard Gui	169
The Stake	173
The Impenitent Heretic	176
The Relapsed Heretic	177
The Church, the Secular Arm and the Stake	180
Imprisonment	181
The *Murus Largus*	185
The *Murus Strictus*	186
General Condition of the Prisons	187
Note on the Idea of Imprisonment	189

CHAPTER VIII
CROSSES, PILGRIMAGES, AND OTHER SENTENCES

The Wearing of Crosses	192
Pilgrimages	197
Procedure against the Dead	203
Demolition of Houses	208
Confiscation of Property	211
The Expenses of the Inquisition	217

CHAPTER IX
THE INQUISITION IN EUROPE

The Inquisition in France	219
The Inquisition in Spain	226
The Inquisition in Italy	228

xxii CONTENTS

	PAGE
The Inquisition in Germany	233
The Waldenses	239
The Spiritual Franciscans	243

CHAPTER X

CONCLUSION

CONCLUSION 250

APPENDIX. ON THE BELIEFS AND PRACTICES OF THE ALBIGENSIAN HERETICS 265

INDEX 271

LIST OF ILLUSTRATIONS

FACING PAGE

St. Thomas Aquinas . . . . . *Frontispiece*

*The " Practica Inquisitionis " of Bernard Gui . . 38
   (A page of the British Museum MS. describing the beliefs of
   the Albigenses.)

*Simon de Montfort, 5th Earl of Leicester . . . 77

*Pope Honorius III and St. Dominic. The Order of
   Preachers receives Papal Confirmation . . . 93

Beziers 118

The High City of Carcassonne 148

Execution of an Heretic 174
   (A pencil sketch made by a notary of Count Alphonse of
   Poitiers in the margin of a proposed edict against heresy.
   The date is somewhere between 1249 and 1254.)

*The Main Gate of the House of the Inquisition at
   Toulouse 202

St. Peter Martyr 230

* Reproduced by permission of the Director of the British Museum.

ERRATA

p. 231, line 4.   *For* " 1261 " *read* " 1251 "
p. 246, line 33.   *For* " 1323 " *read* " 1317."   *For* " April "
     read " October "
  „   line 34.   *For* " 13 " *read* " 7th "
p. 253, line 8.   *For* " XXII " *read* " XXI "

THE INQUISITION

CHAPTER I

THE SPIRIT OF THE MIDDLE AGES

THERE are two methods, equally muddle-headed, of
writing about the Inquisition; and unfortunately, during
the last half-century, we have had several examples of
both. The one is ink-slinging; the other is whitewash.
They fail with equal completeness, since they are plainly
unhistorical and based upon loose thinking.

One of the primary purposes of historical knowledge,
as Mr. Chesterton has remarked somewhere, is the
enlargement of experience by imagination. Or, as Mr.
Belloc puts it:

" Your business in writing of the past is to make the
past comprehensible. . . . Anyone, however ignorant,
can discover what is repulsive and absurd in standards
different from their own; and one's learning, no matter
how detailed, is wasted if one gets no further than that.
The whole art of history consists in eliminating that
shock of non-comprehension and in making the reader
feel as the men of the past felt."

Such an attitude to the historical sciences is clearly
impossible to one who, in some vague fashion, confuses
history with propaganda and discussion with controversy.
If the writer imagines that by vilifying or praising the
Inquisition—to take an example—he is thereby vilifying
or praising the Catholic Church, and hence depreciating
from or strengthening the power of her claims, then his
work, though probably valuable and suggestive, cannot

be more than second-rate.   The history of the mediæval period is, even now, loosely connected in the minds of many people with religious controversy ; and it is thanks to the extravagantly propagandist manner of such writers as Froude, Freeman, Lecky and the more unbalanced of the continental anti-clericalists that the main task of the historian in these fields to-day is, as Mr. Belloc has said, the shovelling-off of rubbish inherited from the immediate past.

Yet, in shovelling off the rubbish, one must be careful not to wield one's spade too vigorously.   One must proceed with caution lest, by one's too violent efforts, one begins to chip fragments off the structure that one is seeking to disinter.   A romantic and undiscriminating mediævalism is one of the most futile of poses ; and such scholars as Dr. Coulton and M. Langlois, who take care to preserve the rough edges and the unsightly excrescences along with the finished masterpieces of decoration, have the gratitude of all who prefer the many-sidedness of historical reality to the uniformity of historical romance.

The problems raised by the study of religious persecution in history are among the most fascinating and the most difficult that confront the student.   It may be said, in broad summary, that religious persecution has always appeared when the interests of Church and State were identical.   The Romans persecuted the Jews and early Christians, not because they cared two straws about the religious beliefs of either, but because the holding of those beliefs seemed to them incompatible with the best interests of the Empire.   The Imperial religion was the ceremonial expression of loyalty to the central government—nothing more.   Under Constantius and Valens the Arians persecuted the Catholics, because those Emperors were Arians and because Arianism after the death of Constantine was never much more than a mere political convenience.   Theodosius turned the tables upon the heretics, and decreed exile of their persons and confiscation of their property.   But the death-penalty for heresy was unknown under the Christian Emperors ;

and when, in 385, Priscillian, the heresiarch, was killed by the orders of the Emperor Maximus—an absolutely isolated instance—the bishops to a man rose up and denounced the atrocious and un-Christian savagery of the action. With the exception of St. Augustine, who was prepared to sanction a " temperate severity " in dealing with heresy, all the Fathers declared that coercion in matters of religious belief was flatly contradictory to the spirit of the Gospels. Several, however, admitted that the aid of the secular power might be accepted. St. John Chrysostom urged that the breaking-up of heretical public meetings was clearly desirable; St. Augustine thought that the State had the right to decree exile or fine ; and St. Leo I gave a qualified approval to the severe laws of the Theodosian Code. All, without exception, upheld the position that the Church does not, under any circumstances whatever, desire the death of a sinner.

After the collapse of the central government in the West there was no religious persecution in Europe for five hundred years. You come across isolated little outbursts of heresy, such as the Adoptianism of Elipandus, Archbishop of Toledo, and Felix, Bishop of Urgel, at the end of the eighth century ; but after their opinions had been examined and formally condemned by Pope Adrian I, the authors retracted and no more was heard of the matter. In the ninth century a monk Godescalcus was denounced by the Councils of Mainz and Quierzy for erroneous teaching concerning the Atonement. He was sentenced to be flogged and imprisoned for life in the monastery of Hautvilliers. But there was no question of appealing to secular legislation ; the sentence was not a punishment imposed by the State, but a penance imposed by the Church. Archbishop Hinkmar, in ordering that he should be flogged, expressly cited the Rule of St. Benedict as justifying the punishment.[1]

---

[1] There are several references to corporal punishment in the Rule of St. Benedict. Thus : " Nor let him (the Abbot) conceal the sins of the erring. . . . The more honest and intelligent minds, indeed, let him rebuke with words, with a first or second admonition. But the wicked

And imprisonment for a monk meant little more than the strict confinement required by conventual regulations.[1]

During all these five centuries we find heresy effectively dealt with by the penitential discipline of the Church. There is no sign of organized resistance to the Church's authority. For it was a time not of thought, but of action; a time of intense military activity, when Europe was being held like a fortress against the successive onslaughts of Islam, the northern pirates and the eastern Slavs. Learning was crystallized and preserved in the monasteries. There was proceeding, in the midst of the clash of arms on the frontiers, a silent consolidation of tradition and morals, a fixing and arrangement of a great legacy. The Dark Ages, which may be described as the ages about which we are most completely in the dark, added little or nothing of their own devising to the legacy of the past—no great literary masterpieces, no distinctive monuments of architecture. The characteristic figures of the age are those of Charles Martel hammering and beating back the hordes of Islam at the battle of Tours, and of Charlemagne posting from end to end of his dominions, the anointed defender of Europe, in a ceaseless whirl of campaigns against the invader. The whole habit of mind of that period was preservative rather than speculative. On the one hand one sees the great fighting princes saving Europe from destruction by her enemies; on the other, the quiet arrangement of canonical and patristic documents in the monasteries. And when the eleventh century dawned in a blaze of promise as dazzling as it was unexpected, the full fruit of these patient monastic labours became apparent. For in the years between 600 and 1000 the Catholic Faith had become wholly one with Europe.

---

and the hard-hearted and the proud, or the disobedient, let him restrain at the beginning of their sin by castigation of the body, as it were with whips." "Rule of St. Benedict," para. 2 in E. F. Henderson's *Select Historical Documents of the Middle Ages*, pp. 274 ff.

[1] " It is interesting to note that imprisonment for crime is of purely ecclesiastical origin. The Roman law knew nothing of it." E. Vacandard, *The Inquisition*, p. 25.

The great Renaissance of the tenth and eleventh centuries is one of the most extraordinary phenomena in history. In 927 the promulgation of the Cluniac Rule by Abbot Odo marked the real beginning of the Middle Ages. In 936 Otto the Great completed the conquest of the Eastern Slavs. In 987 Hugh Capet ascended the throne of France and the evil days of the later Carlovingians were passed for ever. At the end of the century Pope Sylvester II began the great work of reform and reorganization, which Hildebrand was to complete. It was as though man had suddenly remembered how to act and how to think; Europe, in the classic phrase of an old chronicler, clothed herself anew in a white mantle of churches. In the midst of the destructions and horrors of the ninth and tenth centuries the dawn had come.

" Just why this sudden and unpredicted regeneration should then have shown itself with power," says Dr. Cram finely,[1] " is hard to understand. It is sufficiently easy to understand why the eleventh century should have begun in vigour to close in glory, for by that time all things had been prepared ; but why out of the horror of the ninth century should suddenly arise the first beginnings in the tenth is one of those phenomena that baffle the evolutionists and are comprehensible only to those who believe that the destinies of the world are under the guidance and the control of a Supreme Omniscience Who walks not by the ways of man, but otherwise."

So we pass to the great eleventh century—an age characterized as no other age had been by a spirit of conquering energy based upon an already cemented moral unity, an age of confidence, of hope, of promise.

On the other hand, there was none of the modern muddle-headed illusion about the necessary excellence of change and the existence of a supposed " law " of progress. Moralists denounced ; Popes reformed ; sovereigns legislated with vigour and sometimes with ferocity. With the troubadour poets came refinement of manners

[1] Ralph Adams Cram, *The Substance of Gothic*, p. 64.

and the birth of lyric poetry.   The Normans conquered
England and Sicily and set up systems of government
fitted to be models for all Europe.   The Church, in-
vigorated and purified by the genius of Hildebrand, filled
men with a new sense of unity and common purpose—a
purpose which hurled Europe against Asia in the great
tidal wave of the First Crusade.   Finally came the fuller
development of the chivalric tradition, the blurring of the
rugged, austere lines of Norman architecture, the beginnings of the soaring audacity of the Gothic—a vast
movement which might be described in summary as the
transition from Mont St. Michel to Chartres.

The civilization of mediæval Europe was unique in
that it was based upon a unity of culture—the closest form
of unity in which man can possibly be bound ; and of
which political and social unity are simply by-products
or off-shoots.   Unity is the keynote of the European
story during the Middle Ages ; and unless we can, to
some extent, grasp the significance of this conception,
we can never hope to understand the period.

Presiding over the whole was, of course, the Church.
She was the supreme dominating factor in the minds of all.
With her vast prestige in the field of politics and her
tremendous influence over the individual conscience she
could afford to be, and was, easy-going and tolerant.
She had a just confidence in her own power and she looked
on without protest at the annual horseplay on All Fools'
Day, when the Mass was burlesqued by one dressed as a
priest before the Altar itself.   When some too venture-
some scholar strayed from the paths of orthodoxy, he
was, as a matter of course, excommunicated.   But there
was no flourish of trumpets about the affair.   Very few
people knew anything about it ; and in nine cases out of
ten the defaulter would ultimately retract his error,
receiving a warm welcome—and a thumping penance—on
his return to the true Faith.   Even the great Abelard,
after his condemnation by the Council of Sens, was warmly
received by Peter the Venerable into the Abbey of Cluny
and passed the remaining days of his life as a Benedictine

monk. The Church was unquestioned; she was part of the atmosphere which everybody breathed.

The monasteries were the hotels of the Middle Ages; and their boundless charity in feeding the hungry and succouring the poor became ultimately an abuse, since it almost placed a premium upon vagrancy. Of course it must be remembered that all the material benefits—forestry, agriculture and the like—which the monastic system gave to the civilization of Europe were simply by-products. A monastery is primarily a spiritual power-house, where praise and worship are continually offered to God and whence a constant incense of prayer and intercession rises to the Eternal Throne. All else is incidental. All the huge system of public service, which the monasteries provided in the Middle Ages, was incidental to the central purpose. And if, in our blindness, we are unable to appreciate the beauty and the splendour of this great spiritual force, at least we may contemplate in some admiration this huge manifestation of organized Christian charity—a sort of universal system of hotels and tourist-agencies, whose services were entirely gratuitous, whose doors were open alike to rich and poor, to King and peasant.

Hospitality was the duty of all monasteries. St. Alban's had stabling accommodation for 300 horses; Abingdon had a special endowment to meet the cost of re-shoeing the guests' horses. In the ordinary way, free hospitality was provided for two days; but many of the monasteries used to care permanently for a number of poor or sick people in the Almonry. Great Malvern had thirty resident poor people and Barnwell had a hospital and a school for their use. The monastery at Barnwell was occupied by Augustinian Canons; and it was part of the Hosteller's duty:

" To be careful that perfect cleanliness and propriety should be found in his department, namely, to keep clean clothes and clean towels; cups without flaws; spoons of silver; mattresses, blankets, sheets not merely clean but untorn; proper pillows; quilts to cover the beds of full length and width, and pleasing to the eye of those who enter the room ; a proper laver of metal ; a bason clean both inside and out ; in winter a candle and candlesticks ; fire that does not smoke ; writing materials ; clean salt in salt-cellars that have been well scrubbed ; food served in porringers that have been well washed and are un-broken . . . the whole Guest-House kept clean of spiders-webs and dirt, and strewn with rushes underfoot . . . keys and locks to the doors and good bolts on the inside, so as to keep the doors securely locked whilst the guests are asleep." [1]

By her powers of excommunication and interdict the Church contributed largely to policing and the main-tenance of the peace. By the " Truce of God " she put a powerful check on the vigorous pugnacity of barons and princes. Thus we have a typical proclamation by the Archbishop of Cologne in 1083, enjoining that :

" From the first day of the Advent of Our Lord through Epiphany, and from Septuagesima to the eighth day after Pentecost and through that whole day, and on the fast days of the four seasons, and throughout the year on Sunday, Friday and Saturday and on all days canonically set apart, this decree of peace shall be observed ; so that both those who travel and those who remain at home may enjoy security and the most entire peace, so that no one may commit a murder, arson, robbery or assault, no one may injure another with sword, club or any kind of weapon, and so that none may presume . . . to carry arms, shield, sword, lance or any kind of armour." [2]

A bristling catalogue of penalties for the infringement of the decree follows : banishment for a noble, execution for a serf who had committed murder, and so forth. It is easy to sneer at the ingenuous confidence in human nature which is displayed in such a pronouncement as this ; nor should we forget that the very terms of the decree reflect the exceedingly lax condition of public security. But the point is that in the Middle Ages the initiative

[1] " Monks, Friars and Secular Clergy " in *Mediæval England*, p. 372.
[2] Quoted in *The Ideas that have Influenced Civilization*, Vol. IV. p. 342.

in such matters came almost always from the Church. She was not an alien despotism, trampling on the souls of men and terrifying them with threats of hell-fire. She was the animating spirit of society, and the guardianship of the peace was one of her countless functions, gladly recognized by everybody. She was, as Luchaire puts it, the mainspring of all national organizations.

"Her doctrine of the equal worth of souls before God," says Mr. Nickerson,[1] " together with the common observance of her worship, made strongly for friendship and confidence between classes. Her universality, her cosmopolitan officialdom and her use of Latin made for understanding and community of feeling between localities. So she gave to the time, with its accepted division of mankind into classes and its poor communications, a greater measure of fraternity than we possess to-day, with all our talk of ' equality ' and all our devices permitting men to meet or to speak together. This she did, not by any forced, mechanical scheme of union, but by the presentation of a body of doctrine which all accepted and, by accepting, bound themselves to be members one of another."

So mediæval civilization rose steadily to the great heights of the thirteenth century—the greatest of all centuries in the annals of our race. The world of study has never been so perfectly united, so harmonious, so conscious of a common purpose as in the Golden Age of Scholasticism. Lanfranc, St. Anselm, St. Bonaventura and St. Thomas Aquinas were Italians ; John of Salisbury, Roger Bacon, Duns Scotus and Occam were Englishmen ; Hugo of St. Victor and Blessed Albert the Great were Germans ; William of Champeaux, Roscellin, Abelard, St. Bernard and Gerbert were Frenchmen. All these men, in their respective times, taught or studied in the schools of Paris. Their national distinctions were meaningless ; they were simply citizens of the Christian commonwealth. John of Salisbury for a number of years occupied the bishopric of Chartres ; Lanfranc, after a

[1] H. Nickerson, *The Inquisition*, p. 23.

career of extraordinary eminence, became Archbishop
of Canterbury and built the cathedral in that city. The
famous Peter of Blois was Chancellor to the Archbishop
of Canterbury and died as Archdeacon of London. It is
only quite recently that it has been possible to fix the
birthplace of Alan of Lille—" Alanus de Insulis " as he
was known to his contemporaries; and in the meantime
he has been identified, by one authority or another, with
almost every island between Cyprus and Ireland. Landino
says that Hugo of St. Victor hailed from Pavia; Venturi
calls him a Saxon, and Alexander Natalis describes him
as a native of Ypres. There were no nations and no
frontiers.

If there was ever a time in our history when the
Eastern and Western minds came near to full understanding and sympathy, it was in these great days of
Paris University, when the Schoolmen discussed the
philosophy of Aristotle with the Arab doctors, and when
Oriental sovereigns frequently sent their sons to study at
the French capital. So when the Children's Crusade
ended in the merciless " shanghai-ing " of thousands of
boys and girls to the slave-markets of Alexandria, the
Caliph, remembering his own undergraduate days at
Paris, himself saw to it that they were kindly treated.

The twelfth and thirteenth centuries were a period
when men were at their strongest and most vigorous.

" Never before or since," says Henry Adams,[1] " have
they shown equal energy in such varied directions or such
intelligence in the direction of that energy."

The whole tendency and thought of the age was
centripetal. Never has the human intellect raised such a
gigantic monument of reasoned thought as the *Summa* of
St. Thomas—the crown of scholasticism. Never have
human hands constructed so magnificent and so satisfying a gateway to the home of the soul as the Gothic
cathedral. Never have the depths of mystical experience
been sounded with such sureness and beauty as in the
Imitation of Christ. Never, perhaps, has poetry carried

[1] Henry Adams, *Mont St. Michel and Chartres*, p. 246.

the emotions to more sublime heights than in the inspiration of Dante—Dante whom Dr. Cram so finely hails as
" the eternal synthesis of Mediævalism." Yet the
flashing analogies of St. Thomas, the tense spring of the
flying buttress, and the dazzling splendours of the *Divine
Comedy* were all parts of a greater whole. The spire of
the cathedral pointed to Dante's Seventh Heaven; St.
Thomas Aquinas laid his foundations with the same
exquisite care as the architects of Rheims and Amiens.
The exterior of the cathedral expressed the spirit of
energy, vigour and joyous adventure. But within, the
tapering vaults over the Sanctuary, the soft light from the
rose windows, the lamp which burned dimly by the Altar
and the great sweep of the arches, springing upward
from the capitals until lost in the majestic gloom of the
roof spaces, spoke of those great Mysteries which St.
Thomas à Kempis had approached so closely. The
Church pointed the way; and scholars, poets, architects,
artists and mystics followed.

Herein lies the real grandeur of the Middle Ages.
There was nothing Utopian about the twelfth and thirteenth centuries; indeed it is almost the whole point of
the story that, although the men of those times strove
so mightily for so mighty a purpose, they failed in the
ultimate achievement.

" You may know "—I quote Dr. Cram again [1]—" You
may know a crescent epoch from one that is decadent by
this test—if its tendency is centripetal rather than centri-
fugal. If scattered units are being gathered up into
greater wholes instead of the reverse process, then greater
fortunes lie beyond and the future has much to give.
If, on the other hand, things once united and consistent
are resolving themselves into their component parts, if a
Church is disintegrating into sects, a philosophy into
personal followings, each fashioning for itself its own
aggressive propaganda and its own scheme of offence and
defence; if literature and the arts are ceasing to be a
great popular voicing and are becoming the personal

[1] Ralph Adams Cram, *The Great Thousand Years.*

idiosyncrasies of over-differentiated egoists; and if, finally, the human personality is breaking up into its component parts, so that each man lives not a dual but a multiple existence (his religion, business, politics, domestic life all separated by inviolable frontiers), then you may know that an epoch is drawing to its close, and if you are wise you will look all around for the signs of a new day, the grey dawn of which must be visible along the hills."

Now the dominating characteristic of mediæval society was that it was based first and foremost upon a unity of culture.   Europe was the Church.   Life had no meaning apart from the Church.   The blackest disaster that could fall upon a town or district was to be laid under interdict ; for the interdict might well involve temporal ruin as well as spiritual destitution.   The most irretrievable ruin that could fall upon a man was excommunication ; for that might well lead to exile and loss of citizenship.   To be deprived of the Blessed Sacrament was worse than to have your property confiscated.   To strike at the Church was to strike at the hub of everything ; so that whilst the heathen, admittedly a gentleman and a sportsman, was the natural enemy of society, the heretic was the traitor within the camp.   A modern heresy strikes at the Church, but it does not strike at the foundations of the social order, since the social order is not based upon a consciousness of moral unity.   In the mediæval environment heresy was necessarily the ultimate sin, the scourge of Satan.   It was a pollution of the very atmosphere, stifling alike the spiritual and corporate life of Christendom.   It was blasphemy against the Most High, defiance of His Church, insult to Our Lady and the Saints.   But it was more, even, than this.   It was an assault upon society, for it struck at the Church which was the foundation of society.   Thus Pope John XXII declared that Communism was a heresy ; and, as such, the Communism of the Spiritual Franciscan Extremists was dealt with.   To-day, Communism is regarded, very rightly, as a threat to the Constitution.   It strikes at the nation, which is the focus of social unity.   In the Middle Ages the appeal was to a religious principle; to-day the appeal is to a political theory.

" The weakness of the Middle Ages," it has been well said, " lay in four things. First, there was insufficient organization of public powers and of communications. . . . Second, there was very little natural science, *i.e.* detailed knowledge of the properties of the material world. . . . Third, there was cruelty; and fourth, there was the contrast between the vast assumptions made by the Church and the shortcomings and weakness of man himself—layman and churchman alike." [1]

Thus we hear nothing in mediæval discussion of the so-called " economic virtues," so loudly extolled to-day. A well-known publicist recently declared that " an efficient selfishness is the highest form of patriotism "— an opinion which all mediæval thinkers would have unhesitatingly denounced as blasphemous and unmoral. A unity of culture implies a universally recognized code of ethics; and under the reasoned ethical system propounded by the Church the sin of avarice is included amongst the seven most serious moral offences. Avarice, in short, is a deadly sin and not a cardinal virtue; and as such it was recognized by all mediæval thinkers. Accordingly you get the unanimous condemnation of usury—that is, the taking of interest on an unproductive loan; the frequent denunciation of alchemy—that is, the claim of the travelling charlatan to effect the transmutation of metals into gold and silver; and the innumerable complaints of extortion against kings, noblemen, monastic communities and even Popes.

For it need not be supposed that, because avarice was one of the seven deadly sins, it was never practised by anybody. It was rampant in the very citadel of the Church herself; and from the thirteenth century onwards a loud chorus of denunciation arises, ever increasing in volume, against the insatiable rapacity of the Papal curia. By the fifteenth century the Papacy had become, perhaps, the greatest financial institution in Europe, and " what is

[1] Nickerson, p. 209.

followed is the gospel, not according to St. Mark, but according to the marks of silver." Dante, as Mr. Tawney reminds us, put the money-lenders of Cahors in hell; but a Pope gave them the title of " peculiar sons of the Roman Church." [1] Cathedral chapters lent money at a high rate of interest; priests took part in usurious transactions; and of an Archbishop of Narbonne, Innocent III declared that he had a purse instead of a heart. Later, in the sixteenth century, the head of the house of Fugger died in the odour of sanctity, "a good Catholic and a Count of the Empire, having seen his firm pay 54 per cent. for the preceding sixteen years." [2]

Having emphasized the central and indispensable part which the Catholic Church and the Catholic Faith played in the civilization of the Middle Ages, it will be well to conclude with a note of caution. To speak vaguely of the Church doing this or decreeing that is often misleading. Thus we are often invited to picture the Middle Ages as ages of cringing superstition and religious terrorism—to conjure up a picture of an entire civilization held down and enslaved by a vague and elusive " chimera " known as " the Church "—a feat which no institution in recorded history has ever achieved or could ever achieve. We have, for instance, the resounding indictment of Lecky: [3]

" The agonies of hell seemed then the central fact of religion and the perpetual subject of the thoughts of men. The whole intellect of Europe was employed in illustrating them. . . . There was no respite, no alleviation, no hope. The tortures were ever varied in their character. . . . A ceaseless shriek of anguish attested the agonies that were below.

" We may estimate the untiring assiduity with which the Catholic priests sought in the worst acts of human tyranny and in the dark recesses of their own imaginations,

[1] See R. H. Tawney, *Religion and the Rise of Capitalism* (John Murray, 1926), pp. 28, 29.
[2] Tawney, *ibid.*, p. 79.
[3] W. E. H. Lecky, *Rise and Influence of Rationalism*, pp. 317 ff.

new forms of torture, to ascribe them to the Creator.
We can never conceive the intense vividness with which
these conceptions were realized, or the madness and
misery they produced. . . . The sense of Divine good-
ness being destroyed, the whole fabric of natural religion
crumbled in the dust. . . . It centred entirely upon the
priests, who supported it mainly by intimidation."

Now this lurid picture of mediæval times as the long
tyranny of a horde of ambitious, fanatical priests over a
simple and credulous civilization simply does not bear
examination. It is, of course, true that many of the
greatest men of these times were priests and that many of
the greatest women were nuns. Still, one notes the
presence of such terror-stricken rabbits as Simon de
Montfort, St. Louis IX, Philip Augustus, Dante, Giotto,
Cimabue, Gaddi, Queen Blanche of Castile, Eleanor of
Guienne, Henry V of England, William of Lorris, Jean
de Meun, St. Elizabeth of Hungary—to mention but a
very few. And what of that gay troubadour, Fulk of
Toulouse, who, terrified presumably by the threats of
the priests, was browbeaten into joining their number
himself and lived to become Bishop of Toulouse? One
seems to detect in some of these nineteenth-century
historians a certain lack of what may be termed the
historian's sense of humour. And by the historian's
sense of humour I mean, not the power of being able to
laugh at the men of the past, but the power of recognizing
that, if the men of the past had the chance, they would
probably laugh at the historian.

The truth is that when we speak of the Church in the
Middle Ages, we must understand by the term the corporate conscience of Europe, a living reality with a living
voice. It used to be fashionable during the last century
to refer to the *Divine Comedy* as the " Inferno "; and one
still comes across people who associate Dante's masterpiece with the naked figures of men writhing helplessly
in the torments of hell, and seem never to have realized
that there was such a thing as the " Purgatorio " or the
" Paradiso." Hence, presumably, arose the extra-

ordinary suggestion that Dante took his place among that
" intellect of Europe " whose whole time was spent in
illustrating the tortures of the damned; and that the
Divine Comedy was intended and received primarily as
an instrument of religious terrorism. To anyone who
has read the poem the idea is surely too childish to be
discussed. It is much nearer the truth to say, with
Henry Adams, that the men of the Middle Ages troubled
themselves about pain and death much as healthy bears
did in the mountains. We know, for instance, that Satan
himself was often characterized in the mediæval pageants
and miracle plays, and that his appearance on the stage
was always greeted with roars of laughter.[1]

Indeed this toughness of the mediæval mind in its
attitude to physical suffering is one of the main obstacles
of the modern student to anything approaching a sympathetic comprehension of the period. Whatever admiration he may feel for their achievements in literature,
architecture, philosophy and so forth, however much he
may be able to sympathize, whether as an outsider or as a
co-religionist, with the Faith that was the very cement of
their whole social order, he is yet repelled and disgusted
by their frequent lapses into callous and apparently
calculated cruelty. Clearly the wrong way of approaching
the matter is to indulge in a torrent of abuse or ridicule
and to leave it at that. Such procedure is destructive,
of the whole purpose of historical study; and when one

[1] " The people of the Middle Ages, of whom the chroniclers relate
innumerable acts of turbulence, so jealous of their liberties, so gay even
in their churches—these people terrified? What an idea! These strong,
restless men, carrying East and North and South the plenitude of their
warlike activity, represented as groaning beneath the discipline of the
monks? Well, well! We do not pretend that there was no misery in
their time, that there were not abuses of power, terrible plagues; but we
need not believe that such things were the special lot of a people whose
general welfare and joy of living and splendid independence are witnessed
by a thousand and one documents. . . . When were the universities so
vigorous, so daring, so full of the spirit of debate? When have men discussed so many questions of all kinds and put forward so many metaphysical,
philosophical, social and economic theories? " (Th. de Cauzons, *Histoire
de l'Inquisition en France*, Vol. II, p. xxii, Author's trans.)

comes across in historical text-books such phrases as "pious butchery," "the saintly homicides," and so forth, one simply draws the conclusion that the writer has lost touch with his subject.

Moreover, it is evident that any attempt to present an intelligible study of the past consists as much in ridding oneself of the prejudices and abnormalities of the present as in apprehending the peculiar characteristics of the past. The present has its *Zeitgeist* like any other age. Much of our modern sensitiveness to physical suffering is probably due to a certain moral advance, an increased appreciation of gentleness and kindliness, an increased reluctance purposely to inflict pain upon another. But there is also a far less wholesome element in the matter. For nothing is so characteristic of the present age as its intense preoccupation with the things of the body and its corresponding lack of serious interest in those that concern the soul, except in so far as the latter are conceived as subservient or auxiliary to the former. It is, we believe, a plain matter of statistics that, outside the Catholic Church, the only religions which show increased memberships to-day are those which promise the healing of bodily ills.[1] There is a constant outcry against the supposed cruelty of capital punishment. The very idea of hell is more than many people can bear. And one notes with astonishment that, in spite of the emphasis with which the sixteenth-century reformers repudiated the doctrine of Purgatory, many religious bodies to-day have virtually substituted Purgatory for hell. Even on the tremendous story of the Passion and of Calvary there has fallen a gloss of unreality, a convention of timid reticence.

" Nervousness . . . for no one knows exactly what is this disease from which everyone is suffering; it is certain nowadays that people's nerves are more easily shaken by the least shock. Remember what the papers say about the execution of those condemned to death;

[1] See *e.g.* an interesting article, " Healing Religions in the United States," by Dr. J. J. Walsh, in *Studies*, December 1924.

they reveal that the executioner works timidly, that he is on the point of fainting, that he suffers from nerves when he decapitates a man. What misery! When one compares him with the invincible torturers of old time! They used to enclose people's legs in wrappings of wet parchment, which shrank when placed before a fire and slowly crushed the flesh; or they drove wedges into the thighs and so broke the bones; they crushed the thumbs in vices worked by screws, raked off strips of skin with a rake, rolled up the skin of the stomach as if it had been an apron, put you in the *strappado*, roasted you, watered you with burning brandy; all this with an impassive face and tranquil nerves, unshaken by any shriek, any groan. These exercises being a little fatiguing, they found themselves with a great hunger and a fine thirst. They were full-blooded, well-balanced fellows, whereas now . . ." [1]

Even this boisterous irony leaves the whole question more or less in the air. Granted Huysmans' " nervousness," granted, if you will, a real moral advance, there is yet a deep difference between the fundamental philosophies of the two periods. If we attempt to explain or analyze it, we must do so with hesitation and diffidence.

" Men believed something," says Mr. Belloc, " with regard to the whole doctrine of expiation, of penal arrangements, which they have not described to us and which we cannot understand save through the glimpses, sidelights and guesses through what they imagined to be their plainest statements."

We have noted the fact that the Church and all that she stood for was central and indispensable to the mediæval order. To attack the Church was to attack the European commonwealth, to strike at the very foundations of society. Thus religious persecution might be, and frequently was, a mere vent for political animosity. Other considerations were present, besides those of mere difference of religious belief. Possibly one might find

[1] *Là Bas*, by J. K. Huysmans, quoted by Nickerson, *The Inquisition*, p. 59.

rough parallels in the treatment of conscientious objectors during the war or in the lynchings of negroes in the Southern States of America. Yet even in these cases the motive to violence was not so all-embracing or so deeply-rooted. The men of the Middle Ages hated heresy first and the heretic second.

Even so the ferocity of their action appals and revolts us. The recognized punishment was one of the most painful deaths that can possibly be inflicted. The heretic was burnt alive at the stake.

Several extenuating features must, however, be noted. The penalty was by no means the most severe that could be imposed, nor was it confined exclusively to heretics nor instituted specially for their benefit. In the reign of Henry VIII, the recognized punishment for the poisoner was to be boiled alive in a cauldron. In Holland, after the establishment of the Protestant ascendency, it was decreed that Gerard, the assassin of William the Silent, should have " his right hand cut off with a red-hot iron, his flesh torn from his bones in six different places, that he should be quartered and disembowelled alive, that his heart should be torn from his bosom and flung in his face, and finally that his head should be cut off." [1] Burning at the stake was the regular punishment for witchcraft throughout the seventeenth and eighteenth centuries ; and as late as 1807 a beggar was tortured and burnt alive for sorcery at Mayenne.

In the Middle Ages it is fairly clear that, in burning heretics, nothing was further from the intentions of these men than the deliberate infliction of pain. Other considerations, about whose nature we can only guess, were uppermost. Constantly we find instances in which the people and judges showed complete indifference as to whether the criminal was burnt alive or after death. Savonarola is a case in point ; and in the even more familiar instance of St. Joan the chroniclers denounce the savage cruelty of the English, who had deliberately built the faggots and scaffold so high that the executioner was

[1] J. L. Motley, *Rise of the Dutch Republic*, iii. 612.

unable, as he usually did, to approach closely enough to hasten the end of the victim. There seems to have been some almost symbolic idea attaching to the consuming of the body by fire. For in many cases—Arnold of Brescia, for instance—it was thought worth while to disinter the body of some long-defunct heretic and to commit it to the flames. It may even be suggested that in the later Middle Ages the burning of a heretic took on a partially ceremonial character, almost wholly unaccompanied by hatred of the accused. When that fiendish ruffian Gilles de Rais was about to be burnt for his numerous crimes he was overcome by remorse.

" Among other edifying signs of contrition, he begged the people whose little boys he had kidnapped, and then debauched and then tortured to death by hundreds, to pray for him. Whereupon they marched in procession . . . chanting and praying earnestly for the soul of the monster whom their authorities, with the fullest approval of the paraders, were to burn on the morrow." [1]

Why these things should be we cannot say. We have to accept the fact that these men clearly saw no moral problem in the matter at all; and that, in spite of Papal and Episcopal protests, which gradually became less insistent and finally ceased altogether, they regarded the burning of heretics as a just and obvious duty. St. Louis himself, the Christian monarch *par excellence*, reaffirmed statutes ordering that heretics handed over to the secular arm should be burnt. Whilst St. Elizabeth of Hungary, gentlest and most lovable of saints, had for her spiritual director that same Conrad of Marburg, whose fame rests mainly on the intense and often excessive zeal with which he belaboured the heretics as an inquisitor.

Probably we may approach the root of the matter if we realize that no other age has matched the Middle Ages in the depth and intensity of two fundamental religious experiences—the consciousness of sin and the confident belief in a life beyond the grave. Plainly these beliefs, intimately bound up with the whole question of

[1] H. Nickerson, *op. cit.*, pp. 57, 213.

punishments and expiation of guilt, exercised a profound influence on their attitude to heresy. When heresy is seen, not so much as the unchecked freedom of inquiry in theological matters, but as blasphemy against the Most High, defiance of His Church, insult to the Saints, when the salvation of the soul is regarded as appreciably more important than the comfort and well-being of the body, then many things are possible which are not dreamed of in our philosophy. And amongst those things we must count not only the organized prosecution of heresy, but the building of a Chartres Cathedral and the writing of a *Divine Comedy*. " Corruptio optimi pessima."

But whilst it is absurd to ascribe to the men of the Middle Ages an ingrained cruelty and vindictiveness of mind which human nature has now outgrown, it is obviously mistaken to represent them as vague, other-worldly sentimentalists who cared nothing for the ordinary affairs of life. Although we are all creatures of circumstance, human nature itself does not change; and as Mr. Nickerson says : " We must beware of trying to understand the past too well when we cannot even understand the present."

As far as the question of actual cruelty is concerned, we need not look very far in the modern world for examples which challenge comparison with the worst mediæval excesses. Towards the end of 1921 the *New York World* conducted a careful investigation of charges made against the Ku-Klux-Klan. It was reported that between October 1920 and September 1921 the Klan had perpetrated four murders, one " irreparable mutilation," one branding with acid, forty-one floggings, twenty-seven cases of tarring and feathering and five kidnappings. The present writer numbers amongst his friends one who had himself taken part in the lynching and burning alive of a negro for assault upon a white woman. He is himself familiar, upon unimpeachable evidence, of cases where torture and mutilation have been inflicted by the hooded brethren of the Klan upon their victims ; as, for instance, the tarring, feathering and beating with a wet rope of a woman in Teneha, Texas, because she had married a second time. During 1923 a Texas lawyer, in a letter to a U.S. Senator, estimated that " Texas has had, within the last eighteen months, five hundred tar-and-feather parties and whipping bees, not to mention a number of homicides, assaults and other offences."

Now it is clear that the activities of the Ku-Klux-Klan provide a parallel—very superficial, it is true, yet none the less instructive—to those of the mediæval peoples in dealing with heresy. Of course we set on one side all consideration of the rightness or wrongness of the principles concerned. It has been maintained by many that the unity of mediæval Europe was not worth pre-serving and that the Reformation which destroyed it was a blessing to society ; on the other hand, some of us may be disposed to think that 100 per cent. Americanism, the shibboleth of the Klan, is very great nonsense. That is not the point. The point is that in each case you have an intense consciousness of the unity or solidarity of a certain institution—in the one case the American Republic, in the other the Christian commonwealth of mediæval Europe. In each case you conceive of certain societies or sects within that institution as constituting a menace to its prosperity, its health, its continued operative unity. Thus the Klansman is convinced that Catholics, Jews and negroes are anti-social societies, as he under-stands the term. He is little interested in the truth or falsity of Catholic teaching. If the Catholic likes to believe in Purgatory, the Invocation of Saints and so forth, what is that to him ? But he is intensely con-cerned by his belief that the Catholic Church, considered as a society, is un-American ; that she claims a loyalty which cannot be other than subversive of the proper loyalty of the American citizen to his own country. The same principle he applies, with a suitable differentiation of terms, to the Jew and the negro. He regards them as the Roman Emperors regarded the early Christians ; he objects to them as societies possessing a unity and an

organization of their own, not as adherents of a religion
with which he himself may happen to disagree.   Indeed,
in the case of the negro, there is no point of religion at
issue.   The idea is merely that of keeping a dangerous
barbarian element in its proper place.

In like manner the ordinary mediæval Catholic bothered
himself little with the theological aspects of heresy.   It
is only when we move amongst the great philosophers,
canonists, preachers and missionaries—men like St.
Thomas Aquinas, St. Bernard, St. Dominic, St. Raymond
of Pennafort, St. Bonaventura, Albert the Great—that
we find the refutation of heresy conducted on a dignified
plane of reasoned debate.   To such men heresy appeared
primarily as defiance of revealed truth ; to the common
people it appeared primarily as defiance of the Church.
Of course this is merely a rough-and-ready generalization.
But, as we shall have occasion to note in the next chapter,
the revival of religious persecution in the Middle Ages
comes not from the Church, but from the secular authorities.   Heresy was seen first and foremost as an anti-social
conspiracy.

" The (mediæval) Church," says Dr. Tout,[1] " was more
than a Church ; it was a state also—in a way it was a super-
state."

Hence it is true to say that when religious persecution reappeared in the eleventh century, it was inspired
rather by loyalty to the Catholic Church as the universal
society of which all men were members, than by loyalty
to the Catholic Faith, of which the Church was the
Guardian and the Teacher.   In other words, an institution is defended by conduct which is in flat contradiction
to the very principles for which that institution stands.
And that is the meaning of fanaticism.

Exactly the same phenomenon is presented by the
Ku-Klux-Klan.   The Klan is so American that it is un-
American, for it seeks to uphold by religious intolerance
a society which reposes explicitly upon the principle of
complete religious toleration.   Not that *complete* religious

---

[1] T. F. Tout, *France and England in the Middle Ages and Now*, p. 25.

toleration is either desirable or even possible. It is clear that constraint in matters of religious belief, which includes matters of moral judgment, must under certain circumstances become necessary to the good of society.[1]

" Justice forbids and reason itself forbids," said Pope Leo XIII,[2] " that the State should be godless ; or that it should adopt a line of action which would end in godlessness—namely, to treat the various religions (as they call them) alike, and to bestow upon them promiscuously equal rights and privileges. . . . Yet, with the discernment of a true mother, the Church weighs the great burden of human weakness ; and well knows the course down which the minds and actions of men in this

---

[1] Dr. Johnson hit this particular nail on the head with his usual accuracy.

Johnson. Every society has a right to preserve publick peace and order, and therefore has a good right to prohibit the propagation of opinions which have a dangerous tendency. . . . *Mayo.* I am of opinion, Sir, that every man is entitled to liberty of conscience in religion. *Johnson.* Sir, I agree with you. Every man has a right to liberty of conscience, and with that the magistrate cannot interfere. People confound liberty of thinking with liberty of talking ; nay, with liberty of preaching. Every man has a physical right to think as he pleases ; for it cannot be discovered how he thinks. He has not a moral right, for he ought to inform himself and think justly. But, Sir, no member of a society has a right to *teach* any doctrine contrary to what that society holds to be true. . . . *Mayo.* But, Sir, is it not very hard that I should not be allowed to teach my children what I really believe to be the truth ? *Johnson.* Suppose you teach your children to be thieves ? *Mayo.* This is making a joke of the subject. *Johnson.* Nay, Sir, take it thus : that you teach them the community of goods ; for which there are as many plausible arguments as for most erroneous doctrines. You teach them that all things were at first in common, and that no man has a right to anything, but as he laid his hands upon it. Here, Sir, you sap a great principle of society— property. And don't you think the magistrate would have a right to prevent you ? Or suppose you should teach your children the notion of the Adamites, and they should run naked in the streets, would not the magistrate have a right to flog them into their doublets ? . . . *Toplady.* Sir, you have untwisted this difficult subject with great dexterity. (Boswell's *Life of Johnson*, Vol. i. pp. 511–513, O.U. Press, 1922.)

[2] Encyclical *Libertas Præstantissimum*, June 1888. I take this quotation from a letter written to *The Nineteenth Century and After*, September 1925, by Mr. J. W. Poynter.

our age are being borne. For this reason, while not conceding any right to anything save what is true and honest, she does not forbid public authority to tolerate what is at variance with truth and justice, for the sake of avoiding greater ills. . . . But to judge aright we must acknowledge that the more a State is driven to tolerate evil the further is it from perfection."

Further, within the limits defined by the Natural Law, the purpose of civil government is the highest good of the community and the happiness of individuals as they are members of the community. Thus the civil government must be in some degree opportunist. A man familiar with the social conditions of Imperial Rome in the first century would appreciate the circumstances which led the Emperors to levy taxes on celibacy; but he would not thereby commit himself to a belief that men ought to be bred under supervision like cattle. In like manner it is readily conceivable that, under certain circumstances, State interference in the liquor traffic might become necessary to the good of society; though, in recognizing this and in recognizing that the Federal Government of America were confronted by such a crisis in 1919, we do not tie ourselves to a belief in the essential wrongness of " drink " at all times and in all places.

In the two following chapters we shall attempt to demonstrate that in the thirteenth century a measure of coercive legislation against heresy was essential to the preservation of law and order. Such judgment is altogether aside from the general principle of toleration; nor is it in any way to be regarded as a justification of the methods that were employed, first by the Episcopal, and later by the Monastic Inquisition.

CHAPTER II

The Gathering of the Clouds

THE earlier mediæval heresies arose primarily from erroneous speculation about theological matters. They were initiated and received their first explicit statement in the course of debate, in the lecture-room or the refectory. They were based upon no moral protest against the conduct or constitutions of the Church. Probably the outside world heard nothing about them until long after, when the whole thing had been settled; and it is certain that, even if they had heard about them, the ordinary lay-folk would have been quite unable, in nine cases out of ten, to understand the intricacies of the discussion or to appreciate the point at issue in any but its broadest implications. Usually these early scholars who had fallen foul of ecclesiastical authority would ultimately become convinced of their errors and would seek reconciliation with the Church. They had started no movement, instituted no new school of thought. Penance was imposed by the ordinary Church discipline and the whole matter was forgotten. Thus with Godescalcus in the ninth century; and thus with Berengar of Tours in the eleventh. Each had a few followers amongst his friends, acquaintances and pupils; and William of Malmesbury tells us that Berengar on his death-bed was overwhelmed with remorse at the thought of those whom he had led astray by his erroneous theories about the Real Presence and Transubstantiation.[1] But the general

[1] William of Malmesbury's *Chronicle of the Kings of England*, p. 314 (Bohn's edition).

public knew and cared very little about such things. Heresy had not yet become a weapon wherewith to attack the Church.

It is worth while in this connection to quote a passage in which Henry Adams, with his almost miraculous insight into the mediæval mind, brings out very clearly the essentially academic character of these early heresies.   He is describing a debate in the schools between William of Champeaux and his brilliant young pupil, Abelard.

William, skilfully using as an illustration of his theme the exact nature of a little crystal pyramid which lies upon his table, is defending the Realist position.   Abelard, the Nominalist, is pointing out that William's realism, if pressed to its logical conclusion, can only end in Pantheism.

" ' (On your showing),' he concludes, ' humanity exists therefore, entire, identical, in you and me, as a subdivision of the infinite time, space, energy, or substance which is God.   I need not remind you that this is Pantheism and that, if God is the only energy, human free-will merges in God's free-will ; the Church ceases to have a reason for existence ; man cannot be held responsible for his own acts, either to the Church or to the State ; and finally, though very unwillingly, I must, in regard for my own safety, bring the subject to the attention of the Archbishop, which, as you know better than I, will lead to your seclusion or worse.'

" . . . ' Ah ' (rejoins William), ' you are quick, M. du Pallet, to turn what I offer as an analogy into an argument of heresy against my person.   You are at liberty to take that course if you choose, though I give you fair warning that it will lead you far.   But now I will ask you still another question.   This concept that you talk about— this image in the mind of man, of God, of matter—for I know not where to seek it—whether is it a reality or not ? '

" ' I hold it as, in a manner, real.'

" ' I want a categorical answer—Yes or No ! '

" ' *Distinguo*.'   (I must qualify.)

" ' I will have no qualification. A substance either is or is not. Choose ! '

" To this challenge Abelard had the choice of answering yes or of answering no, or of refusing to answer at all. He seems to have done the last; but we suppose him to have accepted the wager of battle and to have answered :

" ' Yes, then.'

" ' Good,' William rejoins ; ' now let us see how your Pantheism differs from mine. My triangle exists as a reality, or what science would call an energy, outside my mind, in God, and is impressed on my mind as it is on a mirror, like the triangle on the crystal, its energy giving form. Your triangle, you say, is also an energy, but an essence of my mind itself; you thrust it into the mind as an integral part of the mirror ; identically the same concept, energy or necessary truth which is inherent in God. Whatever subterfuge you resort to, sooner or later you have got to agree that your mind is identical with God's nature, as far as that concept is concerned. As a doctrine of the Real Presence peculiar to yourself, I can commend it to the Archbishop together with your delation of me.'

" Supposing that Abelard took the opposite course and said :

" ' No ! My concept is a mere sign.'

" ' A sign of what, in God's Name ? '

" ' A sound ! A word ! A symbol ! An echo of my own ignorance.'

" ' Nothing, then ! So truth and virtue and charity do not exist at all. You suppose yourself to exist, but you have no means of knowing God ; therefore, to you, God does not exist except as an echo of your ignorance ; and, what concerns you most, the Church does not exist except as your concept of certain individuals, whom you cannot regard as a unity, and who suppose themselves to believe in a Trinity which exists only as a sound or symbol. I will not repeat your words, M. du Pallet, outside this cloister, because the consequences to you would certainly be fatal; but it is only too clear that you are a materialist, and as such your fate must be decided by a Church Council, unless you prefer the stake by judgment of a secular court.' " [1]

In quoting only a portion of the debate, we of course lose the thread of the actual argument. But the above passage demonstrates very clearly the point which we would wish to emphasize—namely, how extremely easily a purely academic discussion might encroach, and, indeed, must encroach, over the ground of Natural Theology; and how a scholar, pursuing a particular line of thought, might suddenly find himself in the blind alley of heretical statement. We have been accustomed to hearing the whole of the mediæval period dismissed as an age of intellectual apathy and childish superstition. The truth, of course, is exactly the contrary; for the twelfth and thirteenth centuries were ages of an unsparing and almost ruthless rationalism. All the tremendous intellectual ferment of early scholasticism, the speculation and counter-speculations, the never-ending debates, the seemingly futile quibbles and subtleties, the erratic brilliance of an Abelard, the ponderous scholarship of an Alan of Lille—all these things formed part of a vast intellectual movement which received its final crown in that stupendous synthesis of religion and philosophy, the *Summa* of St. Thomas Aquinas. St. Bernard regarded Abelard as a snake in the grass, a second Arius, a plague-spot within the Church, and thundered against the madness of the schools. But his real quarrel was with the method in that madness; and it may be doubted whether the methods of St. Thomas would have impressed him any more favourably than did those of Abelard.

It is of the highest importance to note that the great mediæval heresies were, as far as the main tide of contemporary thought and learning was concerned, nothing more than insignificant side-shows.[2] Who could have

---

[1] Henry Adams, *Mont St. Michel and Chartres*, pp. 299 ff.

[2] " The philosophic ideas of such seem gathered from the flotsam and jetsam of the later antique world. . . . Such mediæval heresies present

been more strikingly indicated as a great heresiarch in embryo than Abelard, with his vast following in the schools, his brilliance and originality, his determined enemies within the Church itself? Yet though he came under grave suspicion and was even condemned by a Council, Abelard never stood apart from the stream of orthodox academic endeavour. If we look round for the men who were at that time raising the standards of revolt against the Church, we find half-crazy fanatics like Tankelm and Eon de l'Etoile, illiterate popular agitators, who went up and down the country-sides denouncing (often with justice) the corruption of the clergy and the inordinate riches of the Church. In many cases the new heresy which such men as these proposed—if, indeed, they had anything constructive to say at all—was merely a revival of some preposterous old pagan superstition, which the Fathers of the Church had encountered and refuted in the first and second centuries, some quaint survival of pagan folk-lore, which the schools of Paris would have considered too childish for discussion.

But supplying the driving-force and giving an altogether disproportionate significance to these fragments of bygone beliefs was a general spirit of grumbling discontent with the condition of things within the Church. Sometimes the denunciations of these popular preachers took the form of abuse of established ecclesiastical practice, as when they denounced symbolism in the churches as tending to idolatry. Sometimes they urged that the Sacraments were wholly inefficacious when administered by unworthy priests. Their whole line of protest was not intellectual but moral.

---

no continuous evolution like that of proper Scholasticism. . . . It has been said, to be sure, that the heresy of one generation becomes the orthodoxy of another; but this is true only of tendencies like those of Abelard, which represent the gradual expansion and clearing up of scholastic processes. For the time they may be condemned, perhaps because of the vain and contentious character of the suspected thinker; but in the end they are recognized as admissible." (H. O. Taylor, *The Mediæval Mind*, Vol. II. p. 313, note.)

" The early twelfth-century shouters," says Mr. Nickerson,[1] " began by playing lone hands, like our own Billy Sunday and his tribe. Their stormy careers left little definite trace. At most they set in motion a general criticism of the wealth and pride of the Church, in comparison with the poverty of her Founder and the humility which she taught."

It is, then, a grave error of judgment to suggest that the revival of heresy in the Middle Ages was, in any considerable degree, the outcome of the great intellectual renascence of the eleventh and twelfth centuries. The main tide of mediæval thought flowed wholly within the broad channel of orthodox Catholicity. The legacy of the Middle Ages is the legacy of the Faith ; mediæval heresy added nothing to it. The root-causes of mediæval heresy are to be found in the corruptions within the Church, not in that great awakening of the minds of men in the eleventh century. No mediæval heretic left any lasting monument of achievement, either in literature, philosophy or the arts. If one were asked to jot down a list of the twenty most distinguished men of the eleventh, twelfth and thirteenth centuries, men pre-eminent either in intelligence or in administrative ability or in artistic talents, it would be difficult to include a single heretic.

Indeed the activities of these early heretical tub-thumpers and platform orators, each setting up his little local whirlpool of heresy and revolt against the Church, have little interest for the historian, except as showing the potential popularity of anti-sacerdotal propaganda. Such men as Eon de l'Etoile and Henry of Lausanne came not to fulfil but to destroy. The very crudity of their denunciations, the essentially negative character of almost all that they had to say, made it impossible that their influence should have been other than local and ephemeral. But during the twelfth century these little streamlets of heresy began gradually to converge into two or three main currents, each of which, moving along its own course, steadily gathered momentum. It is true that the element

---

[1] H. Nickerson, *The Inquisition*, p. 42.

of more or less violent hostility to the Church was prominent in each. The Church was the hub of everything; and those who criticized her wealth, denounced the conduct of her priests and ridiculed her Sacraments were necessarily working along converging lines.[1] But the constructive philosophies which the various new sects proposed in opposition to Catholicism differed widely.

The Waldenses

Before turning to the Albigensian heresy, which was by far the most important of them all and with which we shall be primarily concerned throughout, it will be convenient briefly to note the rise and significance of the Waldensian or Vaudois heresy. The sect was founded in 1170 by a certain Peter Waldo, a rich but illiterate merchant of Lyons. Having prepared and made public a translation into the vernacular of the Gospels and several other books of the Bible, he disposed of all his property and, anticipating St. Francis of Assisi, embraced a life of complete poverty. He had no thought at this time of breaking away from the Church; he was a reformer, not a heretic. From the first he attracted a large following. He and his disciples were accustomed to preach in the streets and public places; and enormous numbers thronged to hear them. For the widespread neglect of the preaching office by the Catholic clergy lent to their discourses the added charm of novelty.[2]

[1] Perhaps this partially accounts for the way in which the different heretical sects were confused in the minds of the people and even, sometimes, of the Inquisitors. So that, in the later period, "Cathari," "Manichees" and "Albigenses" became generic terms covering all heretics.

[2] Such neglect seems to have been fairly general. See Luchaire, *Social France under Philip Augustus* (Eng. trans., A. Krehbiel), p. 52:

"A great many of the *curés*, profoundly ignorant, did not preach at all, and for a good reason. Still, as it was necessary for the people to be instructed, they imported professional preachers. There were clerics, and even laymen, who made a business of itinerant preaching. Fortunately for the incompetent *curés*, these moved from parish to parish for

Still, this kind of thing, the preaching of the Gospel by men for the most part uneducated and lacking any kind of theological training, could not long escape ecclesiastical censure. In 1179 the Archbishop of Lyons forbade the continuance of their sermons; and, since his injunctions were completely disregarded, he excommunicated Waldo and a number of his followers. Forbidden thus to preach by their own bishop, the Waldenses appealed boldly to the Lateran Council; and Alexander II restored them to the communion of the Church, insisting only that their meetings and sermons should have the sanction of the local bishop. Not until five years later, after more complaints of their conduct from the Archbishop, were they finally excommunicated by Pope Lucius III at the Council of Verona; and even as late as 1218 a sort of Waldensian Council was held without interruption at Bergamo—a fact which demonstrates the easy-going attitude of the Catholic authorities towards them.

The only instance of specific legislation against them was the savage proclamation, in 1198, of Pedro II of Aragon. He issued an edict, banishing the Waldenses and all other heretics from his dominions, and ordering that, after a certain date, all heretics found in the kingdom were to be burnt at the stake. The severity of this enactment, particularly in the threat of the capital punishment, was quite unprecedented. Of course the penalty of the stake was held out only as a threat. The King had prescribed banishment and confiscation of property. Those heretics who refused to leave the country were to be punished, not as heretics, but on the purely general

---

a pecuniary consideration. They even gave rise to an occupation of a peculiar character; they formed ' preaching companies,' which contracted by the year for all the sermons of the diocese, or of a group of parishes, and furnished preachers to those who required them. There is proof that this strange organization actually operated in Normandy.

" The Church was alarmed. . . . She feared, and not without reason, that these strangers would spread the seed of false doctrine amongst the people. . . . The Council of Paris in 1212 forbade all sermons by strangers, unless they were authorized by the bishop of the diocese."

principle that they had wilfully disobeyed a royal proclamation. The thing was not a mere equivocation. Not long after we find the lighthearted sovereign arrayed in battle on the side of the heretics against De Montfort's crusaders. Mr. Nickerson is probably right in suggesting that, had the Waldenses been the only heretics in the field, there would have been no Albigensian Crusade and, perhaps, no Inquisition.

Cut off finally from the unity of the Church, the Waldenses adopted an anti-Catholic tone as violent as that of any other sect. From having claimed the right to exercise the preaching office of the clergy, they passed to a sweeping denial of the whole idea of ordination, declaring that every " good man " had the power of hearing confessions and granting absolution. They rejected the majority of the Sacraments, attaching to those, such as baptism, which they preserved a completely new meaning. They repudiated belief in Purgatory, in miracles, in the invocation of Saints, in fasts and abstinences. Finally they maintained the duty of literal truth-telling under all circumstances and they rigidly opposed the taking of oaths in any form whatever. In a society which practically reposed upon oaths of allegiance, feudal and ecclesiastical, this kind of thing savoured of anarchy. And as Mr. Nickerson neatly puts it:

" To forbid even ' white lies ' is harmless enough, although, if pushed to an extreme, it partakes of the character of impossibilism and eccentricity, which the Catholic Church has always avoided." [1]

We do not possess much information about their actual religious ceremonies. But, according to Bernard Gui, their worship consisted chiefly of readings from the Scriptures and other sacred writings, of sermons and of recitations of the Lord's Prayer, which they would often repeat eighty or a hundred times on end.[2]

Like most of the contemporary heretical sects, the

[1] *Op. cit.*, p. 43.
[2] See also Tanon, *Histoire des Tribunaux de l'Inquisition en France*, pp. 93 ff.

Waldenses were often accused by their enemies of gross sexual immorality amongst themselves. But such stories need not be taken very seriously. In general it would seem that they were distinguished by the simple piety of their lives and their strict adherence to the rules of poverty which they had set up for themselves. An inquisitor went so far as to say that they were to be recognized—

" by their customs and speech, for they are modest and well-regulated. They take no pride in their garments, which are neither costly nor vile. They do not engage in trade, to avoid lies and oaths and frauds, but live by their labours as mechanics—their teachers are cobblers. They do not accumulate wealth, but are content with necessaries. They are chaste and temperate in meat and drink. They do not frequent taverns or dances or other vanities. They restrain themselves from anger. They are always at work; they teach and learn, and consequently pray but little. They are to be known by their modesty and precision of speech, avoiding scurrility and detraction, light words and lies and oaths." [1]

Of course it would be easy to exaggerate the contrast between the simple virtues of a new heretical sect, filled with zeal and conscious of a great mission of reform, and the general degradation of the Catholic priesthood as a whole. The constant fulminations of the Pontiffs show that simony was widespread and that there was an immense amount of immorality amongst the priests. Still it is necessary to take the denunciations of professedly hostile critics, and even of zealous reformers like St. Bernard, with a pinch of salt. There was still much of the beauty of holiness in a Church which could produce St. Norbert, St. Thomas of Canterbury, St. Francis, St. Dominic, St. Anselm, St. Elizabeth of Hungary and St. Clare. There was plenty of recreative energy, of vigorous reforming activity in a Church which could give birth to the Cistercians, the Premonstratensian Canons

[1] A. S. Turberville, *Mediæval Heresy and the Inquisition*, p. 21.

and the Austin Friars.   Even so there is probably much
truth in Mr. Turberville's suggestion that—

" It is, perhaps, not too much to say that the distinctive
dangerousness of the (Waldenses) lay in the fact of such
excellence, such fruits of the spirit being brought forth
among a sect which arrogated to itself apostolic functions
without lawful authority." [1]

Indeed the most interesting point in connection with
the Waldenses is the question as to why they became
heretics at all.   It is very striking to notice that Peter
Waldo, with his voluntary assumption of poverty and his
zealous revival of popular preaching, anticipated the
distinctive reforms both of the Franciscan and the
Dominican Orders ; and that for fourteen years he and
his followers remained in full communion with the
Church, their vows of poverty receiving Papal benediction
at the Lateran Council of 1179, and the continuance of
their preaching activities being sanctioned with the very
natural reservation that they should recognize the authority
of their bishop.   Yet within five years of this time they
were formally excommunicated by the Pope ; in 1198
we find Pedro of Aragon threatening them with the
stake ; and in 1212 a number of them were burnt alive
at Strasburg by an infuriated populace.   The Poor Men
of Lyons became outcasts upon the face of the earth :
the Poor Men of Assisi and the Watch dogs of the Lord
became the mightiest reforming forces in Christendom.

The essential point of divergence lay, we fancy, in the
fact that St. Francis knew how to obey and that Waldo
did not.   St. Francis founded his Order on the triple
vow of poverty, chastity and obedience ; Waldo omitted
the latter, declaring, like many who were to come after
him, that his conscience was his guide and that he pre-
ferred to follow God rather than man.   Implicit in such
doctrine was, of course, a repudiation of the whole Catholic
tradition, the whole idea of the Church as the Divinely
appointed Guardian of the Faith, the whole teaching of
the Apostolic succession.   From whom, demanded

---

[1] A. S. Turberville, *Mediæval Heresy and the Inquisition*, p. 22.

Moneta, did the Poor Men of Lyons receive their Orders ?
From Waldo himself ?   And who had ordained Waldo ?
No one.   And yet Waldo " glorified himself to be a
bishop; in consequence he was an Antichrist, against
Christ and His Church." [1]   Waldo, says another
chronicler, Richard of Cluny, was " proud in his own con-
ceit and, possessing a little learning, assumed to himself
and usurped the office of the Apostles." [2]

The force of such reasoning as this may or may not
appeal to the reader.   Yet, if he is to understand the
question of mediæval heresy and the actions of those who
laboured to suppress it, he must try to realize that in the
mediæval environment the logic of Moneta and Richard
would seem quite impregnable.   Granted that there were
many and grave abuses within the Church, what could
justify a man in confusing the abuse with the system
itself ?   You will find no more violent anti-clericalist than
St. Bernard, if the term implies nothing more than a
denouncer of clerical abuses.   But St. Bernard treated
such things always as abuses, as stains upon the ineffable
dignity of the priestly vocation.   Waldo simply swept
the whole idea of priesthood aside.   St. Bernard was
the reformer, Waldo the schismatic.

The Albigensian Heresy

The heresy which was later to become known as the
Albigensian heresy (from the fact that the town of Albi in
Languedoc was one of its earliest strongholds) began to
filter into Europe from the Eastern Empire about the
beginning of the eleventh century.   Much controversy
has raged round the question of the actual origin of the
sect, some historians having maintained that it was in a
direct line of descent from the Manichees of the pagan
Empire, others that it was a dualist sect, though distinct
from that of the original Manichees.   For our purpose
it is sufficient to note that dualism was the dominant note

---

[1] Turberville, *op. cit.*, p. 19.
[2] *Ibid.*, p. 19.   See also H. O. Taylor, *op. cit.*, Vol. I. p. 381, note.

of its philosophy and that almost all the contemporary writers regarded it purely and simply as a revival of Manicheeism. Roger of Chalons and Abbot Guibert of Nogent in the eleventh century, the Council of Rheims in 1157, Moneta of Cremona, Luke of Tuy, Stephen of Bourbon and Innocent III in the thirteenth, and Bernard Gui in the fourteenth centuries refer to the Albigensian heretics simply as modern Manichees.[1] And St. Thomas Aquinas, dining one evening at the court of good King Louis, profited by a lull in the conversation to announce solemnly to the assembled company, " I have a conclusive argument against the Manichees—*conclusum est contra Manichæos.*" Perhaps, as Henry Adams observes, the dinner-table was not much more used then than now to abrupt interjections of theology into the talk about hunting and hounds. But at any rate there was no need for anybody to ask the great Doctor who the Manichees might be.

The Manichee heresy was, of course, an old enemy of the Church. Eusebius mentions its existence in his history; in its furrows St. Augustine had sown some of his spiritual wild oats; and even the Arian historian Philostorgius speaks emphatically about " the mad heresy of the Manichees." [2] The Emperor Justinian legislated against them; and in 556 a number of Manichees were stoned to death by the people of Ravenna. To say the least of it, they were never popular, either under the pagan or Christian dominion.

First and foremost they asserted this principle of dualism—of a dual universe created jointly by two gods, the one good and the other evil. Matter was evil and spirit good; and all existence took the form of a conflict between these two principles. There was some difference

---

[1] *Practica Inquisitionis*, pp. 131 ff. (British Museum, Egerton MSS. No. 1897), where a full account is given of their practices and beliefs. The most easily accessible edition of Guibert's *Autobiography* is in the Broadway translations.

[2] Eusebius, *H.E.*, vii. 31. Philostorgius, *H.E.*, iii. 16, 17. Socrates has an account of Manes, the founder of the sect (*H.E.*, i. 22).

THE "PRACTICA INQUISITIONIS" OF BERNARD GUI.

A page of the British Museum MS., describing the
beliefs of the Albigensian heretics.

of opinion amongst them as to whether the good and the evil deities were equally powerful. It was urged by some that God had two sons, Jesus and Satan; and that the latter, revolting against parental authority, was turned out of heaven and proceeded to create a material world with Adam and Eve as its first inhabitants. Others regarded Satan merely as a fallen angel, who had persuaded two other angels—Adam and Eve—to share his exile. In order the better to secure their allegiance to him, he had lighted upon the idea of awakening the carnal appetite, which is original sin, and which had proved the chief source of his continued power.

From this dualistic conception arose several important considerations. Believing all material creation to be essentially evil, they found it unthinkable that our Lord should have assumed a human body during His earthly life. On the other hand, they regarded Him as inferior to God Himself and merely the highest of the Angels. Denying His Divinity, they also denied His humanity. It followed immediately that His body could not be injured, least of all killed by any human process. Therefore there could have been no Crucifixion and, hence, no Resurrection. The whole story of the Passion and the Crucifixion was a delusion.

They said that the Blessed Virgin possessed the same form of celestial body as Christ Himself. They said that she was only apparently a woman, but was actually sexless.

So much for the theological teachings of the sect, which, like those of most heretical bodies, were chiefly negative. For the Catholic Church herself they professed the heartiest contempt and hatred. The Popes, they declared, were the successors of Constantine, not of St. Peter, who had never been near Rome in his life. The Church was the Scarlet Woman of the Apocalypse, " drunk with the blood of the Saints and with the blood of the martyrs of Jesus." The Sacraments were childish impostures. Transubstantiation was a mad blasphemy, for the Church dared to assert that Christ Himself could be present under the forms of material bread and wine, the

creations of the evil spirit.   The Catholics dared to claim
that they received the Body of Christ in the Sacrament,
as though Christ could possibly enter a man's stomach.

The new heretics were particularly emphatic in their
contempt for all forms of symbolism and for the veneration
of relics, especially of the Cross.   Admitting, for the
sake of argument, that there had been some sort of
Crucifixion, by which the celestial body of Christ had
been tortured, though not, of course, killed, they maintained that the Cross itself should be treated with loathing
as a mere piece of wood, upon which Christ had been made
to suffer.   The Cross should not be reverenced, but
despised and insulted.   " I would gladly," said one of
their writers, " hew the cross to pieces with an axe, and
throw it into the fire to make the pot boil." [1]

In many respects the tenets of the neo-Manicheeans
resembled those of the great modern dualist heresy called
Christian Science.   But the former possessed, as the
latter do not seem to possess, the characteristic genius of
the Middle Ages for following things to their logical
conclusions.   They had a kind of priesthood known as
the " Perfect " and a ceremony called the " Consolamentum " for the spiritual nourishment of their lay-folk, the
" Believers."   Since matter was inherently evil, all sexual
relations were clearly the blackest of sins.   The " Perfect " were forbidden to eat meats, eggs, cheese or
anything that was the result of sexual procreation.   (Fish
was excluded from the ban, since it was thought that fish
were not bi-sexual !)   They believed that those who died
without the " Consolamentum " might pass either to
eternal punishment or to the habitation of the body of an
animal.   Hence, since the body of an animal might be
the dwelling-place of a human soul, they refused under all
circumstances to take animal life—a feature of their beliefs
which often led to their exposure.   At Goslar, for

[1] N. Eymericus, *Directorium* (Venice, 1607), pp. 273, 274, 277, 278 ;
B. Guidonis, *Practica Inquisitionis* (Paris, 1886), pp. 236 ff.   See also
Turberville, *op. cit.*, pp. 24 ff.   E. Vacandard, *The Inquisition* (Eng.
trans. Bertrand Conway), pp. 55 ff.

instance, a number of them were condemned for having refused to kill and eat a chicken—a clear indication in the minds of the Catholics that they were Manichees.

Clearly, however, if it was wrong under all circumstances to kill an animal, it was an even greater crime to kill a human being. All killing, they said, was murder. And the man who strangled his grandmother to rob her of her last sixpence was not a greater criminal than the soldier fighting in battle against his country's enemies. They denied that the State had the right to inflict capital punishment under any circumstances whatever; and when a prominent heretic was elected consul of Toulouse, a certain Peter Garsias wrote to remind him that " it is not God's will that human justice condemn anybody to death." Some of the extremists went even further than this, denying the State's right to punish at all. Vacandard cites the *Summa contra hereticos*, which declares that " all the Catharan sects taught that the public prosecution of crime was unjust and that no one had the right to administer justice."

Proceeding logically upon the dualistic principle, they maintained that the procreation of children was the work of the devil. A woman with child was a woman possessed of an evil spirit; and if she died in this state of impurity, she could not possibly be saved from eternal damnation. The married state was a perpetual state of sin, worse than adultery or fornication, since the married felt no shame. So, too, anything which could interrupt the natural processes of birth was commendable; even incest and perversion were preferable to marriage, since the great sin of bringing children into the world was thereby avoided. Nobody, therefore, could receive the " Consolamentum " who had not first renounced all marital relations. And for the " Perfect," that is, those who had received the " Consolamentum," it was considered a sin even to touch a woman. " If a woman touches you," said one of their oracles, Pierre Autier, " you must fast three days on bread and water; if you touch a woman, you must fast nine days on the same diet."

I hasten to add that the Albigensian heretics loudly proclaimed themselves the true Church of Christ, without which no man could be saved. The Pope was Anti-christ; and the Catholic Church was the whore of Babylon.

Finally, there was their genial ceremony known as the " Endura." The " Consolamentum," besides being a sort of caricature of the Church's Sacrament of Extreme Unction, was also the standard form of initiation into the number of the " Perfect." You generally received it upon your death-bed and were thereby guaranteed eternal beatitude, whatever might have been the obliquity of your past life. Thus any sick person who had received the " Consolamentum " was clearly running a grave risk of damnation if he showed signs of recovery. Under such circumstances the " Perfect " would forbid the family to feed the patient or would even remove him to their own house, where, as Mr. Nickerson puts it, they might starve him to death in peace. All this was done, of course, for the salvation of the patient's soul, since it was feared that, in the event of recovery, he would be almost certain to lapse from the rigid asceticism demanded of the " Perfect," to whose number he had, in virtue of the " Consolamentum," automatically become admitted. Nor was the practice by any means exceptional. It has been maintained, indeed, that the " Endura " put to death more victims in Languedoc than the stake or the Inquisition. One of the " Perfect " named Raymond Belhot, after administering the " Consolamentum " to a sick girl, ordered that under no circumstances was any food to be given to her. He returned frequently to see that his instructions were being obeyed, and the girl died in a few days. Many submitted to the " Endura " quite voluntarily. A woman named Montaliva starved herself to death in six weeks; a woman of Toulouse, after several unsuccessful attempts to consummate it by blood-letting and taking of poison, killed herself by swallowing pounded glass; a certain Guillaume Sabatier starved himself to death in seven weeks.[1]

[1] See *Liber Sententiarum Inquisitionis Tolosanae* (Ed. P. A. Limborch, Amsterdam, 1692), pp. 104, 143, 190, etc.

Such was the extraordinary agglomeration of pagan dualism, distorted Gospel teaching and nauseously anti-social ethics which, proclaiming itself a return to the pure Christianity of the early Church, entered Europe through Bulgaria and Lombardy, spread thence all over Northern Italy, Languedoc and Aragon, and then swept northward through France, Belgium and Germany to the shores of the Baltic. It will be convenient to defer until the next chapter an examination of the circumstances under which the Albigensian heresy grew to power in Languedoc, its first and greatest stronghold. For the present we may briefly discuss its progress in the northern kingdoms, where, in striking contrast to those of the south, its appearance was everywhere greeted by savage popular hostility.

Spread of the Heresy in the North

In 1018 we hear of the Albigenses at Toulouse, in 1022 at Orleans, in 1025 at Cambrai and Liège, in 1045 at Chalons; and by the middle of the century the heresy had penetrated as far as Goslar in North Germany. When their presence at Orleans first became known, King Robert the Pious hastily summoned a council to decide what should be done. So great was the fury of the common people that the Queen herself was stationed at the door of the church where the heretics were being tried, to save them from being dragged into the streets and lynched. Thirteen of them, including ten resident canons of the collegiate Church of the Holy Cross, were condemned to be burnt alive; and as they came out of the church, the Queen, recognizing amongst them a priest who had been her confessor, sprang forward and jabbed him in the face with a stick, putting out an eye. They were then bundled ignominiously through the streets amidst the curses and imprecations of the people. Outside the walls of the city fires were started and they were all burnt alive.

This outburst of violence is of interest as being the first

recorded instance in European history proper of the burning of heretics. The punishment by the stake was a
complete innovation. It was decreed by no law, for as
yet the crime of heresy did not exist in the eyes of the law.
We have simply the summoning of a sort of extraordinary
general meeting by the King, at which the clergy seem
simply to have testified to the existence of heresy amongst
them; and the subsequent decision, endorsed by all
present, that death at the stake was the only appropriate
punishment for these pernicious wretches.

If it is asked why burning was specially chosen as a
means of death, we can only reply with vague suggestions.
M. Julien Havet has noted that—

" In the early Middle Ages the penalty of the stake
was an ordinary method of inflicting capital punishment,
perhaps, even, the most usual after hanging. . . . Burning, moreover . . . was the ordinary punishment for
poisoners, sorcerers and witches, and it might have
seemed obvious to liken heresy to witchcraft or poisoning.
Finally, the stake, more destructive than the gallows, more
cruel, more theatrical, might have appeared more likely
to awaken a salutary terror in the hearts of the condemned,
who had the choice either of abjuration or of punishment."[1]

Moreover, it seems to be in the nature of men that,
when they are roused to the limits of fury and hatred
against their fellows, their minds turn always to the lurid
glare of the flames and the horrors of death by burning.
Negroes in America are sometimes hanged by the mobs,
just as heretics in the Middle Ages were sometimes
hanged. But much more often it is a matter of stake,
faggots, old furniture and a gallon of kerosene.

In 1039, in spite of the protests of the Archbishop
of Milan, the civil magistrates of that city arrested a
number of heretics. They were invited to reverence the
cross held before them or to be sent to the stake. A few
recanted, but the majority, covering their faces with their
hands, cast themselves into the flames.

[1] Julien Havet, " L'hérésie et le bras séculier au moyen-age " in
Œuvres, Vol. II. pp. 130, 131 (author's trans.).

In 1051 the presence of Albigensian heretics was discovered at Goslar. They were convicted of belonging to the sect by their refusal to eat chickens, which were given them by the authorities. The Emperor Henry III himself convened a Council and, expressly stipulating that the verdict was given " with the consent of all, in order that the leprosy of heresy may be prevented from spreading and from contaminating a greater number of persons," ordered that they should be hanged. Here again we note the absence of legal precedent for the sentence. It was merely a measure of public safety, ratified, since it was an innovation upon the laws of the Empire, by the consent of people and nobles.

In 1076 a heretic of Cambrai was arrested and brought before an assembly composed of the bishops and the leading clergy of the diocese. They were unable to reach any decision in the matter. But, as he left the Council, the unfortunate man was seized upon by the people and some of the minor clergy, and nailed up in some sort of wooden chest, which was then set on fire.

At Soissons in 1114 the bishop arrested and imprisoned several heretics, until he should be able to decide what to do with them. During his absence at Beauvais the populace burst into the prison, dragged forth the captives and burnt them all. In 1144 at Liège there was a furious explosion of popular wrath against them, and the bishop had the greatest difficulty in preventing a regular holocaust; but many perished in spite of his efforts. Instances of similar excesses could be multiplied. But the important point to be noted is that, in all these cases, covering a period of more than a century, the Church either held aloof or plainly manifested her disapproval. Of course you find persecuting bishops like Theodouin of Liège and, later, Hugh of Auxerre. But these men were exceptions. Pope Gregory VII protested against the excesses at Cambrai in 1076 and ordered that those Catholics who had taken part should be excommunicated. At this time the ecclesiastical authority recognized no precedent for seeking the aid

of the secular power in combating heresy. Vaso, Bishop
of Liège, declared that the employment of the civil
authority against the Manichees was contrary to the
spirit of the Gospels and the traditional precepts of the
Church. The only punishment that should be inflicted
upon them, he said, was excommunication. Such men as
Peter Cantor and St. Bernard wrote in the same strain.

In 1145 the half-witted fanatic, Eon de l'Etoile, began
his crazy agitations in the diocese of St. Malo. Proclaiming himself the Son of God, he seems to have made
a number of converts amongst the local peasants, who,
not content with denying the Faith, began to loot churches
and break into monasteries. Eon himself, recognized
to be insane, was placed in the kindly hands of Abbot
Suger of St. Denis, and ended his life in a monastery.
But his followers were hunted down by the people, and
several perished at the stake.

Probably, even in St. Bernard's time, the common
people as a whole made little mental distinction between
the various brands of heresy that were appearing amongst
them. To them heresy was primarily attack upon the
Church, the centre of organized charity, of education and
even of administration. Deny the Church's right to
sanction oaths and you struck at the whole feudal system.
Repudiate her Sacraments and, since marriage was a
Sacrament, unaccompanied by any civil ceremony, you
made marriage identical with concubinage. Moreover,
was not the Church the one gateway of salvation, the
guardian of the true Faith of Christ, once and for all time
delivered to the Saints ?

Even so the main tenets of the new Albigensian heresy
must have been familiar to most. Horrible stories were
told of their gross immorality—stories of closed doors,
extinguished lights and hideous orgies of lust and
promiscuity. And whilst it would be uncritical to accept
all such stories on their face value, it would be absurd to
reject them all as the malicious fabrications of enemies.
As Mr. Turberville reminds us :

" The critic's objection, ' what abomination may not

one expect of those who hold incest no worse a crime than marriage ? ' is pertinent and sound." [1]

Indeed it is difficult to exaggerate the horror and disgust which the doctrines of the new heresy must have excited in the minds of the mediæval peoples—particularly in those districts where the Church was still pure and vigorous. Repulsive as it was in its essence, the Albigensian heresy was not merely anti-Christian ; it was flatly anti-social. We may well shudder at the ferocity of King Robert the Pious, and of the mobs at Cambrai and Soissons. But, if one were to give free rein to one's imagination, one would find difficulty in concocting a system of philosophy and ethics which could be better calculated to excite the almost frantic horror of the mediæval mind than the actual thing which was called Albigensianism. We may shudder, I say, at these local and occasional excesses during the eleventh and twelfth centuries. But need we be very surprised ? Far more important and far more difficult to answer is the question as to why the heresy spread at all—why so plainly unnatural and revolting a philosophy should have engaged the serious attention of anybody.

Reasons for the Spread of the Heresy

In the first place it would seem that asceticism, however wild and misdirected, has always exercised a great fascination over the minds of men. To-day in America we may note the rancid Puritanism which has directed and consummated the Prohibition movement, and has already made the sale of cigarettes illegal in certain States of the Union. In the fourth and fifth centuries there was always a tendency amongst the people to venerate those anchorites whose mortifications and vigils were most tremendous and sustained, to a greater degree than those whose piety was most serene and well-ordered. Even amongst the early monks themselves we find traces of the same spirit—instances of actual rivalry in the devising

[1] *Op. cit.*, p. 31.

of new fasts and austerities; and this by men wholly untainted by fanaticism, great Saints who never regarded such austerities as other than means to an end.[1] The latter feature, leading, as it must often have done, to grave abuses, is not discernible in the twelfth century. But it is certain that the austerities of such men as St. Bernard made a tremendous impression upon the people and added in no small degree to the prestige which the monastic reformers enjoyed. Lea tells a story of how St. Bernard,

"After preaching to an immense assemblage . . . mounted his horse to depart; and a hardened heretic, thinking to confuse him, said, ' My Lord Abbot, our heretic of whom you think so ill has not a horse so fat and spirited as yours.' ' Friend,' replied the Saint, ' I deny it not. The horse eats and grows fat for itself, for it is but a brute and by nature given to its appetites, whereby it offends not God. But before the judgment-seat of God I and your master will not be judged by horses' necks, but each by his own neck. Now, then, look at my neck and see if it is fatter than your master's and if you can justly reproach me.' Then he threw down his cowl and displayed his neck, long, thin, and wasted by macerations and austerities, to the confusion of the misbelievers." [2]

It is for us, perhaps, a little difficult to repress a smile as we visualize the scene. But we may be perfectly certain that none of those present—heretic or orthodox— saw anything the least bit amusing in St. Bernard's retort. It is not an exaggeration to say that much of St. Bernard's extraordinary influence over the men and affairs of his time [3] was ascribable to the dominantly ascetic character

[1] Thus St. Macarius of Alexandria, " having heard that the monks of Tabennisi all through Lent ate only food that had not been near a fire, decided for seven years to eat nothing that had been through a fire; and except for raw vegetables and moistened pulse, he tasted nothing." (Palladius, *The Lausiac History*, Cap. XVIII.)

[2] H. C. Lea, *A History of the Inquisition in the Middle Ages*, Vol. I. p. 71.

[3] Henry Osborn Taylor observes justly that " St. Bernard . . . for a

of his whole life. We find this note of sternness and austerity in every reforming and every heretical movement throughout the period. It must be remembered that, at the time of which we have been writing, the Poor Men of Lyons had not yet appeared upon the scene, whilst St. Francis of Assisi was yet unborn. It is not, therefore, surprising that the rigid asceticism of the Albigensian " Perfect " should itself have exercised a real attraction towards heresy and should, in the early days at any rate, have constituted a genuinely high moral appeal. Were not the bishops to be seen riding about in luxury and magnificence ? Were not the monasteries rolling in riches, and were not the parish priests distinguished often by the easy-going indolence of their lives ? " To-day," thundered St. Bernard, " foul rottenness crawls through the whole body of the Church." The people listened to him and thronged to hear his words. But when these others arose, preaching that the Catholic Church was not only utterly corrupt but an imposture and a usurpation, challenging St. Bernard himself in their lofty contempt for the things of this world, was it not natural that many should have listened, should have wavered and should have followed ?

To an altogether different type of mind the Albigensian heresy made an altogether different kind of appeal. I refer to its Epicureanism. Provided that the " Believer " received the " Consolamentum " upon his deathbed he had nothing to fear, for he was automatically promised eternal beatitude thereby. Therefore, during his lifetime he was at liberty to do exactly as he pleased, to ignore all the prescribed rules of conduct, to fight, accumulate riches and to eat what he liked. Such a philosophy was simply a *reductio ad absurdum* of the Catholic attitude towards death-bed repentances. It was a direct invitation to hypocrisy. In short, whilst en-

---

quarter of a century swayed Christendom as never holy men before or after him. An adequate account of his career would embrace the entire history of the first half of the twelfth century." (*The Mediæval Mind*, Vol. I. p. 408.)

joining so rigid an austerity upon the "Perfect," the Albigensian heresy practically banished the moral code from the life of the "Believer." And a philosophy which may be twisted into providing an apology for vice will find adherents in any age.

But that particular aspect of their teaching which embraced the "Endura" and which commended and sought to accelerate suicide presents a more difficult problem. Perhaps a sort of half-answer is to be found in the absolutely logical character of the mediæval mind. Henry Adams notes that, in the Middle Ages, " words had fixed values like numbers ; and syllogisms were hewn stones that needed only to be set in place in order to reach any height or to support any weight." [1] The great scholars of the Middle Ages were amongst the most exact thinkers who have ever lived ; and possessed, to a degree that is almost inconceivable in an age like our own, of loose thinking and slapdash philosophy, the power of following their convictions to their logical conclusions. Some of the earliest followers of St. Francis, in their enthusiasm for a life of poverty and a community of goods, rushed to the extreme of denouncing the whole idea of property. And perhaps, likewise, once you had convinced a man of the inherent evil of matter, you would find him prepared to go to almost any lengths in manifesting his hatred and contempt for it.

The Catholic Church has never had any great affection for extremes and has always recognized that even logical extremes are often extremely dangerous things. The same fact was bound to be recognized by the Albigensian heretics. You could not expect the vigorous and sustained propagation of a sect which aimed explicitly at the destruction of the race—not, that is, if you upheld its teachings in all sincerity. You could not declare that the procreation of children was the grossest of sins, and that suicide was the highest of the virtues, and then insist that you had a message for all generations of men.

" The consequence was," as Mr. Turberville well puts

[1] *Mont St. Michel and Chartres*, p. 290.

it, " —and herein lies the greatest condemnation of the sect—that it went on proclaiming an impracticable ideal, while admitting that it was impracticable; sanctioning a compromise, itself antithetical to its essential dogma, whereby alone the heresy was able to continue at all." [1]

The whole thing, in fact, was a monstrosity. In its completeness it could make no sort of real appeal to human nature. It was essentially diseased, unwholesome, antisocial. It could only continue by encouraging hypocrisy. It was based upon a quibble. If, finally, we must attempt some sort of summary for the reasons of its propagation, we should suggest that there were three. First, this more or less overt insincerity, turning a blind eye to contradictions necessarily inherent in the system. Second, its ascetic appeal, an exaggerated spurning of the things of the world, a reaching-out into the realms of pure spirit. Third—and perhaps most powerful of all—its open disgust for the riches and corruptions within the Catholic Church and its promise of a renewed spiritual life within the supposed true Church of Christ.

Of course the heresy never obtained a real hold in the north. In 1139 Innocent II, presiding over the Second General Council of the Lateran, established a significant precedent by calling upon the secular princes to aid in the suppression of heresy; and five Papal Councils within sixty years declared the heretics excommunicate. In 1163 the Council of Tours decreed that " if these wretches are captured, the secular princes are to imprison them and confiscate their property." But all these pronouncements and exhortations were addressed primarily to the powerful noblemen of the southern kingdoms, of Aragon, Languedoc and Lombardy, where the heresy was almost wholly unopposed.

In the north it was different. You found there the little local and sporadic outbursts of popular fury, accompanied by lynchings and burnings. More important, you found the practice of putting heretics to death by burning at the stake gradually assuming the force of an

[1] *Op. cit.*, p. 30.

established custom.   It is certain that the great bulk of
public opinion was strongly and even ruthlessly anti-
heretical.   Still there was, as yet, nothing to excite the
alarm of the secular rulers.   These heretics were doubtless a great nuisance, but heresy, after all, was the Church's
affair, not theirs.   And they saw nothing in the organization or numbers of the heretics to justify them in taking
measures to safeguard the commonweal.   For nearly
two hundred years following the executions at Orleans
no northern State made any official anti-heretical gesture
—with one exception.   That exception, curiously enough,
was England.

It appears that in 1166 a number of Albigensian
heretics landed in England from Germany and at once
began vigorous proselytizing.   They had short shrift.
Henry II, hearing of their presence, immediately summoned them to appear before a Council at Oxford.   They
were convicted of heresy and the King ordered that they
should be branded with a hot iron, publicly beaten and
driven out of the city ; and that no citizen was to harbour
them or give them any assistance.   Terrified by the
threat, their only convert, a woman, made full abjuration.
But the rest submitted to the punishment, and, without
an exception, all perished of cold and starvation in the
country-sides.   It was the first, as it was to be the last,
appearance of the heresy in England.   Later in the same
year the Assizes of Clarendon enacted that anyone who
should presume to shelter heretics should have his house
destroyed.[1]   England was the first European country
to legislate against heresy.

[1] " The Lord King forbids, moreover, that anyone in all England
receive in his land, or his soc, or the home under him, any one of that
sect of renegades who were excommunicated and branded at Oxford.
And if anyone receive them, he himself shall be at the mercy of the Lord
King ; and the house in which they have been shall be carried without the
town and burnt." (" Assize of Clarendon," stat. 21, in *Ideas that have
influenced Civilization*, Vol. IV. p. 400.)

CHAPTER III

THE scene changes to the sunny lands of Southern France; and the change is a vivid and startling one. The difference is not only in the setting, but in the very atmosphere. In some degree it persists down to the present day. Will not the northern Frenchman still tell you that the men of the *midi* are noisy, ostentatious and superficial? And do not the northern regiments still affect a certain contempt for the fighting abilities of the southern? Yet Marshal Foch comes from the French Pyrenees; from Marseilles came the battle-song of the Revolution; and the great Provençal name of De Castelnau has flashed in the pages of French history from the days of Count Raymond VI of Toulouse down to the battle of the Marne in our own time. The contrast is one of temperament, of *timbre*. And, as so often happens, men come to emphasize such contrasts by dwelling upon particular distinctions, which they themselves probably recognize as superficial and even inexact, but which enshrine a consciousness of real and deeper divergences of character. Thus we have our own quaint theories that the Scotch have no sense of humour and the Irish no sense of logic. Nobody seriously believes these things. Yet they serve as useful generalizations covering certain distinctive characteristics that are far more difficult of analysis.

So it is in the case of Languedoc and the French " meridional." North and south of the Cevennes a real difference of social atmosphere is apparent even to the most casual traveller; and at the time of which we write it was far more clearly marked, far more readily recognized alike by northerner and southerner. The French nation, as we understand the term, was not even a theory until the days of Philip the Fair, and not even the most shadowy of realities until after the Hundred Years' War.

The Roman Tradition in Languedoc

Long before the great days of the Empire, Languedoc had its cities, its foreign trade, its vigorous urban administration—a city civilization rather like that of Asia Minor in St. Paul's time. Narbonne was prosperous many years before the coming of Julius Cæsar. The great harbour of Marseilles was thronged with vessels from Constantinople, Carthage and the Near East when the city was still a colony of the Republic ; and this Mediterranean trade was never wholly interrupted, even during the long nightmare of the Dark Ages. Marseilles has always been one of the most cosmopolitan cities in the world. Under the Republic it had a large Greek population, particularly amongst the shopkeeping class. Yet it was first and last a Roman town. No district in Europe has so thoroughly maintained the impress of Rome and of the Imperial system as this coastal strip of country between the Rhone delta and the Pyrenees. The great triumphal arches, the bridges and aqueducts, the circuses, the roads and even the paving-stones of the Roman Empire are here more thickly scattered even than in Italy itself.

By the time of the First Crusade, Aquitaine and Languedoc had again become, as in Roman times, the most brilliant and in some ways the most cultured parts of Europe. Of all countries they had been least affected by the restless migrations and infiltrations of the fourth and fifth centuries. The Teutonist historians of the last century were accustomed to maintain that the traditional respect for women, which is such a radical and distinctive feature of European civilization, was brought into Christendom by the bands of barbarians who raided and plundered and in many cases encroached permanently over the frontiers of the old Empire. The argument cannot be sustained. Chivalry, romance, courtesy do not appear for nearly seven centuries after the collapse of the central government; and, as Mr. Belloc has noted, they appear in precisely those districts which had been least affected by the passage of these barbarians.[1] What is more important still—we shall return to this point in a moment —is the fact that they appear in precisely those districts which had been most affected by the thought and manners of Islam.

The Roman Empire perished from within, losing under the growing corruption and ineffectiveness of her colonial administration that marvellous power of assimilation upon which her triumphs had been built. Alaric was a mutinous Roman general, not an invading German War-lord. In Languedoc the Imperial tradition survived in remarkable completeness—effete and inoperative, it is true, a mere ghost of its former self, yet none the less essentially Roman. Even in the thirteenth century the chief magistrates of Toulouse were called consuls; and the town was dominated by its municipal building, the Capitol, rather than by its churches, which, as Mr. Nickerson notes, " are fitted in like after-thoughts in the town plan."

Contact with the Eastern Empire

Through their Mediterranean trade with Constantinople and the Syrian ports, and thence with the great emporia of Baghdad and Damascus, the southern noblemen were introduced to the glittering luxuries of Byzantine and Oriental civilization. We have only to read between the lines of the angry and bewildered letter, which Bishop Luitprand of Cremona addressed to the Emperor Otto II, describing his humiliating diplomatic mission to Constantinople in 968—we have only, I say, to read between the lines of this remarkable epistle to realize something of the magnificence of the tenth-century Byzantine capital. Here was the Roman Empire

[1] See also A. L. Guerard, *French Civilisation*, p. 234, where the same point is developed.

in all its pristine splendour, with the great public baths
of old time, with its schools and universities, its riches
and its great military organization which stood as an
impregnable barrier against Islam for seven centuries.
For the pugnacious, uneducated tribes of Western Europe
the citizens of this great Empire professed the heartiest
contempt. To this day the Orthodox Patriarch of Jerusalem styles himself the Roman Patriarch, whilst the
Catholic Patriarch in communion with Rome is referred
to as the Latin Patriarch. The Roman Empire was not
overthrown by Alaric and Radagasius. It had moved east
nearly a century previously and was to remain guarding
the doorway of Europe for more than a thousand years.

Nothing surprised the Crusaders of Innocent III's
time so much as the incredible splendour and spaciousness
of all that they saw in the city which they had sacked.
As Guerard says, discussing the great revival of the
eleventh century :

" The luxury of the East was a revelation to the
Westerners, just awaking from the uneasy slumber of
the Dark Ages. Silk, satin, velvet, brocade, muslin,
gauze, carpets, dye-stuffs, glass, paper, candies, sugar,
spices, hemp and flax—most of the amenities and some
of the necessities of life were introduced at this time.
The economic expansion which, in any case, was bound
to accompany the general renaissance was immeasurably
hastened by this intercourse with Byzantine and Arabic
civilization." [1]

Moslem Influences

With its Roman traditions of administration and with
its age-long associations with pagan and Christian East
through the Mediterranean trade-routes, Languedoc came
in the eighth century into direct contact with the Moslem
invaders of Spain. They never captured Toulouse, but
they held Narbonne for forty years. Saragossa was in
their hands for nearly four centuries, as well as all the
mainland behind it, like a great handful of Asia thrust

[1] Guerard, *French Civilisation*, p. 259.

up into the heart of Europe. Naturally these Arabs, who brought Aristotle and the study of medicine back into Europe, exercised an enormous influence upon the thought and manners of those amongst whom they had established themselves. Many of the noblemen of Languedoc seem to have owned Saracen slaves at a time when slavery was practically unknown in the rest of Western Christendom ; whilst large numbers of Christian slaves, taken as prisoners of war, served in the court and in the army of the Emir of Cordova. The belabouring of the infidel by the arms of Christian princes was exceedingly spasmodic, and seems often to have been regarded almost as a kind of winter sport. Thus noblemen and princes, who found the affairs of their own dowry a little tedious or who wished to move to a warmer climate for the winter, would pack up to go crusading in the south of Spain, and would have a thoroughly enjoyable time in the intervals between the occasional battles.[1]

Indeed, it would be a great mistake to suppose that the relations between the Christian and Moslem populations of Spain at this time were consistently hostile or even antagonistic. On the contrary, a great mass of evidence goes to show that the two peoples lived together on terms of the closest intimacy and inter-association. During the tenth and eleventh centuries Moslem Spain was the admitted centre of Western culture. The reigning houses of Aragon and Castile became allied by marriage with the families of the Moorish kings.[2] Moslem fashions and habits were introduced into every phase of private life. From all over Europe came students and travellers, eager to drink at the fountain of the new classic culture from the East. Translations of the Koran and of the great philosophical treatises of the Arab doctors began to circulate freely in the schools of Europe. In

---

[1] I speak, of course, of the later period, not of the stirring and supremely critical days of Charles Martel and of Roncesvalles.

[2] According to one tradition Abdelrahmen I married a daughter of the Duke of Aquitaine,—a surprisingly early instance of intermarriage between Christian and Moslem.—Ballesteros, *Historia de España*, t. II, p. 9.

the time of King Alphonso the Wise the fusion of the
two civilizations received the royal favour, when there
was founded at Seville a Latin and Arabic university, at
which Moslem doctors and Christian professors collabo-
rated in the teaching of medicine and the sciences.

But in all this great intellectual movement the Christians were admittedly the pupils, whilst the Arab doctors
were the teachers. The superiority of the latter in
realms of philosophy was openly acknowledged by many
Christian thinkers and loudly proclaimed by the Arabs
themselves. In his History of the Sciences the Moslem
doctor, Said of Toledo, observed that those who lived in
the far lands of the north—by whom he meant all who
lived north of the Pyrenees—" are of cold temperament
and never reach maturity; they are of great stature and
of a white colour. But they lack all sharpness of wit
and penetration of intellect." [1]

The whole tendency of modern scholarship is towards
a fuller recognition of the vast debt owed by European
culture to the Arab doctors of Spain and Sicily. Nothing
that one may say in this connection can detract from the
creative splendour of the achievements of the Schoolmen.
The boldness and the brilliant originality of a St. Thomas
is unchallengeable. Yet the roots of the whole movement were in Islam. And to the present writer it seems
that, when we recognize in Scholasticism an adaptation
and a development along Christian lines of Moslem
rationalism, we are only adding another jewel to the
diadem of mediæval achievement. Indeed there is a
strange paradox in the thought that the legacy of Islamic
thought, purified and systematized, should have been
inherited by the Christian Church and permanently
enshrined in her treasury of learning.

It is established beyond question that Moslem coinage
circulated freely in Languedoc. Then the great school
of Montpellier, the oldest in Europe with the exception
of Paris, became devoted primarily to the study of

[1] Quoted by Miguel Asin, *Islam and the Divine Comedy* (Eng. trans. by
Harold Sunderland), p. 258.

medicine. It was in the University of Montpellier towards the end of the thirteenth century that the famous English doctor, Gilbert, made his investigations into the proper treatment of small-pox; and insisted, amongst other things, that the rooms of patients suffering from that disease should be hung with red curtains and the windows covered with heavy red hangings—a discovery which was re-discovered in the nineteenth century by Dr. Finsen and gained for him the Nobel prize. Clearly in the great medical schools of Montpellier we may discern the influence of Arab science and may argue therefrom, as from other considerations that have been noted, a vigorous interchange of thought, manners and customs between the peoples of Languedoc and the Spanish Moslems.

The Troubadours

At the beginning of the eleventh century we find the Counts of Toulouse amongst the most powerful and wealthy princes of Europe. In contrast with the almost tortured activity of the contemporary north we find an atmosphere of luxury, ease and, perhaps, lethargy. In contrast with the warlike barons of the north, the southern noblemen seem to have had little appetite and, as the northern Frenchman would hastily have added, little aptitude for fighting. The architecture of the eleventh-century south shows a certain lightness of design and elegance of detail, which contrasts vividly with the massive simplicity of the Norman manner. In this refined and easy-going society, with its many Oriental affinities and with its unbroken traditions stretching back beyond the Golden Age of Rome, there arose two things of immense significance. The one was the great distinctive contribution of Languedoc to the central traditions of Europe; I mean, of course, the poetry of the troubadours. The other, filtering in from the plains of Lombardy and from the East, was the Albigensian heresy. And although, as M. Tanon says, there was nothing in common between the ideals of courtesy and chivalry and the basic doctrines of the heresy, yet the two things overlapped. We are all familiar with the declamations of such writers as Lecky, who declare that the Albigensian Crusade "quenched the lamp of liberty in blood," "crushed the fair promise of the Albigenses," and so forth. The truth is that the crushing of the fair promises of the Albigenses was the work, not of the Crusaders—it had been done long before that—but, to a much greater extent, of the heresy which, soaking like a poison into the veins of this brilliant but slightly anæmic civilization, corrupted its whole system and made of it a very plague-spot within the heart of Europe.

It was in the courts of Narbonne, Toulouse, Montpellier and the other great cities of the "meridional" that the ideas of "courtly" love first took shape. The troubadour style is fully developed in William IX, Duke of Aquitaine, who died in 1127. He is the earliest troubadour known to us, but the ease of his versifications and the symmetry of his poetic forms suggests the existence, even at the beginning of the century, of a well-developed tradition. The whole troubadour movement was essentially aristocratic in its appeal. Many of the great troubadours, like the martial Bertrand de Born and the proud Raimbaud d'Aurenga,[1] were themselves noblemen. Richard Cœur-de-Lion, "the least English of all the English kings," left a number of exquisite poems in the troubadour manner. Yet, although their art made little or no appeal to the middle and lower classes, the troubadours themselves were drawn from all ranks of society. Fulk of Marseilles, who lived to become Bishop of Toulouse, was the son of a wealthy merchant. Bernard de Ventadour was the son of a stoker in the baronial castle at Ventadour. Peire Cardenal and the famous Monk of Montaudon were professed religious.

With the easy skill and the almost incredible variety of their rhymed couplets, the troubadours were the

---

[1] "Since Adam ate the apple," remarks Raimbaud in one of his poems, "there is no poet, loud as he may proclaim himself, whose art is worth a turnip compared with mine."

creators of European lyric poetry.   Further—and herein
lies their chief significance in the history of society—
they brought back into Europe the traditions of good
manners and refinement, of politeness and courtesy.   The
poetry of the troubadours, as Mr. Nickerson observes,
was the most cultivated and civilized thing that had
happened since Rome had fallen asleep.   For the philosophies of courtly love and romance spread outwards
with amazing vigour, and the troubadour influence may
be traced in the mediæval literature of every European
country.

It is a curious and unique thing, this " courtly " love
of the southern troubadours—delightfully artless and
irresponsible, yet perhaps lacking in ballast.   I say that
it is unique ; for the same note was never struck by the
poets of the sterner and more vigorous northern countries.   There you had courtesy, gallantry and refinement,
but cast in a more virile mould.   There is something
effeminate and almost grotesque in the earlier love-poems
of the south, charming though they be.   Certainly they
present a remarkably convincing picture of the easy-
going worldliness of the southern courts, little interested
in anything but their own pleasures, skirting daintily on
the surface of many things, yet seriously pursuing none.

A recognition of this rather unwholesome element in
the troubadour poems must not, however, blind us to
the supreme excellence of their technique and the very
great beauty of their ideals.   The whole troubadour cycle
in the classical age is remarkable for its perfect purity
and lack of grossness ; for a certain elvish gaiety and
lightness of touch.

" Love is the medium through which alone the hero
surveys the world around him, and for which he con-
temns everything that the age prized ; knightly honour,
deeds of arms, father and mother, hell and even heaven ;
but the mere promise by his father of a kiss from Nicolette inspires him to superhuman heroism ; whilst the
old poet sings and smiles aside to his audience, as though
he wished them to understand that Aucassin, a foolish

boy, must not be judged quite seriously, but that, old as
he was himself, he was just as foolish as Nicolette." [1]

Critics have exhausted all their ingenuity and scholarship in seeking the origins of the troubadour movement
and of the almost mystical ideals of courtesy in love.
For the most part they have been singularly unsuccessful ;
and one theory after another has gone to the wall as the
accumulation of fresh evidence has rendered it obsolete.
It has been left to a group of modern Spanish scholars at
last to set the thing upon a firm basis and to show conclusively that the origins of courtly love are to be found
in the mystical poetry of Islam—or rather to show that
Islam was the bridge across which these ideas were
brought into Western Christendom. Courtly love is
explained and extolled by Ibn Daud of Ispahan, who
wrote in the ninth century. Ibn Hazm of Cordova,
who lived in the eleventh century, has left in his *Necklace
of the Dove*, an elaborate treatise on the subject, com-
parable to the first part of the *Romance of the Rose*. The
beautiful poem, *Aucassin and Nicolette*, is based upon
traditional Arab tales.

" The common prejudice," writes Don Asin,[2] "—common both by its wide diffusion and the absence of all
logical foundation—denying all idealism to the conception of love of the Arabs, and of Moslems in general,
is quite contrary to fact. The Yemen tribe of the Banu
Odhra, or ' Children of Chastity,' were famous for the
manner in which they upheld the tradition of their
name. . . . The romanticism that prefers death to the
defilement of the chaste union of the souls is a feature
of all the melancholy and beautiful songs of these poets.
The example of abstinence and perpetual chastity set by
the Christian monks of Arabia may well have influenced
the Banu Odhra. The mysticism of the Sufis, directly
inherited from the Christian hermits, also drew its
inspiration from the lives and writings of the romantic

[1] A passage quoted by Henry Adams, *Mont St. Michel and Chartres*,
p. 231. The critic is discussing that most entrancing of all troubadour
tales, *Aucassin and Nicolette*.   [2] *Op. cit.*, pp. 272–5.

poets of Arabia.   Regardless of the fact that neither the Koran nor the life of Mahomet himself furnishes the slightest ground for so idealistic an interpretation of love, they do not hesitate to attribute to the Prophet the saying, ' He who loves and remains chaste unto death dies a martyr.' . . . Later, when to the asceticism inherited from the Christian monks the Sufis applied a pantheistic and neo-Platonic form of metaphysics, the idealization of sexual love reached the acme of subtlety and abstruseness.   This has been shown in the erotic poems of Ibn Arabi, in which the beloved is a mere symbol of Divine wisdom, and the passion felt for her is allegorical of the union of the mystic soul with God Himself."

It is a far cry from the cave of St. Antony the Hermit to the delicate fancies of Christian of Troyes.   It may seem fanciful to regard the anchorites of Sinai as the heralds of chivalry.   Yet from the inspiration of these early monks the imaginative genius of Islam was enabled to develop those lofty ideals of human love, which Islam itself was not big enough permanently to assimilate and which we now regard as part of the legacy of the Christian Middle Ages.

The Social Significance of Mediæval Heresy

There seems to exist in all human societies of which we have historical record a certain corporate instinct of self-preservation.   It does not repose upon respect for existing laws, for most often it anticipates legislation. Moreover, however violent and unprincipled may be its manifestations—in riots, popular risings and so forth—it is almost always proved right in the end.   It is a sort of corporate sixth sense, which enables a society to recognize things which threaten its continued well-being, things which it cannot safely assimilate.   Further, it is evident that the vitality of a particular society may be gauged to some extent by the effectiveness of this preservative instinct in directing its constitutional policy; so that, instead of undisciplined expressions of popular feeling, you swiftly get the controlling and directing power of official legislation. Thus, within a few months of the appearance of heretics in England, Henry II, who was himself a southern Frenchman and had doubtless seen something of heretical activity in his Aquitainian domains, had set the machinery of State in motion against them. Had his statesmanlike action been followed or anticipated by the other sovereigns of Europe, had heresy been elsewhere nipped in the bud, it is at least arguable that the Albigensian Crusade would never have been summoned and the Inquisition never have come into being.

Now, as we have seen, there was one thing which the Catholic society of mediæval Europe could not safely assimilate and whose appearance was everywhere greeted by violent popular hostility—namely, heresy.

" Heresy," says Guiraud,[1] " in the Middle Ages was nearly always connected with some anti-social sect. In a period when the human mind usually expressed itself in a theological form, socialism, communism and anarchy appeared under the form of heresy. By the very nature of things, therefore, the interests of Church and State were identical. This explains the question of the suppression of heresy in the Middle Ages."

It is, I think, in the complete absence of this self-preservative instinct in the southern civilization of Languedoc that we may see its essential weakness. It was essentially spineless and lethargic. Luxury and outward magnificence there may have been. Energy and the promise of greater things there certainly were not.

" In spite of the acknowledged brilliancy of this civilization," says Guerard, " it may well be doubted whether, if unchecked, it would have enjoyed a very healthy development."[2]

As in the northern kingdoms, though to an immeasurably greater extent, the spread of the heresy in Languedoc was vastly assisted by the feebleness and corruption of

[1] Quoted by Vacandard, *The Inquisition*, p. 184.
[2] *Op. cit.*, p. 235.

the Catholic priesthood and episcopate. William of Puy-Laurens forcibly expresses the contempt in which the priests were generally held.

"They were classed with the Jews. Nobles who had the patronage of livings took good care not to nominate their own relations to the livings ; they gave them to the sons of peasants or their serfs, for whom they naturally had no respect." [1]

About the middle of the twelfth century St. Bernard visited the country, which was at that time much excited by the preaching of the heretic, Henry of Lausanne ; the Saint gloomily summarized the conditions in Languedoc thus : the churches without people, the people without priests, the priests without the respect due to them, the Christians without Christ. In 1209 the Council of Avignon declared that " priests do not differ from laymen, either in appearance or in conduct." Early in his pontificate Innocent III found it necessary to remove Bishop Raymond of Raberstein from the see of Toulouse on account of his open support of heresy. Then there was Berengar II, who was Archbishop of Narbonne from 1192 to 1211. This almost incredible prelate, at the time of his final suspension, had not visited his diocese for sixteen years and would often pass weeks together without entering a church. In his diocese, declared Innocent in 1204, it was almost a regular thing for monks and canons to lay aside their cloth, to take wives, live by usury, and to become lawyers, actors or doctors. Berengar, said the Pope, had a purse instead of a heart and served no other god but money. Even the troubadours occasionally laid aside their cap and bells and hurled invectives at the rapacity and immorality of the priests.

" Eagles and vultures," cried the fiery Peire Cardenal, " smell not the carrion so readily as priests and preachers

[1] Cited by A. Luchaire, *Social France under Philip-Augustus* (English trans., A. Krehbiel), p. 49.

It should, perhaps, be noted that the monastic orders very often affected a superior and critical attitude to the secular priesthood. One has to make some allowance for this.

smell out the rich ; a rich man is their friend and, should a sickness strike him down, he must make them presents to the loss of his relations.   Frenchmen and priests are reputed bad, and rightly so ; usurers and traitors possess the whole world." [1]

All these instances, it is true, concern the later period, almost immediately prior to the summoning of the Crusade.   Still it is not surprising that we find amongst most of the earlier troubadours an atmosphere of good-tempered scorn for the priesthood and the ceremonies of the Church, a sort of genial and well-bred profanity. Thus the troubadour Raimbaud d'Aurenga declares that the smile of his lady gives him more pleasure than the smiles of four hundred angels.   More famous is the cheerful outburst of Aucassin :

" In Paradise what have I to do ?   I do not care to go there unless I may have Nicolette, my very sweet friend whom I love so much.   For to Paradise go none but such people as I will tell you.   There go the old priests and old cripples and the maimed, who all day and all night kneel before altars and are clothed in old worn-out capes and old tattered rags, who are naked and sore, who die of hunger and want and misery.   These go to Paradise and with them I have nothing to do. But to Hell I am willing to go.   For to Hell go the fine scholars, and the fair knights who die in tourneys and in glorious wars, and good men-at-arms and the well-born.   With them I will gladly go.   And there go the fair and courteous ladies, who have friends, two or three, beside their wedded lords. . . . With these I will go, so only that I may have Nicolette, my very sweet friend, by me." [2]

Of course this kind of thing is not heresy and need not necessarily have ended in heresy.   It was mere indifferentism.   A rather similar note is struck by the

[1] H. J. Chaytor, *The Troubadours*, pp. 85, 86.   Note the bracketing of priests with " Frenchmen," *i.e.* northern Frenchmen.

[2] *Aucassin and Nicolette and Other Mediæval Romances* (Everyman Library).

Monk of Montaudon, a very popular troubadour in the later period, who was accustomed to bestow all his earnings upon his own priory and who was a thoroughly good religious in every way.   Two of his satirical poems deal with the vanities of women, and particularly with the feminine practice of painting the face.   In one the setting is before the throne of God; and the poet discusses the question with a lady, whilst the Almighty acts as judge.   The action of the other takes place in Heaven and consists of a dialogue between God and the poet. " In neither poem," remarks Mr. Chaytor, " is reverence a prominent feature." [1]

The Albigensian Heresy in Languedoc

Entering Languedoc about the beginning of the eleventh century, the Albigensian heresy encountered practically no resistance of any kind and remained unopposed alike by ecclesiastical and secular authorities for more than a century and a half.   Following on the summary action of King Robert the Pious at Orleans in 1022 there seem to have been anti-heretical demonstrations in Toulouse.   Almost exactly a century later the heretical teacher, Peter of Bruys, was burnt alive by the mob at St. Gilles.   Certainly he had asked for trouble; and it seems that the hostility of the people was aroused less by his actual teaching than by the fact that he had shown his contempt for Catholic symbolism by burning a Crucifix in the public square and roasting meat over the flame.   These are absolutely isolated incidents.   Up to the beginning of the thirteenth century, according to M. Julien Havet,[2] the municipal registers of the cities in the *midi* make no mention of heretics and seem quite unaware of their existence.   There is nothing very surprising in this; for everything in Languedoc was favourable to the spread of the heresy—the easy-going

[1] *Op. cit.*, p. 71.
[2] Julien Havet, " L'hérésie et le bras séculier au moyen-âge " in his *Œuvres*, Vol. II. p. 150.

life of the courts, the corruptions within the Church, the ascetic zeal of the " Perfect " and the accommodating elasticity of the new philosophy. Manichæism, whether pagan, Albigensian or Christian Scientist, has always made a great appeal to vague and superficial minds; and, unless its tenets are followed out to their proper logical conclusions, it may well remain a comparatively innocuous form of misbelief. To these southerners, wealthy, easy-going and pleasure-loving, with their intimate Moslem and Jewish affinities—one chronicler refers to the country as " Judæa secunda "—heresy, as Mr. Nickerson says—

" may well have seemed like a grateful mist, a twilight serving to blur and soften the clear, unmistakable lines of Catholic Christianity. And if, to such a people, the life of an Albigensian believer seemed easier and more natural than that of a Catholic layman, on the other hand, their self-mortifying eccentrics found in the life of the Albigensian ' Perfect ' a stricter and more fiercely inhuman rule of conduct than that of any Catholic Order." [1]

To the rapacious noblemen and robber-barons of the south the Albigensian heresy came also as a welcome novelty. It was exceedingly pleasant to be told that the bloated riches of the monasteries and episcopates were abominations in the sight of God, that the Catholic Church was an imposture and a usurpation; and, hence, that plundering her properties was part of the just war against Antichrist. The baiting of ecclesiastics had long been one of the favourite, though rather furtive, sports of the more pugnacious noblemen; and here was the express permission to carry on the good work. Some of these noblemen were veritable brigands; they lived surrounded by gangs of hired hooligans, who were ready to commit any outrage that their lord might desire. Thus, at the beginning of the thirteenth century, the monks at St. Martin-du-Canigon drew up a huge list of misdeeds committed by Pons of Vernet, a nobleman of Rousillon.

[1] H. Nickerson, *The Inquisition*, p. 61.

" He broke down our fence and seized eleven cows. One night he entered our property at Vernet and cut down our fruit trees. . . . Another time he killed two cows and wounded four others on the farm of Col-de-Jou, and he carried away all the cheeses that he found there. . . . At Eglies he took a hundred and fifty sheep, a donkey and three children, whom he refused to give up without a ransom of one hundred sous, some capes, some tunics and cheeses. . . . And after he and his father, R. du Vernet, had sworn in the church of Ste. Marie of Vernet that he would leave the abbey in peace, he stole eight sous and seven hens from our men of Avidan, and he forced us to buy over again the boundary-line of Odilon, which his father had sold to us. . . . He then seized two men of Odilon, whom he ransomed for fifteen sous and one of whom is still in captivity." [1]

In Beziers the heretics harassed the clergy and even molested the dean and chapter in the cathedral itself. In Toulouse, according to Guy de Puy-Laurens, the bishop was unable to travel about his diocese without an armed escort, provided by the nobles through whose land he was passing. His ecclesiastical dues were regularly appropriated by heretics and robbers ; and he himself was reduced almost to destitution. A gang of brigands, having raided the cathedral of Ste. Marie at Oloron, trampled the Host underfoot, dressed themselves up in the priestly vestments and conducted a wild burlesque of the Mass. These genial goings-on were accompanied by their usual ebullitions, burning down churches and capturing priests to be held for ransom.

By the middle of the twelfth century the heresy was firmly established in Languedoc. St. Bernard visited the country in 1147 and declared that almost all the nobility were heretical. His mission met with scanty success and on one important occasion he failed to get a hearing at all. In 1163 the Council of Tours had called upon the secular princes to aid in the suppression of heresy. Four years later the heretics felt so sure of their position as to hold a council of their own under

[1] Luchaire, *op. cit.*, pp. 249, 250.

the presidency of a Manichee prelate from Constantinople; many "bishops" of the sect were present and
the "agenda" included the election of the new bishops
of Carcassonne, Toulouse and Val d'Aran.[1]   There were
heretical convents for women at Cabaret, Villeneuve,
Castelnaudary and Laurac.   There was also a highly
organized system of workshops and elementary schools,
where the young were apprenticed both to a trade and
to the practice of the Manichee doctrines; in the town
of Fanjeaux alone there were a number of these estab-
lishments.   The heresy, indeed, had long since ceased
to be the placidly epicurean fad of the nobility, and had
taken on all the trappings of a powerful and fiercely
anti-social organization.   It had started, like Arianism
eight centuries previously, as a fashionable philosophy
of the moment, a stylish court heresy.   It fitted in well
with the easy indifferentism of the southern courts and
the general contempt into which the organization and
teaching of the Church had fallen.

But it was impossible that it should long have remained
in this fluid and formless shape; and as a fact it did not
do so.   The men of the Middle Ages were, as a whole,
better educated than we are, more truly scientific in
temper, more daringly logical, less conventional.   Therefore it was natural that, as the heresy gained in power,
numbers and solidarity, the vagueness of its dualistic
teachings should have become crystallized and developed
into a full, coherent system—a system which, in its logical
completeness, aimed explicitly at the destruction of the
race and the undermining of all morality.   By the middle
of the twelfth century it had fastened its sinister strangle-
hold upon the civilization of Languedoc and was leading
it headlong to its destruction.   It is of capital importance
that this point should be clearly apprehended.   Even
Lea, " almost always accurate on points of fact even when
he is most exasperating in his utter lack of the realizing
imagination so necessary to the modern historian of the
Middle Ages "—even Lea, I say, admits that—

---

[1] The official minutes of this function are given in Bouquet, *Recueil
des Historiens des Gaules*, Tom. XIV, pp. 448–50.

" The cause of orthodoxy was in this case the cause of civilization and progress. Had Catharism become dominant or even had it been allowed to exist on equal terms, its influence could not have failed to prove disastrous. . . . It was not only a revolt against the Church, but a renunciation of man's dominance over Nature." [1]

The poetry of the contemporary troubadours brings out the same point. Gone is the spontaneous gaiety of the earlier period; and instead we find savage satires and denunciations, gloomy moralizings on the degeneracy of the times, and regrets for the splendours of the past. Guiraut de Bornelh, perhaps the greatest of all the troubadours, lamented the decline of the true spirit of chivalry and condemned the pugnacity of the nobles. The Monk of Montaudon and, later, Peire Cardenal, thundered against the corruptions within the Church and the godlessness of the people. In 1177 Count Raymond V of Toulouse addressed a letter to the Chapter-General at Citeaux, declaring that the heresy had penetrated everywhere, introducing discord into families, dividing husband from wife, son from father, step-mother from step-daughter. The Catholic priests had been corrupted in large numbers, and churches were everywhere abandoned and unused. For himself, he was powerless to cope with the situation, mainly because many of his most distinguished subjects had been seduced, and had led others astray with them.[2]

Up to this time the spread of the heresy in Languedoc had been almost wholly unopposed. St. Bernard's mission in 1147 had been a mere flash in the pan and had left no lasting impression. The secular rulers had manifested either a complete indifference or an overt favouritism of the heretics. The decrees of Councils had been openly scouted. But in reply to Raymond's letter we get the first suggestion of ordered action. In 1178 Pope Alexander III despatched a number of priests and bishops, under the leadership of Cardinal Peter of St. Chrysogonus, to Languedoc to investigate the conditions.

[1] H. C. Lea, *A History of the Inquisition in the Middle Ages*, Vol. I. p. 106.　　　　　　　　　[2] Tanon, *op. cit.*, p. 21.

" When the mission reached Toulouse," says Mr. Nickerson,[1] " they were insulted from the streets. Nevertheless they went on to draw up a long list of heretics, and finally determined to make an example of a rich old man named Peter Mauran, who seems to have been one of the first citizens of Toulouse. They proceeded against him under the Canon promulgated by the Council of Tours, which prescribed imprisonment for convicted heretics and confiscation of their property. After much palaver and wordy shuffling by the accused, he was adjudged a heretic. To save his property he recanted and offered to submit to such penance as might be imposed."

Accordingly the Bishop of Toulouse and the Abbot of St. Sernin proceeded in person to the prison, where he had been temporarily detained and, having caused him to be stripped to the waist, led him through the streets of the city to the cathedral, scourging him vigorously the while. Arrived before the High Altar, he was granted absolution and, as a penance, ordered to undertake a three years' pilgrimage to the Holy Land, to be daily scourged in the streets of Toulouse until his departure, to restore all Church lands occupied by him and to pay to Count Raymond five hundred pounds of silver in redemption of his forfeited property. The penance is sufficiently vigorous. But of the effectiveness of such measures in attempting to deal with the situation we may judge by the fact that, after his return from Palestine, Mauran was three times appointed chief magistrate of Toulouse; and the city was then more solidly Manichee than ever.

It was evident that the ecclesiastical authorities were no longer in a position to deal unaided with heresy on a large scale. Even had the Catholic bishops and clergy of Languedoc possessed an energy which they certainly seem never to have exhibited, it is doubtful whether much could have been done. The opportunity had been lost a century previously. The time for such mild cor-

[1] *Op. cit.*, p. 64.

rectives as pastoral visitations was long past.   In 1181
Henry of Clairvaux placed himself at the head of a little
Crusade, but after the slightly sensational capture of the
town of Lavaur, his forces dwindled away and the enterprise was abandoned.   In 1195 a Papal legate at Montpellier denounced the heretics with crushing vigour, but
the thunders of his eloquence died away without an echo.
To all intents and purposes the heresy in Languedoc
seemed impregnable.   So matters stood when, in 1198,
Innocent III, the giant of the whole mediæval story,
ascended the Pontifical throne.

Pope Innocent III

Within two months of his accession the new Pope
had taken Languedoc in hand.   Two legates had been
despatched to investigate the conditions and to seek the
co-operation of the secular authorities in enforcing the
prescribed penalties against heresy.   Throughout his
reign Innocent made no alteration in these laws.   Contrary to the confident statements of a number of nineteenth-century historians—Lecky and Duruy are two
whose names occur at once—he did not establish the
Inquisition nor give Papal sanction to the infliction of
the death penalty for obduracy or relapse.   Banishment
and confiscation of property remained the extreme
penalties which the secular rulers were empowered to
enforce.

It is hard not to linger over the character and achievements of the great Pope.   The almost incredible range
of his activities, the masterly statesmanship with which
he guided the Church through the seventeen crowded
and supremely critical years of his pontificate, these
things alone mark him as one of the most remarkable
men that have influenced the course of history.   But to
see him only as the man who raised the prestige of the
Papacy to the highest point it has ever reached is to see
only one side of his character.   A scholar and graduate
of the University of Paris, one of the most learned and

widely-read lawyers of his day, the author of several mystical treatises of a deeply devotional nature, he is to be remembered not only as the Pope of the Crusades, but as the Pope of the Universities and the Pope of the Hospitals.

"There is something conciliating and fascinating," said the German historian, Virchow,[1] "in the fact that at the time at which the Fourth Crusade was inaugurated through his influence, the thought of founding a great organization of an essentially humane character was also taking form in his soul; and that in the same year (1204) in which the new Latin Empire was founded in Constantinople, the newly erected hospital of the Santo Spirito, by the old bridge across the Tiber, was blessed and dedicated as the future centre of this universal humanitarian organization. . . . It may be recognized and admitted that it was reserved for the Roman Catholic Church, and above all for Innocent III, to establish institutions for the care of those suffering from diseases."

Finally, Innocent was a great gentleman. Even in the full heat of the Albigensian Crusade we find him interfering on behalf of an accused canon of Bar-sur-Aube. Severe as was his treatment of Raymond VI of Toulouse, it never exceeded the bounds of equity; and the Pope expressly stipulated the restoration of certain confiscated lands to the Count's heir, should he abjure his father's errors. It would be easy to cite half a dozen instances in which, in dealing with sporadic cases of heresy in other parts of Christendom, he showed a similar leniency and kindliness. It was characteristic of him that, in spite of the pressure brought to bear upon his action by bishops and legates, he waited nearly ten years before finally summoning the Albigensian Crusade.

The Papal Mission

From the first the Papal legates in Languedoc fared no better than had the secular clergy. Their practice

[1] Quoted by J. J. Walsh, *The Thirteenth Greatest of Centuries*, p. 343.

of travelling about the country in magnificent equipages and surrounded by retainers cut very little ice with the peoples of Languedoc, to whom the luxury of the priesthood had long been a matter for ridicule and contempt, and in whose eyes the austerity of the Albigensian " Perfect " seemed so impressive a guarantee of sanctity and integrity.   Things went from bad to worse.   The renegade Berengar II, Primate of Languedoc and Archbishop of Narbonne, broke boldly with the legates and refused to assist their mission in any way.   His lordship the Bishop of Beziers manifested a complete lack of interest in the proceedings.   Long accustomed to seeing the heresy flourishing all around them and to living the lives of ordinary noblemen, these prelates, perhaps naturally, had little sympathy with the activities of these interfering Cistercian monks, whose very presence was a reflection upon the conduct of their own diocesan affairs.

About midsummer 1206 the little band of legates, assembled at Montpellier, talked despairingly of resigning their mission.   There had been small successes and great reverses.   Some of the nobles had thrown open their castles to be the scenes of wordy debates between the Catharan apologists and the Catholic missionaries.   But however complete had seemed the dialectical triumphs achieved, the results had been negligible.   Even the arrival of Didacus and St. Dominic—that amazing man— and the adoption by the legates of apostolic poverty had been attended by scanty success.

An incident at Champ-du-Sicaire throws some light on the general situation.   The labourers, in accordance with heretical doctrine, were accustomed to carry on their work without interruption on Sundays and festivals. On the feast of St. John the Baptist, St. Dominic, who was staying in the village, ventured to reproach one of the workers for this.   So hostile was the attitude of the people at this interference that the Saint barely escaped with his life.

In 1207 the senior legate, De Castelnau, took a critical step—the culmination of a long series of evasions and quibblings on the part of the slippery Count of Toulouse. He excommunicated Raymond and laid his lands under interdict; and Innocent, without any hesitation, confirmed both sentences. On January 15th of the following year De Castelnau was assassinated by one of Raymond's retainers.

The crime made Innocent master of the situation, and he acted with prompt and smashing vigour. Within three months of the murder the bugles of the Vatican sounded through Europe.

"Flaming circular letters went to every bishop in Raymond's lands, recounting the crime and the strong presumption of the Court's complicity therein, directing that the murderer be excommunicated, that Raymond be re-excommunicated and that the interdict laid upon Raymond's lands be enlarged so as to include any place that either he or the murderer might curse and pollute with their presence. This masterpiece of malediction was to be solemnly published, with bell, book and candle, in all churches, and to be republished until further notice on all Sundays and feast-days." [1]

Raymond's person was outlawed, his vassals and allies were released from all oaths of allegiance to him, and he was forbidden to seek reconciliation with the Church until he had banished all heretics from his dominions. Meanwhile Arnaut Amalric summoned a chapter-general of the Cistercian Order and, in a characteristically fiery address, called on the faithful throughout Christendom to join in the Crusade. Innocent wrote in the same strain to the French bishops. The tardy capitulation of Raymond caused no hitch in the management; and, even had he been able to do so, the Pope had no intention now of calling off the Crusade. The count, who, after all, was no heretic but, in the eyes of the Pope, merely an insufficiently energetic Catholic, was solemnly reconciled to the Church of St. Gilles. Less than a week after this humiliating ceremony the Crusading army marched south from Lyons.

[1] H. Nickerson, *op. cit.*, p. 96.

SIMON DE MONTFORT,
5TH EARL OF LEICESTER.

Commander of the Albigensian Crusade.

The Crusade and the Albigensian War

The Albigensian Crusade lasted a bare two months ; the Albigensian War dragged on sporadically for more than twenty years.   The period prescribed for the gaining of the Crusading indulgences was forty days ; so that, after the great westward drive, which included the captures of Beziers and Carcassonne, the vast proportion of the crusading army prepared to return home, " gorged with spiritual graces and not altogether lacking in temporal booty," as Mr. Nickerson puts it.[1]   From that time onward Simon de Montfort remained in command with the triple object of consolidating the occupied territory, of subjugating the Languedocian nobility, and of providing a kind of police security for the spiritual labours of the Preaching Friars.

The religious aspect of the conflict, predominant at the outset, became gradually obscured by the political considerations that necessarily arose.   King Pedro of Aragon, who in 1204 had been decorated by the Pope with the title of " First Standard-Bearer of the Faith," appeared in battle against De Montfort and as an ally of Count Raymond, to whom he had become related by marriage.   The erratic sovereign was killed in the famous battle of Muret in 1213—a zealous Catholic fighting against the armies of the Church.

Muret settled the fate of Languedoc.   In 1224 De Montfort met a soldier's death before the walls of

[1] The looting, arson and massacre which accompanied the capture of Beziers are the events for which the Crusade is chiefly remembered by many people.   There are two definite reasons for doubting the completeness of the massacre.   First, that the civic life of the town was so quickly reconstituted thar it was soon able to resist the Crusaders again ; and second, that as Mr. Nickerson pointed out, " the Church of St. Mary Magdalene, where the slaughter is supposed to have been heaviest, is so small that not a third of the 7,000 supposed to have been killed there could possibly have packed into the place."

These total destructions of mediæval cities must not always be taken at their face value.   Thus De Montfort formally demolished the walls and destroyed the fortifications of Toulouse twice within a period of eighteen months.

Toulouse. The war dragged on in desultory fashion for another five years, when a treaty was signed providing for the complete absorption of the Duchy of Toulouse by the French Crown.

The political nature of the struggle is worth noting. None of the leaders of the southern forces were heretics. Raymond had been a Catholic all his life and died with all the consolations of the Faith. Pedro was the " First Standard-Bearer of the Faith " and had zealously be-laboured the Moslem infidels in Spain, besides legislating with unprecedented severity against the heretics in his own dominions. Raymond Roger had dabbled in Catharism, as a man might dabble in the fashionable cult of the moment; yet, although his wife and one of his sisters were Cathari and another sister a Waldensian, he had never openly embraced heresy himself. In its latter stages, at any rate, the war had been fought, not between the forces of a united Christendom and the united armies of an heretical country, but between the French Crown and the southern nobility.

Still, it would be a mistake to regard the resistance offered to the Crusaders as that of a downtrodden people, roused to a frenzy of patriotism by the onslaught of foreign invaders upon their hearths and homes. There was no sense of national solidarity amongst the peoples of Southern France. No leader appeared to organize their resistance. Raymond himself showed as little interest in the claims of the Church as in the facile attractions of heresy. Like most of the other noblemen, his chief desire was to be left alone ; and he resented the Crusaders, not because they personified the swelling arrogance of Rome, but rather because they interfered with the easy routine and pleasures of court life. The general feeling was one of annoyance rather than of indignation, of resentment at being interfered with rather than of patriotic anger at being invaded. Thus the troubadour, Raymond of Miraval, welcomed the arrival of Pedro II in Languedoc in 1213, remarking that " the King has promised me that in a short time I shall have Miraval again and my Audiart shall recover his Beaucaire; then ladies and their lovers will regain their lost delights." [1] After the battle of Muret St. Dominic himself lost all interest in the progress of the war, which had become a hopeless tangle of intrigues and counter-intrigues and had long lost all semblance of a Crusade against heresy.

Both sides employed mercenary troops pretty freely— hired bands of brigands who perpetrated many horrible excesses. "Without their aid," remarks Luchaire, "the Counts of Toulouse and Foix would never have been able to resist the chevaliers of Simon de Montfort for long." Still De Montfort himself was not above employing them; and we hear of the people of Toulouse complaining to Pedro that, "they (the Crusaders) excommunicate us because we use brigands; yet they themselves use them."

The real driving force behind the war was the envy of the north for the riches and luxury of the south and their hatred for a civilization wholly different from their own—more Oriental than European. Languedoc became a happy hunting-ground for all the brigands and vagabonds in Europe; and the fighting, which centred chiefly round the cities and the baronial castles, became a mere series of marauding expeditions against the southern noblemen. Naturally the war did not crush the heresy, which seems to have been as rampant and widespread at the end as at the beginning. Even St. Dominic, after eleven years of missionary exertion, gave way to momentary expressions of despair and, like St. Bernard more than seventy years before, cursed the country and its inhabitants.

"For many years," he declared in 1217, "I have exhorted you in vain with gentleness, preaching, praying and weeping. But according to the proverb of my own country, ' Where blessings can accomplish nothing, blows may avail.' We shall rouse against you princes and prelates who, alas, will arm nations and kingdoms against this land; and many will perish by the sword, the country will be laid waste, the walls thrown down and you—oh,

[1] See Farnell, *Lives of the Troubadours*, pp. 186, 187.

grief!—you will be reduced to servitude. And thus blows will avail where blessings and gentleness have been powerless." [1]

The Saint's words are a curious commentary on the essentially local and spasmodic character of the later war. It was nine years since the first capture of Beziers and four years since the battle of Muret. Languedoc was in an uproar. Marseilles had driven out its Bishop and publicly outraged the Consecrated Host. The people of Toulouse had risen in revolt, expelled Bishop Fulk, the ex-troubadour, and were eagerly planning the formal restoration of Count Raymond—an event which was actually to take place less than three weeks after the preaching of St. Dominic's sermon. From the Church's point of view the whole work of the Crusade had been undone. Yet to the people of Prouille (a village near Fanjeaux in the heart of the occupied territory) the idea that swords and staves might be used against them was still apparently a threat.

The political decision achieved in 1229—an important step towards the establishment of the French nation, as it has existed down to the present day—marked the end of organized resistance to the prosecution of heresy. And although it is impossible to pin down any particular date as fixing the establishment of the monastic Inquisition, yet that year forms a convenient landmark. Like all considerable institutions in history the Inquisition was not born in a day. Almost all the features of distinctive Inquisitorial procedure may be noted years before the Albigensian Crusade. In 1184 Lucius III had decreed that all bishops or their accredited representatives should visit every parish in their dioceses at least once a year. Where the existence of heresy was suspected, they were empowered to demand the denunciation of every suspect or of any whose manner of living differed conspicuously from that of the ordinary Catholic. These were then to be questioned by an episcopal tribunal; if they confessed their guilt and persisted in their errors,

[1] Jean Guiraud, *St. Dominic*, p. 88.

they were to be excommunicated and handed over to the secular arm.

These measures, and others that we have noted, had proved hopelessly ineffective.   During the years between 1189 and 1229 we may trace a regular, clearly discernible process, by which the stiffening of the attitude of the secular power was accompanied by the development of an ecclesiastical machinery, capable at once of co-operating with and controlling the activities of the secular authorities.

CHAPTER IV

THE ESTABLISHMENT OF THE INQUISITION

St. Dominic and the Inquisition

I⊤ will be convenient at this point to examine the evidence connecting St. Dominic with the Inquisition.

That famous Protestant scarecrow, the " bloody-minded Dominic," as he appears for the first time in the pages of Llorente (who wrote nearly six hundred years after the Saint's death), may be at once dismissed without serious consideration. The picture finds no support in contemporary evidence and has long been abandoned by all serious historians. Nor was St. Dominic the founder of the Inquisition, though, in a sense, he was perhaps its herald. Pope Sixtus IV is reported to have once referred to him as " the first Inquisitor," but this isolated remark is not in agreement with the evidence and can scarcely be regarded as having any historical value. In like manner a man might describe Wyclif as the first Protestant or Icarus as the first airman.

As far as St. Dominic is concerned, we possess two documents written by the Saint himself. In the first of these he instructs a friend in Toulouse to shelter a certain converted heretic, pending the arrival of the Cardinal legate. The second is a formula of reconciliation with the Church of one Pons Roger, together with the penance imposed upon him—one of those thumping penances which the mediæval Church was wont to lay upon her erring children. The unfortunate man—

" is to fast for ever from flesh, eggs, cheese and all that comes from flesh, except at Easter, Pentecost and Christmas. . . . He is to keep three Lents a year, fasting and abstaining from fish, unless from bodily infirmity or the heat of the weather he shall be dispensed. . . . He is to be beaten with rods on his bare back three Sundays running by the village priest; he is to wear a distinctive dress marked with crosses, to designate him as a former heretic; to hear Mass every day, if possible, recite seventy Paternosters a day and twenty during the night. . . . Finally, once a month he is to show the parchment on which all this is written to the village priest." [1]

There is also an incident related by Constantine of Orvieto, who wrote less than twenty-five years after St. Dominic's death, and (in almost identical words) by Theodoric of Apuldia, whose *History of St. Dominic and the Dominican Order* was completed about 1288.[2] It appears that a number of heretics had been handed over to the secular arm and condemned to be burnt; and that St. Dominic, looking upon one of them, ordered that he should be released.

" Then, turning with great gentleness to the heretic, ' I know, my son,' he said, ' that you need time, but that in the end you will become good and holy.' "

Twenty years later this man, whose name was Raymond Gros, sought admission to the Dominican Order and died in the odour of sanctity.

Finally, we have a scrap of evidence in the official register of Bernard of Caux, Inquisitor of Toulouse between 1244 and 1246. It is noted that several relapsed heretics, whom Bernard examined, had been reconciled with the Church by St. Dominic nearly thirty years previously.

The whole discussion is well summarized by Guiraud : [3]

" Comparing with all these documents the canon of the Council of Verona, renewed in 1208 by the Council of Avignon, which ordered that apostates who, after

---

[1] Nickerson, *op. cit.*, p. 197 ; Th. de Cauzons, *Histoire de l'Inquisition en France*, Vol. I. p. 420.

[2] See Lord Acton, *History of Freedom and other Essays*, p. 554 ; Jean Guirard, *St. Dominic*, p. 40.

[3] *Ibid.*, p. 40.

being convicted of heresy by the bishops or their representatives, should obstinately persist in their errors should
be delivered over to the secular arm, it would seem
that it must be concluded that, in virtue of the delegated
authority of the Cistercian monks, St. Dominic was to
convict the heretics; and that, in convicting them, he
delivered them up, indirectly but surely, to execution,
unless he suspended by an act of clemency the action of
that docile instrument of the Church, the secular arm.
Doubtless he did not himself pronounce the fatal sentence;
but during their trial he played the part of an expert
in the matter of orthodoxy; or even of a juror trans-
mitting to the court a verdict of ' guilty,' whilst capable
at the same time of signing a recommendation to mercy."

On the other hand, it should be remembered that
St. Dominic did not finally leave Languedoc until 1217,
and that he had been working in the district for nearly
twelve years. Now the whole *raison d'être* of the Albigensian War was that in Languedoc the secular arm was
anything but a " docile instrument " of the Church.
De Montfort himself never achieved anything approaching to a real conquest of the country; he was always
the hostile commander of an army of occupation. During the whole of St. Dominic's sojourn in Languedoc,
coercive action against the heretics was hopelessly mixed
up with considerations of military and political expediency
and was more often than not the result of mere lack of
discipline amongst the troops. Very rarely is there any
sign of judiciary proceedings, of examinations, condemnations and so forth. And, in spite of his close
personal friendship with De Montfort, St. Dominic
made no secret of the fact that his interest lay in his
own work of preaching and organizing his new Order
rather than in the military struggle. So much has been
written by others who would represent him as the presi-
dent of an iron tribunal, created by himself, acting in the
closest co-operation with the Crusading army and constantly urging the troops to all sorts of bloody massacres,
that it is well to emphasize the point. We have no

direct evidence that St. Dominic ever condemned any single heretic; we know only that he received many back into the household of the Faith.

Clearly, then, as we understand the term, St. Dominic was not the founder of the Inquisition. That is to say, he was not the founder of that tribunal, Dominican and Franciscan, which was specially commissioned by the Popes with the extirpation of heresy. After all, the endeavour to extirpate heresy is one of the most obvious functions of the priesthood and episcopate; and in that sense the Inquisition may be said to date from the Apostolic age. To convert the heretic is to help him to save his soul; and, as guardian of the Faith, the Church necessarily claimed and has always exercised the right of determining what was heresy and who was heretical. Beyond that point her jurisdiction does not and cannot extend; and the essential characteristic of the developed inquisitorial procedure—I speak of the Monastic tribunal, the Holy Office, in its plenitude of development—was the full co-operation of the spiritual and secular authorities, the officials of the former acting as experts in the whole inquiry, whilst the coercive power was recognized as belonging exclusively to the latter.

It is thus evident that, when the Council of Tours in 1163 and of the Lateran in 1179 had appealed for the co-operation of the secular arm, and when Pope Lucius III had formally recognized the Episcopal (as distinct from the Monastic) Inquisition, the anti-heretical machinery had been in theory complete, although it had remained a dead letter in practice. Hence the Albigensian War, which had, so to speak, brought the Languedocian secular power into line; and hence the development of the Monastic Inquisition—a series of official Papal gestures, by which the trial and prosecution of heretics were made the special function of the newly-formed Dominican and Franciscan Orders, acting in proper subordination to the episcopate. It is impossible to pin down the founding of the Inquisition by specific dates; but, as we understand the term, the Holy Office does not become recognizable, even in its vaguest and most tentative form, until at least ten years after St. Dominic's death.

The Return of Roman Law

The great upward spring of the twelfth century was accompanied by the revival of Roman law.

As long ago as 1040 Anselm of Lucca had revived academic interest in the Code of Justinian; and before the end of the next century Roman law formed the basis of the legal training at the University of Bologna. Many puerilities of the Salic law and of the various Anglo-Saxon compilations had fallen imperceptibly into disuse. The old barbaric practice of settling disputes by the ordeal of fire, water, red-hot ploughshares and what-not was legislated out of existence by the Popes. In its relation to heresy the whole phenomenon is of considerable importance, for out of this virtual re-discovery of Roman law arose a complete system of legislation, which was adopted by every country in mediæval Christendom.

The Code of Justinian contained some sixty enact-ments against heresy. It also recognized the burning of Manichees, thus giving some sort of legal precedent for the sporadic outbursts of mob violence that had occurred during the eleventh and twelfth centuries.[1] In 1209 the pantheism of a certain Amaury de Beynes, a master of arts and lecturer in the schools of Paris, was condemned by a Council; and a number of his followers, who refused to recant, were handed over to the secular court of Philip Augustus. The King was absent from the city at the time; on his return he ordered that ten of the ringleaders should be burnt at the stake and

[1] Under Roman law burning alive was the recognized punishment for parricide, sacrilege, arson, sorcery and treason. The first edict against the Manichees was promulgated by the pagan Emperor Diocletian.

the rest sentenced to lifelong imprisonment. The bones of Amaury himself were exhumed and cast outside the cemetery. Such action was still quite outside the province of any statute law; therefore the decision of the King had to be awaited. Meanwhile the popular hatred of heresy in the north remained as violent as ever; eight Cathari were burnt by the people at Troyes in 1200, one at Nevers in 1201, several at Braisne-sur-Vesle in 1204 and one at Troyes in 1220.

It is impossible to determine how far such sovereigns as Philip Augustus and Pedro of Aragon were influenced by the precedent of the early Christian Emperors in their summary treatment of heretics. The famous " Codex " of Gratian, which was compiled about 1140, prescribed only fine and exile. In 1163 the Council of Tours had declared all heretics excommunicate and had called upon the secular princes to imprison them and confiscate their property. In 1179 the Council of the Lateran had re-affirmed these enactments, lumping heretics in with bandits and robbers as social pests. In 1184 Lucius III, presiding over the Council of Verona, ordered that all heretics were to be excommunicated and handed over to the secular arm, which was to inflict upon them the punishment that they deserved.[1] Acting in co-operation with the Pope, the Emperor Frederick Barbarossa decreed the Imperial ban against them, comprising banishment, confiscation and loss of all civic rights. Finally, in a letter to the magistrates of Viterbo in 1199, Innocent III declared that heretics were forbidden to hold any public office, to be members of city councils, to appear in court as witnesses, to make a will or to receive inheritance. The Lateran Council of 1215 incorporated these instructions into the canons of the universal Church.

" This code," says Luchaire,[2] " which seems so pitiless to us, was in reality at that time a great improvement in the treatment of heretics. For its special laws pre-

---

[1] "Animadversio debita "—the stock phrase used in this connection.
[2] Quoted by Vacandard, *op. cit.*, p. 46.

vented the frequent outbreaks of popular vengeance, which punished not only confessed heretics, but also mere suspects."

Up to this time the death penalty had not been mentioned in any official document, secular or ecclesiastical.

Development of Anti-heretical Legislation

Whilst the Albigensian War was desultorily dragging on to its conclusion—a conclusion which had never been in much doubt since the battle of Muret—the anti-heretical legislation throughout the Empire had been developing steadily and inexorably under the joint efforts of Frederick II and Pope Gregory IX. In 1220 the Emperor promulgated a law which, in full accordance with the canons of the Lateran Council, condemned heretics to banishment, confiscation of property and loss of citizenship. A significant comparison is drawn between heresy and treason—significant because, under Roman law, treason was invariably punished by death.

" To offend the Divine majesty," says the Emperor, " is a far greater crime than to offend the majesty of an Emperor." [1]

He did not, however, proceed to draw the logical conclusion.

In 1224 the apparent inconsistency was removed. Frederick enacted a law for Lombardy which declared that relapsed heretics were to be burnt at the stake or, as a lesser penalty, to have their tongues torn out. Vacandard is doubtful whether this law was actually in operation before 1230; in that year Pope Gregory IX inscribed

[1] The comparison was not an original one. In his letter to the magistrates of Viterbo, dated March 25, 1199, Innocent III had declared that " the civil law punishes traitors with confiscation of their property and death; it is only out of kindness that the lives of their children are spared. All the more, then, should we excommunicate and confiscate the property of those who are traitors to the faith of Jesus Christ. For it is an infinitely greater sin to offend the Divine Majesty than to attack the majesty of the sovereign."

it upon the Papal register and at once set about securing its rigid enforcement in the Eternal City. From this time onwards we get a whole series of Papal and Imperial pronouncements, consolidating the position already taken up. The stock phrase, that relapsed and obdurate heretics are to be handed over to the secular arm to receive the punishment that they deserve—the "animadversio debita"—continues to be used, but evidently with a more elastic significance. In February 1231 a number of Patarin heretics were arrested in Rome. Those who refused to abjure were sent to the stake, whilst the rest were sent to Monte Cassino to do penance.

On the other hand, banishment and confiscation seem to have been the extreme secular penalty in many Italian cities until several years later. The first heretics were not burnt in Milan until 1233; and the fact was noted as a complete novelty by a contemporary chronicler. Over the statue of the magistrate Oldrado di Tresseno, who presided at the examinations, the following words were inscribed:

> "Atria qui grandis solii regalia scandis
> Presidis hic memores Oldradi semper honores
> Civis Laudensis, fidei tutoris et ensis,
> Qui solium struxit, catharos, ut debuit, uxit."

This inscription may still be read upon the façade of the *palazzo della Ragione* at Milan. It carries us back in a flash to those turbulent and critical days of the thirteenth century, when our whole European Order was threatened by the Oriental poison of Manichæism. This "guardian and defender of the Faith" "did his duty and burnt the Cathari."

The Emperor was not long in following up his law for Lombardy. In 1231 the law "Inconsutilem tunicam," the first enactment in the Sicilian Code, ordered that suspected heretics were to be tried by an ecclesiastical tribunal and that those who refused to abjure were to be burnt in the presence of the people—*in conspectu populi*. Six years later an Imperial edict, promulgated from Ravenna, condemned all heretics to death without specifying the method of execution. Finally, by three enactments, dated May 19, 1238, June 25, 1238, and February 19, 1239, the Emperor declared that the Sicilian Code and the law of Ravenna had binding force throughout his domains.

" Henceforth," says Vacandard, " all uncertainty was at an end. The legal punishment for heresy throughout the Empire was death at the stake." [1]

Frederick II and the Heretics

Nothing illustrates more strikingly the nature of mediæval heresy and the social problems which it raised than the extraordinary vigour with which Frederick II laboured to ensure its suppression. Utterly indifferent to the spiritual welfare of the Church and continually at loggerheads with the Papacy, a Christian ruler only in name, this Emperor led the way in the systematic severity with which he sought to exterminate the heretics within the Empire. Lea thinks that his legislation " shows the irresistible weight of public opinion to which Frederick dared not run counter." [2]   We find it difficult to accept such a judgment. An acute sensibility to the opinions of other people was not one of the Emperor's most prominent characteristics. He was not the man to care two straws about anybody's opinion but his own. The plain fact is that he realized, like all thinking men of his time, that the whole question was as much a social and political as a religious one. Occasionally, it is true, he attempted to use his persecuting policy as a means of obtaining the favour of the Pope. Thus in 1233 we find him boasting to Gregory IX of the number of heretics whom he has killed; and the Pope replies coldly that he is not greatly impressed by this ostentatious zeal, knowing full well that the Emperor had simply

[1] *Op. cit.*, p. 81.
[2] H. C. Lea, *A History of the Inquisition in the Middle Ages*, Vol. I. p. 325.

been killing off some of his political enemies, many of whom were not heretics at all.

If it had been merely a matter of an occasional act of violence here and there, we might find it easier to accept Lea's judgment. But it is impossible to explain Frederick's steady and ruthless campaign against heresy on the same hypothesis. He was, after all, the first European sovereign to give to the capital punishment the force of written law. On purely intellectual grounds he had far more in common with the Manichee heretics than with the orthodox Catholics. He never attempted to disguise his contempt for the Papacy; and the few casual conciliatory gestures which he made towards the Popes were no part of any settled policy. On the contrary, he showed himself the bitterest and most determined enemy that the Papacy had ever encountered. Why, then, did it not occur to him to protect the numerous heretics in his dominions and make common cause with them against the Pope? If he had wished to make concessions to public opinion, why did he not include the Jews in his repressive activities? Crusading against the infidel would have been just as effective a means of gaining Papal favour as legislating against the Cathari. Yet Frederick protected the Jews, maintained the closest diplomatic relations with the rulers of the Orient, drew upon himself the constant anathemas of Rome—and belaboured the heretics as no sovereign had done before him.

He was, indeed, one of the most remarkable figures in mediæval history. An Italian and not a German, he had been brought up in the almost exclusively Moslem atmosphere of Sicily. Throughout his reign he remained virtually a Moslem free-thinker, keenly interested in Arabian learning and ordering his private life in completely Moslem style. He was surrounded at all times by Arabian counsellors, courtiers, officers and ministers. He affected the Oriental style of dress and kept two harems, one in Italy and the other in Sicily, which were under the charge of eunuchs. He corresponded with men of learning throughout Islam and travelled widely in the Near East. He made a unique collection of Arabian manuscripts, presenting them to the University of Naples, which he founded in 1224. The tunic in which he was buried bore an Arabic inscription. Such was the man who built up the most ruthless system of anti-heretical machinery that had been seen since the days of Justinian. Mediæval heresy may have been an offence against the Church; in that point Frederick was not in the least interested. But he was sufficient of a statesman to recognize that it was also a crime against society and the State.

The penalty of the stake had long been more or less recognized, if not actually legalized, in France and Germany; and it was not altogether unknown in England. In 1212 eighty Cathari were burnt by the people of Strasburg. Philip Augustus, as we have noted, burnt a few heretics from time to time. In 1222 a student at Oxford, who had apostatized to Judaism, was condemned to be burnt at the stake. Thus Frederick II had merely taken a German custom and made it a law of the Empire; and, as regards France, we get the definite legal sanction in the *Institutiones* of St. Louis:

"As soon as the ecclesiastical judge has discovered, after due examination, that the suspect is an heretic, he must hand him over to the secular arm; and the secular judge must send him to the stake."

The Dominicans and Franciscans

The immediate and obvious necessity was the presence of some organized force, capable of regulating the gigantic legal machinery against heresy which the secular rulers had erected. To such a generation, with its intensely logical habit of mind and its keen regard for the newly discovered Roman law, it was intolerable that so weighty a matter as that of variations from the Faith should be dealt with haphazard. It was a clear gain to have replaced lynch law by a regular legal code; but that

POPE HONORIUS III AND ST. DOMINIC.
The Order of Preachers receives Papal confirmation.

was not enough.   At the critical moment, then, the eyes of the Pope fell naturally on the two newly-founded Orders, the Dominicans and the Franciscans.

" The establishment of these Orders," says Lea,[1] " seemed a Providential interposition to supply the Church of Christ with what it most sorely needed.   As the necessity grew apparent of special and permanent tribunals, devoted exclusively to the widespread sin of heresy, there was every reason why they should be wholly free from the local jealousies and enmities which might tend to the prejudice of the innocent, or the local favouritism which might connive at the escape of the guilty.   If, in addition to this freedom from local partialities, the examiners and judges were men specially trained to the detection and conversion of heretics ; if they had also by irrevocable vows renounced the world ; if they could acquire no wealth and were dead to the enticement of pleasure, every guarantee seemed to be afforded that their momentous duties would be fulfilled with the strictest justice—that while the purity of the Faith would be protected, there would be no unnecessary oppression or cruelty or persecution, dictated by private interest or personal revenge."

Even so, the first discernible Papal gestures were extremely tentative.   Lea develops this point with characteristic thoroughness and shows conclusively that the Monastic Inquisition was not a going concern, an established weapon of spiritual discipline, until, at the earliest, the middle of the century.   The extremely delicate question as to the precise relationship between the bishops and the travelling Inquisitors, the gradual supersession of the episcopal Inquisition and its replace-ment—or, perhaps, rather its reinforcing by the intro-duction of the monastic office—these things were worked out gradually and without any definite break with the past or any sweeping innovations.   In 1231 the Senator of Rome referred to the " Inquisitores ab ecclesia datos," and Frederick II spoke in one of his laws in 1232 of

[1] *Op. cit.*, Vol. I. p. 318.

certain "Inquisitores datos ab apostolica sede." In November 1232 a Dominican Friar, Alberic, travelled through Lombardy with the official title of "Inquisitor hereticæ pravitatis." In the same year Gregory IX despatched several Dominican Friars to Henry I, Duke of Brabant; "they will work," he said, "against the heretics in Germany." Again, in 1233, the Pope wrote to the Bishops of Languedoc that—

"We, seeing you engrossed in the whirlwind of cares and scarce able to breathe in the pressure of overwhelming anxieties, think it well to divide your burdens, that they may be more easily borne. We have, therefore, determined to send preaching Friars against the heretics of France, ordering you, as you reverence the Holy See, to receive them kindly and to treat them well, giving them in this, as in all else, favour, counsel and aid, that they may fulfil their office."

But the Pope was so fully anxious to avoid any unnecessary precipitancy, or possibly, as Lea suggests, had so little idea of organizing a permanent and universal tribunal, that when the Archbishop of Sens complained of the intrusion of the Inquisitors in his diocese, Gregory, by a brief of February 4, 1234, promptly revoked all commissions for it and contented himself with suggesting that the Archbishop should call in the assistance of the Dominicans, if he thought that their knowledge and experience might be of value at any time in the future.[1]

Finally, we may note a letter written by Gregory IX on October 11, 1231, to the celebrated Conrad of Marburg. This Dominican priest, who was the con-

---

[1] "Auxiliaries to the bishops," says M. de Cauzons—"that is how Gregory IX regarded the Dominicans." (*Op. cit.*, Vol. I. p. 451.)

He also notes—and the point is important—that "one must be very careful in deciding whether or not the term 'inquisitores,' so often found in mediæval documents, means inquisitorial judges. Without proper care one might easily find many more inquisitors than there actually were. The term Inquisitors . . . means inquirers, supervisers, police agents . . . and, in a very special sense, ecclesiastical judges delegated directly by the Pope. A little critical ability is needful to choose which of these meanings applies to each particular case." [P. 438, note (author's trans.).]

fessor of that gentle and lovable Princess, St. Elizabeth of Hungary, was a personage of considerable importance at the court of Thuringia. He seems to have enjoyed the highest esteem of the Pope and to have occupied in Germany a position rather similar to that of Peter de Castelnau or Arnaud Amalric in Languedoc. A stern, austere man, fanatical alike in his zeal and his piety, he was entrusted by Gregory IX with the work of combating heresy in the whole district. He was the first inquisitor in Germany.

" When you arrive in a city," wrote the Pope, " summon the bishops, clergy and people, and preach a solemn sermon on faith ; then select certain men of good repute to help you in trying the heretics and suspects brought before your tribunal. All who, on examination, are found guilty or suspected of heresy must promise complete obedience to the commands of the Church ; if they refuse, you must prosecute them according to the statutes that we have already promulgated."

Here, at any rate, we have all the distinctive features of the regular Inquisitorial procedure—the time of grace, the denunciation of suspects, the trial, the imposing of penance upon repentant heretics and the abandonment to the secular arm of those who obstinately persisted in their errors. Before passing to a detailed consideration of these features it will be convenient to note one or two general points in connection with the Inquisition, with a view to preserving a proper perspective and to avoiding that distortion and over-emphasis which a narrative unbroken by digression can scarcely fail to give.

Summary

In the preceding chapters we have passed briefly in review a period of rather more than two centuries, witnessing the appearance and spread of heresy in various parts of Europe and the gradual development by European society as a whole of a great system of protective and, as it were, self-defensive legislation against heresy.

We noted first of all the lethargic doctrinal security of the period from the eclipse of the Western Empire up to, say, the year 1000. About this time there begins to filter into Northern Italy and Languedoc an Oriental and dualistic heresy, which is practically a revival of Manichæism; at all events it is referred to as such by all contemporaries. It spreads with quite remarkable rapidity. In the northern kingdoms it is everywhere met by violent popular hostility. In Northern Italy and Languedoc, after one or two trifling little riots, it remains wholly unopposed.

In Germany and Northern France a variety of little heresies are beginning to spring up; and the popular practice of burning these heretics at the stake gradually assumes the force of established custom. They are regarded as social pests; they are loathed and despised. They are of no significance in the history of the time, most of them being merely illiterate, half-crazy agitators, who are up in arms not so much against the Church as against everything and everybody. Still their violent hostility to the claims of the Church and the established order, together with their lurid denunciations of the priesthood, find a sort of grumbling echo of acquiescence in many quarters; and it is clear that more serious upheavals are threatened. Even so, nobody is seriously alarmed. The mind of Europe, in the full tide of its new vigour, is occupied with far more interesting and important matters. The crime of heresy is unknown in any legal code, and the heretics are regarded with the same contemptuous hatred as brigands and witches. The officials of the Church start at the beginning of the period by holding up their hands in genuine horror at the ferocious action of the people. But their attitude steadily stiffens. The little local whirlpools of heresy are beginning to settle down into two or three main channels or streams. Of these the most important are the new Manichæism and the heresy of the Waldenses, the former being by far the more considerable of the two. It is unquestionable that the bishops realized before the secular rulers that heresy was becoming a thing that could not be safely ignored. The period lasts from the beginning of the eleventh to the beginning of the thirteenth century.

In Italy, and particularly in Languedoc, one distinctive heresy, this new dualism from the East, spreads without opposition of any kind. To this phenomenon a number of causes contribute. As it gains in power and solidarity, it loses gradually its character of nebulosity and looseness. Its theology is developed to full, logical conclusions. It assumes the form of a definitely anti-social philosophy, aiming at the literal destruction of society. It rots the life of the pleasure-loving, highly-coloured southern civilization, which has nourished the heresy to its own destruction. The Church, by this time thoroughly alarmed, makes desperate efforts to combat the thing by spiritual weapons. But it is already too late; the help of the secular rulers is sought in vain. Finally, the Pope appeals to the conscience of Europe and the armies of Christendom fall upon the country. A protracted and, in the main, abortive struggle ends simply in huge territorial accretions to the French Crown. The strength of the heresy is virtually unaffected.

During the first third of the thirteenth century the secular rulers of the European kingdoms, convinced at last that the whole structure of society is potentially threatened, build up, in co-operation with the ecclesiastical authorities, an iron system of anti-heretical legislation. By the middle of the century the laws of Europe are unanimous in condemning the impenitent heretic to be burnt alive. Lynch law has been superseded by statute law.

The Nature of Mediæval Heresy

Such in broadest summary are the points that we have endeavoured to set forth in earlier chapters. If we have succeeded in doing so with even the smallest degree of coherence and right proportion, it will have been made perfectly clear that the Monastic Inquisition came into being to fulfil an absolutely necessary function. It was an indispensable adjunct or throttle to the secular powers. The secular significance of heresy depends largely upon the peculiar structure of the society in which it appears. This is so because in any society a subversive doctrine necessarily comes into conflict with the Sovereign Power, necessarily strikes at the Sovereign loyalty. Therefore in a theocracy the scope of what is categorized as heresy is vastly greater than in any other kind of social structure. An opinion that may be termed unpatriotic or even treasonable under a secular monarchy will be termed heretical under a theocracy.

Not that the real nature of heresy is in any way variable. From the Catholic point of view Communism—to take a case in point—is just as much a heresy to-day as it was in the thirteenth century. But the scale of values has changed. There is a different standard of judgments. To-day the Sovereign loyalty is to the nation ; and Communism is seen primarily as subversive of national security rather than as a rejection of one or other dogma of the Christian Faith.

If, however, the interests of Church and State are identical—if, that is, the State exists within the Church rather than vice versa—it is clear that the position will be reversed. Let us take a concrete instance by way of example.

In reaction against the system of industrial capitalism, which is the dominating feature of our present social order, we have a number of men proclaiming the negation of the whole idea of private property. They are called Communists. By the majority they are hated and boycotted. They are summoned before the secular judges and sometimes punished. Their teachings are considered antisocial and treasonable, as indeed they are. In the thirteenth century a powerful and fanatical communistic movement was initiated, and the officials of the Inquisition laboured strenuously to apprehend and examine the ringleaders. They formed an heretical sect ; they were denounced as heretics and punished as heretics. They are known in history as the Spiritual Franciscans.

The Task of the Inquisition

Here, then, is the first point that should be noted in connection with the Monastic Inquisition. It was charged with the task, not only of preserving the integrity of the Faith, but of preserving the security of society. Its failure to do so would have involved a complete collapse of Western Christendom. As a fact, of course, it did not fail. The mediæval Inquisition was one of the most thoroughly successful tribunals in all history. It succeeded triumphantly in securing the extirpation of the anti-social poison of the Albigenses and, in so doing, preserved the moral unity of Europe for three hundred years.

It is also important to note that none of the mediæval heresies, which the Inquisition set out specifically to combat, were based upon intellectual protest against the Faith. We have remarked in a previous chapter that no mediæval heretic up to the beginning of the fourteenth century left any lasting monument of achievement in literature or the arts. The Albigensian heresy was more like a conspiracy than anything else. There was no trace of ordered apologetic as in the great treatises of Calvin, Beza, Zwingli and Melancthon in the sixteenth century. And this in an age of such terrific intellectual activity as the thirteenth century! In comparison with the great, full stream of mediæval achievement, the heresies seem like muddy, brackish little backwaters. Or it is as if we were watching some mighty procession, with Dante, St. Thomas, Giotto, Innocent III, St. Louis and other giants of the period striding proudly in the van; whilst a turbulent, abusive little element in the crowd are very properly suppressed by the police, with the obvious approval of the mass. From the point of view of mediæval achievement as a whole this is no belittlement of the actual importance of the heresies. A situation may be potentially dangerous without being critical. Thanks to the Inquisition, the Albigensian heresy never assumed the character of a pressing, desperate menace. The work of scotching it was begun in time, though the process occupied nearly a century.

Although they loom in such black impressiveness throughout Lea's huge volumes, the severities of the thirteenth-century Inquisition were both local and infrequent. Furthermore, they were, in the vast majority of cases, directed against the Albigensian heretics, who were deservedly detested by everybody. The Inquisition was almost unknown in Northern France and the Scandinavian kingdoms. It appeared almost momentarily in England at the time of the suppression of the Templars ; Portugal and Castile knew nothing of it before the days of Ferdinand and Isabella. Even in countries like Aragon, Languedoc and Northern Italy, which were its principal fields of activity, it operated almost exclusively in the larger towns and in the few recognized centres of heretical resistance. It was not established in Venice until 1289 ; and the Inquisitorial archives of that city show that the death penalty was inflicted by the secular power on only six occasions. In Rousillon, on the Aragonese border :

"The minute researches of the indefatigable M. Brutails have brought to light only four sentences of the Inquisition. All were directed against robber barons. . . . What happened to two of these wretches is not clear. Those whose fate is known suffered only the penalty of having their dead bones dug up and solemnly burnt, forty years after death in one case." [1]

It is unfortunate that the whole history of the Inquisition has necessarily been so closely bound up with matters of religious controversy. On the one hand, one comes across the type of writer who can never even mention the Catholic Church without referring in parenthesis to " the atrocious cruelties of the Inquisition " ; which is as though a man could not mention the word " monarch " without enlarging upon the villainies of the Star Chamber. On the other hand, there is the apologist, who approaches the Inquisition in

[1] H. Nickerson, *op. cit.*, p. 217.

a somewhat furtive manner, with a pot of whitewash concealed not very skilfully behind his back. He tends continually to lose the thread of his discourse. He discusses at some length the Protestant persecutions of the sixteenth and seventeenth centuries; one feels that he wishes, not so much to make the Inquisition intelligible, as to apologize for it. The truth is, of course, that uncritical abuse and uncritical apology are equally unnecessary. That historian is successful who so presents the facts as to show that the Inquisition came into being in response to a perfectly definite need; that, in the matter of heresy, it introduced law, system and even justice where had been limitless scope for the gratification of political jealousy, personal animosity and popular hatred; and, finally, that the ordinary, normal-minded person to-day, if suddenly dumped in the mediæval environment, would probably have given his heartiest support to its establishment.

"What you need for true history," says Mr. Belloc, "is by no means an agreement with the philosophy of the time that you describe (you may be wholly opposed to that philosophy), but at least a full comprehension of it and an understanding that those who worked its human affairs were men fundamentally the same as ourselves. . . . In the case of mediæval Europe . . . we are dealing with men who are not only of our ' genus,' but of our very stock; wholly of our particular blood, our own fathers, our own family. . . . It is certainly not necessary to agree with the details of their action, as, for example, their lapses into cruelty on the one hand or their fierce sense of honour on the other. . . . But what one must have if one is to be an historian at all, and not a mere popular writer, repeating what the public of the ' best-sellers ' wants to have told to it, is a knowledge of the spirit of our ancestors *from within*."

The Capital Penalty

Unquestionably the main difficulty of the modern reader in attempting to " get inside " the Middle Ages, particularly in the matter of the suppression of heresy, is the infliction of the death penalty. It seems ferocious, fanatical and inhuman. Yet it must be remembered that it is useless to attempt to contrast the so-called religious intolerance of the Middle Ages with the so-called religious toleration of to-day. The unity of the Middle Ages was moral and reposed upon the Church; the unity of to-day is political and reposes upon the nation; churches and religions do not seriously enter into the question. Hence, for a Church confronted, as in the thirteenth century, by the menace of Albigensianism we must see a nation of to-day confronted by some great national crisis. Thus we may compare the clean, spontaneous and comparatively wholesome enthusiasms of the Middle Ages with the pumped-up fanaticism generated by unscrupulous newspaper propaganda on the most prodigious scale, as manifested during the War. We may contrast the Inquisitorial procedure with the summary violence of our own treatment of conscientious objectors—a sect of national heretics. We may compare the vigour of the " anathemas " and denunciations which were launched upon the Albigenses with the fury which led men during the War to anathematize not only Bernhardi and the Hohenzollerns, but Wagner, Beethoven, Mozart, Goethe, Mendel and the whole imperishable flower of German genius. We may compare the Papal condemnation of subversive heretical literature with the rigid prohibition of free speech in any form under the vigilant eye of a modern censorship. If we think upon the matter on these lines, we should be able to understand; or at any rate we shall come nearer to understanding.

One question immediately arises. Upon whom rests the responsibility for having formally introduced and approved the penalty of the stake for relapsed and obdurate heretics ? Clearly it is impossible to give a categorical answer. It is impossible to lay the charge at the door of any particular individual. It is beyond doubt that Frederick II was the first monarch to give the thing the force of written law. But, as M. de Cauzons points out :

" The Imperial law imposing it (the penalty of the stake) first in Lombardy, then in Sicily, and finally throughout the Empire, seems the natural consequence of (1) attempts already made in Aragon, Jerusalem and Toulouse, and perhaps in other signories; (2) the repeated appeals of the Church to the secular arm ; (3) the already agelong custom in the northern countries ; (4) innumerable examples of the punishment, consequent upon the Albigensian War ; (5) the influence of the re-discovered Roman law. The theory which lays upon Frederick II the responsibility for the repressive measures, particularly the stake . . . is not based upon historical documents. It is certain that for two hundred years before Frederick's time the stake had been the regular punishment for heresy, especially in the north. It was the legal punishment for heresy in Jerusalem—that is, in the Latin kingdoms of the East—in Aragon and at Toulouse. It was adopted and carried out in the sight and with the knowledge of Popes and bishops, without any protest on their part." [1]

On the other hand, it is quite unhistorical to lay the full blame upon the Church. Many writers have attempted to do this, and their efforts end in such laughable blunders as that of Mr. H. B. Cotterill who, in his book, *Mediæval Italy*, declares that " Frederick II arrested the heretics and handed them over to Gregory to be burnt "; which is like saying that murderers are arrested by the hangman and handed over to the police to be executed. As a fact, the first formal recognition by the Papacy of the death penalty for heresy occurs in the Bull *Ad Extirpanda*, which Innocent IV promulgated

[1] De Cauzons, *op. cit.*, Vol. I. p. 296, note (author's trans.).

in 1252, nearly a quarter of a century after Frederick's legislation. Up to that time the Church was officially committed to the laws of Innocent III, which prescribed only banishment and confiscation of property.

Not that the committal was anything more than a theory; the phrase "animadversio debita" was a sufficiently elastic one and, after the Lombardy proclamation of the Emperor, everybody, bishops and clergy included, knew perfectly well what it meant. As early as 1229 we find the Council of Toulouse referring casually to those heretics who, "through fear of death or any other cause, return to the Faith" and ordering that such "are to be imprisoned by the bishop of the city to do penance, that they may not corrupt others."

In truth it is useless, as Mr. Turberville points out, to attempt "to read into the mind and conduct of the men of mediæval times a humanitarianism which is the peculiar product of the modern world and which they would not even have understood."[1] Lea comments justly upon "the smile of amused surprise" with which Gregory IX and Gregory XI would have listened to the thesis that the Church could and did have no share in the infliction of the capital punishment for heresy. The heretic was sent to the stake, not for the benefit of his soul nor in order to force him to change his beliefs, but to prevent him from spreading heresy amongst others. His fate was intended to be a salutary warning to the people; witness Frederick's insistence that the ceremony should take place "in conspectu populi." We do not hang murderers to cure them of a proclivity for murdering, but to warn others against the practice.

"The Church and State in the Middle Ages combined to prevent what they held to be immoral and untrue doctrine being preached to the common folk."[2]

The development of the whole great system of anti-heretical machinery was, then, a thing in which the whole conscience of society was concerned. Its driving force

[1] *Mediæval Heresy and the Inquisition*, p. 241.
[2] Bede Jarrett, O.P., *Life of St. Dominic*, p. 59.

was the public opinion of mediæval Europe. To represent it as the special creation of one man or as having been forced upon society by a particular party, whether secular or ecclesiastical, is to miss the point completely.

It is, of course, arguable that the Church, with her enormous prestige in every department of contemporary life, might have protested successfully against the introduction of the death penalty. But such a protest could have been inspired only by a humanitarian sentiment which the age did not possess. We have to remember that the whole position was built upon a foundation of remorseless and impregnable logic. If to-day we have other ideas about liberty of conscience, it is not because we have discovered a flaw in the mediæval line of argument nor because we are better men than they were ; but because, in the present condition of society, the premises, upon which the mediæval canonists based their conclusions, are no longer applicable. Granted the savage criminal law of the time, granted the theocratical structure of European polity, granted the peculiarly repulsive teachings of the Albigensian heretics, and the sequel is clear and inevitable.

CHAPTER V

UNDER Roman law the three recognized methods of procedure in criminal cases were the *Accusatio*, the *Denunciatio* and the *Inquisitio*. From its almost exclusive adoption of the latter method the Holy Office received its name. It was an office of Inquisition, that is, an office of Inquiry.

The Accusatio

In the Roman process of *Accusatio* the accuser definitely pledged himself to prove his case. He submitted to the authorities a written statement of his charges and entered the court on exactly the same footing as the person accused. If he failed to substantiate his charge, he suffered the same penalty as the defendant would have incurred by guilt; this was called the *pœna talionis*. Once handed in, the accusation could not be withdrawn; and the trial took the form of a duel between accuser and accused. The presiding magistrate only interfered when it was a matter of elucidating obscure points, clarifying the evidence to his own satisfaction and so forth. Both sides, of course, were at liberty to summon as many witnesses as they liked and to produce such documentary and circumstantial evidence as might help their respective cases. But neither accuser nor accused could be represented in court by a counsel. Both had to appear in person.

With the revival of Roman law in the twelfth century the procedure by *accusatio* passed naturally into the judiciary routine of both the civil and ecclesiastical courts of Europe. Up to the time of Philip Augustus it remained in France the only recognized method of bringing a criminal before the bar of justice. I say that it was the only *recognized* method. For naturally there were certain restrictions placed upon its employment. In cases of murder, theft, brigandage and such other flagrant crimes against society, it was not necessary for formal accusation to be made or for an individual accuser to institute proceedings. Clearly it was unsuitable for dealing with the more trifling or impersonal offences, in which, on the one hand, nobody would have felt particularly called upon to assume the arduous rôle of accuser, and, on the other, the authorities could not afford to take no notice whatever. A judicial authority must necessarily possess disciplinary powers of its own, must necessarily be able to proceed against delinquents on its own authority. It must be something more than a mere court of appeal.

Hence it is evident that, whatever may have been the official position in the matter, the *accusatio* can never have been, in practice, more than an auxiliary to the administration of justice. The Roman law summarized the power of the magistrate under three heads. He possessed (1) the *imperium*, that is, the absolute right, as an official of the State, to proceed against enemies of society; (2) the power of coercion, that is, the power to enforce obedience to his orders; (3) the power of conducting *quæstiones*, or *cognitiones*, that is, of interrogating those whom he summoned before him. In other words, the magistrate possessed, in virtue of his office, an official authority quite distinct from that of a mere judge. When he exercised that authority, he necessarily proceeded by a method of inquiry or inquisition.

In theory the power of instituting proceedings by an *accusatio* belonged to everybody as a civic privilege. In practice, however, it was not so. In the Middle Ages neither women, children, professional soldiers, excommunicated persons nor suspected criminals could avail themselves of it. Members of a family could not formally accuse one another. Lay-folk could not accuse priests, nor vice versa. Nor could heretics, Jews or pagans institute proceedings against Catholics. These disabilities did not apply when it was a matter of injury done to the property or person of the accuser. In the case of certain crimes, such as treason, there were no restrictions at all. And as soon as the idea of likening heresy to treason became general, the same applied to heresy.

It is not surprising, however, that the officials of the Holy Office made it quite clear from the first that they had no liking for heresy trials under the *accusatio*. Nicolas Eymeric, the great Spanish Inquisitor of the fourteenth century, objected emphatically to the method, saying that it was entirely unsuited to investigation concerning the Faith, that it was exceedingly dangerous for the accusers and that it necessarily involved lengthy and complicated procedure. Bernard Gui, Inquisitor of Toulouse from 1307 to 1323, makes no direct mention of it, but he insists, like Eymeric, that everything should be made as simple as possible. In 1261 Pope Urban IV urged that the Inquisitorial trials should be carried out " in a simple and straightforward manner, without the noisy arguments of advocates." Lea has noted an incident in 1304, when the Inquisitor Fra Landulpho imposed a fine of one hundred and fifty ounces of silver on the town of Theate because it had officially accused a man of heresy and failed to carry the case.[1]

This, of course, was nothing more than the ordinary *pœna talionis* which was incurred by an unsuccessful accusation. Still, taken in conjunction with the other evidence, it illustrates clearly the attitude of the Inquisitors. They frowned steadfastly upon the procedure by *accusatio* and sought always to discourage it. The reasons for this are sufficiently clear.

In the first place, it should be noted that a successful accusation entitled the accuser to a portion, decided upon by the magistrate, of the property of the accused. This undoubtedly acted as a counterweight, an attraction compensating for the unpleasant possibility of the *pœna*

[1] H. C. Lea, *A History of the Inquisition in the Middle Ages*, Vol. I. p. 401.

talionis in case of judgment for the accused.   Still, the immense possibilities of corruption are clearly apparent. We have only to read the *Annals* of Tacitus to see the thing in being.   Even in the Golden Age of the Empire we constantly come across the professional accuser engaged upon his odious task.   A rich nobleman, a suspicious Emperor, a word to some hired spy—and then the elaborate trial, based on some incautious word or gesture, which was exaggerated and distorted by a number of paid witnesses.   For the unfortunate noble-man it was the end.   Everybody was satisfied ; the Emperor had got rid of a dangerous though enviable nuisance, and the " accuser " grew fat upon the spoils of the confiscated property.   And if such things were possible in the splendid security of Imperial Rome, they were inevitable in the freer, less stable environment of mediæval Europe—particularly when the offence in question was only reflected in social conduct, and was primarily a matter of belief.

Again, as Eymeric remarked, the procedure by *accusatio* was exceedingly dangerous for the accuser. Under the *lex talionis* he laid himself open to the possi-bility of the legal punishment for heresy, namely, the stake.   But that was not all.   For if he formally accused a man of heresy, he appeared in court himself and every-body knew exactly what part he had played in the matter, how he had obtained his information and so forth.   All the other heretics in the neighbourhood, therefore, knew him for an informer and a person of whom they would be well rid.   From that time onwards, if heresy was at all widespread in the district, he was a marked man. There could be only one end to the matter ; a dark night, a lonely lane or back street, and he would be found the next morning with a knife between his ribs.   We shall have occasion to return to this point and to note that, even under the Inquisitorial system, where the names of witnesses were always carefully guarded, the heretics frequently avenged themselves upon persons whom they believed to have denounced their brethren.

In fact the attempt to extirpate heresy by legal methods

based upon the *accusatio* would have been utterly hopeless from the first. In districts where the heretics formed a majority, no ordinary person, however zealous in the Faith, could have been expected to court almost certain injury or even assassination by filing a suit against a heretic. And in places where such danger did not exist no Inquisitor, however competent and experienced, could be certain of exposing a careful conspiracy, backed by plenty of perjurious witnesses and faked evidence, to ruin an innocent man. Finally, in face of the obvious necessity for swift and unhampered action against heresy, the procedure by *accusatio* was intolerably lengthy and cumbersome. It may be urged, with a show of reason, that it provided safeguards for the accused, which could not be guaranteed under any other form of procedure. The *lex talionis* was a formidable deterrent to calumny, however cleverly worked up. The accused was confronted by his accuser and had full access to all evidence against him. But the thing presupposes a certain security of the public order which did not exist in the Middle Ages. It was not fitted to deal with an emergency nor to cope effectively with any vital menace to society as a whole.

" It is well enough," says Mr. Nickerson,[1] " for a modern civilized government, strong in the perfection of communications and of all public powers, to safeguard elaborately those accused of crime. Mediæval conditions were in many ways like those of frontier regions where the criminal can easily slip away. When this is so, justice must make herself swift and terrible by rough-and-ready methods. Otherwise she does not exist. . . . The elaborate safeguards of our procedure are defensible only on the theory that it is better to err by letting many culprits escape rather than by punishing one innocent man. And this theory, in turn, is tenable only on the assumption that no serious harm is done to the community by the escape from punishment, through the legal safeguards aforesaid, of a considerable proportion of criminals.

[1] H. Nickerson, *The Inquisition*, p. 210.

" Where, on the other hand, the life or death of the community is felt to be at stake, then matters must take a different course. Perhaps as good an example as our own time can furnish is that of military justice. Clearly it is supremely important to keep up the discipline of an army. Accordingly courts-martial are given wide latitude. And yet the almost unanimous opinion of those competent to judge is that, when administered by experienced officers, miscarriages of justice under the court-martial system are exceedingly rare ; and that, on the other hand, such a procedure as that followed in the civil courts would be destructive of all proper discipline. . . . The wide latitude allowed the Inquisitors undoubtedly produced cases of injustice, but probably no system permitting the ' disputatious wrangling of lawyers ' (as the Inquisitorial manuals put it) would have answered the case."

The " Denunciatio "

However, the fact that the procedure by *accusatio* was completely unsuited to heresy trials had been recognized long before the establishment of the Monastic Inquisition. By the time that Innocent III ascended the Papal throne, the ecclesiastical courts had almost completely discarded it in favour of the process called the *denunciatio cum promovente*. Under Roman law the *denunciatio* did not bind the accuser in any way at all. He simply handed in his testimony and left the whole conduct of the case to the judge. Thus he was not exposed to any *pœna talionis* in case his charges were not substantiated. He acted as a member of society, revealing a crime or offence of some kind to the civil authorities ; and for him the responsibility ended there. Of course he was liable to be summoned to appear at the trial, but he did so only in obedience to the magistrate's orders and not on his own initiative as an accuser.

It was obviously an elastic and rather formless method of procedure. But from the earliest times it had taken its place in the ordinary routine of internal Church discipline. A priest or monk who strayed from the paths of orthodoxy would be " denounced " in this manner to the bishop or abbot ; and such denunciation would invariably be preceded by some sort of semi-official remonstrance and fraternal warning.

But during the twelfth century it became evident that some sort of adjustment and expansion in anti-heretical procedure was unavoidable. The simple *denunciatio* had worked admirably in the days when heresy had been little more than a form of monastic misdemeanour, and exceedingly infrequent at that. But now it was a question which concerned the whole of society, to the suppression of which secular and ecclesiastical powers were committed with equal wholeheartedness. Accordingly we get the development of the procedure called the *denunciatio cum promovente*. It took its origin in the episcopal courts, but by the fourteenth century had become firmly established in the civil as well. The essential innovation consisted in the introduction of a " promoter," who took upon himself the rôle of the accuser in the *accusatio*. In his conduct of the case he simply took over the evidence from the denouncer and had the power of summoning any witnesses he chose, and so forth. He was a sort of public prosecutor.

" The institution of the promoter," says M. de Cauzons,[1] " was, perhaps, the greatest modification introduced into penal judiciary legislation since the days of antiquity. It completely changed the manner in which the suppression of crime was regarded. There was no longer any question of personal vengeance, but rather of the preservation of the social order."

It will be seen that, by relieving the accuser of the burden of formally proving his charges under pain of punishment, the procedure by *denunciatio* removed a considerable obstacle to the rapid and efficient detection of such a crime as heresy. But an accuser was still indispensable, and proceedings could not be instituted against the criminal without him. The heretic, for

---

[1] De Cauzons, *op. cit.*, Vol. II. p. 39, note (author's trans.).

THE INQUISITION IN ACTION (I)   113

instance, had to be denounced to the bishops or clergy
before anything could be said or done to him.

Accordingly, with the establishment in 1184 of what
has been rather loosely called the Episcopal Inquisition,
we get a whole series of pronouncements, demanding
that denunciation should be made and assigning to
certain persons the special duty of so doing. The
Council of Verona, in instructing the bishops or their
representatives to visit at least twice a year all parishes
in which heresy was believed to exist, empowered them
to demand from these persons, (who were called synodal
witnesses,) the name of all suspects, whose conduct or
habits were conspicuously different from those of the
ordinary Catholic. Similar decrees were passed by the
Councils of Avignon in 1209 and of Montpellier in 1215,
and were ratified and approved by the Fourth General
Council of the Lateran. The Council of Narbonne in
1227 went further, ordering the appointment of synodal
witnesses in every diocese and entrusting them with the
task of definitely searching out the heretics in their
haunts. Two years later the Council of Toulouse made
an even more explicit ruling:

" We prescribe that the archbishops and bishops shall
choose in each parish one priest and two or three lay-folk
of good reputation—or more if the occasion requires it
—and shall bind them by oath diligently, faithfully and
regularly to seek out the heretics in the said parishes.
They are to search in houses and cellars which they
consider suspicious. They are to seek for secret attics
and other such hiding-places, which, if found, are all to
be destroyed. And if any heretics are found, let information speedily be given, that they may be punished
as they deserve."

So matters stood at the end of the Albigensian War
and up to the time when Gregory IX officially entrusted
to the Mendicant Orders the special task of combating
heresy. On the one hand were the secular authorities,
unanimously agreed that heresy was a crime against society
and merited the same punishment as treason. On the

other hand were the bishops, the sole judges as to what constituted heresy. Co-operation between the two was provided by the appointment, on the part of the latter, of these synodal witnesses in each parish. Upon those denounced to them the bishops passed judgment, and in the extreme cases of obduracy abandoned the guilty to the secular arm. The synodal witnesses were ordered to act, not only as passive spectators, but as active agents or spies in the service of the Church. On paper the thing sounds tremendously formidable and ruthless. It would seem that the heretics had no possible avenue of escape and that it must be simply a matter of time before they were all denounced and dealt with. But in practice the great machine never worked at all. The bishops, already fully occupied in the cares of their pastoral offices, were quite unequal to shouldering this additional burden without additional assistance. As to the synodal witnesses, their position was clearly invidious and dangerous. It was a compromise between the old procedure by *denunciatio*, under which the denunciation of heretics depended upon individual and spontaneous action, and the fully developed Inquisitorial procedure, under which it was laid down that the duty of denouncing heretics was incumbent upon all the faithful.

The " Inquisitio "

As regards the Roman procedure by *inquisitio* it is sufficient for our purpose to note that the criminal was not formally accused or denounced by anyone. He was cited to appear before the judge as a suspect and was then tried in the ordinary way. The judge, acting upon popular rumour or upon special information which he had received, assumed the office of public prosecutor and of magistrate; in the actual judiciary proceedings he took charge of the whole trial, summoning witnesses and conducting cross-examinations himself.

This procedure, with suitable adaptations to fit the peculiar circumstances, was adopted by the Monastic

Inquisition. It was not, of course, developed into a full, coherent system in a single day or even in a single year. Many pages might easily be filled in tracing that development from its earliest beginnings, in showing how certain features were introduced in response to certain needs or deficiencies, how difficulties were smoothed out, obstacles removed and so forth. But such a study would necessarily be lengthy and would almost certainly be tedious. And we shall now attempt a general description of the developed Inquisitorial procedure as it was functioning about, say, the end of the thirteenth century.

In the first place it is of the utmost importance that several general points in connection with the work of the Holy Office should be clearly apprehended and born in mind throughout. All culpable actions of whatever kind fall into one or more of three categories. An infringement of the moral law is necessarily a *sin* against God; it may also be an *injury* to an individual, or a *crime* against the State, or both. The position of the Inquisition was, therefore, as follows. It was concerned to find out whether the accused was or was not guilty of a certain sin, the sin of heresy and rebellion against God's truth. The Inquisitor acted simply as an official of the spiritual power. But by the agreement of Church and State this particular sin had been declared also a crime, an offence against the State. And since wilful persistence in rebellion against God cannot be punished by man, all penal action against the heretic was that of a secular power punishing a secular crime. Strictly speaking, the Inquisition had nothing to do with it; and the Inquisitor, in abandoning the impenitent heretic to the secular arm, simply withdrew the protection of the Church from a hardened sinner, declaring that he had placed himself in wilful opposition to the law of God and could therefore be punished only by the law of man.

But if the heretic showed any signs whatever of a desire to amend his ways and make full abjuration of his errors, there was no longer any question of a secular crime. The Inquisition was first and foremost a peni-

tential and proselytizing office, not a penal tribunal. Its
one desire was to secure from the accused a promise of
obedience to the Church. It was this feature, no doubt,
which encouraged De Maistre to declare that the
Inquisition was the most merciful tribunal in all history.
The statement sounds fantastic and is unquestionably an
exaggeration of the facts. Yet it is not altogether without
foundation. For all secular justice aims at establishing
the guilt of the accused simply in order to allocate the
proper punishment. The Inquisition, on the other
hand, desired only an acknowledgment of guilt—an
acknowledgment that heresy was a guilty and execrable
thing—in order that the accused might become reconciled
with the Church. The Inquisitor, as Mr. Nickerson
remarks, was in the unique position of a judge who is
always trying to turn himself into a father-confessor.
Actually the Inquisition inflicted no punishments at all;
its whole plan of action was penitential and not penal.
All the Inquisitors invariably spoke of their ministrations
in this sense. They were out to convert and reconcile,
not to condemn. As far as they were concerned, heresy
was not a crime at all, but a sin for which, by sacramental
confession and promise of amendment, one could obtain
full absolution.

I have said that this fact is of the highest importance
to an understanding of the methods and actions of the
Holy Office. Unless it is clearly recognized, the
Inquisition appears, not only as a monstrosity, but as an
unintelligible and meaningless monstrosity. For instance,
we shall have occasion to discuss later the emphasis with
which the Inquisitors frowned upon the introduction of
lawyers and advocates into their examinations of the
heretics. Of course there were, as we shall see, several
reasons for this. But, in the mind of the Inquisitor, the
obvious objection to the employment of lawyers was
simply the fact that the person before him was a sinner
and not a criminal. Why on earth should a sinner need
an advocate to defend him? Note that this does not
involve a presupposition of guilt in the accused; but

merely the premise that the simple decision as to the guilt or innocence of the accused was only part of the Inquisitor's task. In case of innocence there was, of course, no more to be said. For the guilty there were two alternatives. Either he repented and received absolution and penance; or he persisted in his sin and was abandoned to the secular arm. In the former case he was reconciled with the Church; the lost sheep returned to the fold. In the latter he died in open rebellion against God. As far as the Inquisitor was concerned, every heretic abandoned to the secular arm represented a complete failure. He had failed in the primary purpose of his office, and in his professional capacity as a priest of the Church.

Under the Inquisition matters went somewhat as follows. Each Inquisitor had charge of a certain district, often of enormous territorial extent. Thus at the end of the thirteenth century there were two Inquisitors for the whole of Languedoc, two for Provence and four for the rest of France. They had their own headquarters, where the trials were held and the records preserved. Usually the Dominican convent was used for the purpose, but, when this was not possible, as at Pamiers, a room in the Bishop's palace was allotted to the special use of the Inquisitors. At Toulouse the Holy Office established its headquarters at the house given to St. Dominic in the early days by Peter Cella, near the Château Narbonnais.[1]

It is not to be wondered at that the Friars frequently expressed their unwillingness to assume the office of Inquisitors. Not only did the work demand almost superhuman exertion and tremendous vigilance; not only did it lay upon the Inquisitor an enormous responsibility; it placed him in an extremely precarious and dangerous position. But it was laid down by the Popes,

---

[1] In 1376 Gregory XI assigned to the Inquisitor at Vienne a house which had previously belonged to the chapter, situated near the hospital in that city. The reason given was that the Holy Office had no proper headquarters there. (Vidal, *Bullaire de l'Inquisition au xive siècle*, p. 434.)

under pain of incurring irregularity, that the appointment could not be refused by a Friar who had been officially nominated.   Under the Franciscan system no one could hold the office for more than five years at a stretch.[1]   But the Dominicans had no such limitation ; Bernard Gui, for instance, was Inquisitor at Toulouse for nearly sixteen years.

When the Inquisitors first took up the duties of their office in Languedoc, they found the heretics both numerous, powerful and intensely hostile.   In regard for their own person safety, they accordingly conducted their whole business from the headquarters at Toulouse, summoning heretics from the whole district under their charge to appear before them in the city.   But in 1237 the legate John of Vienne visited Languedoc and, after expressing dissatisfaction at the progress that was being made, ordered that in future the Inquisitors should not remain thus in one place, but should personally travel round the country-side, visiting all districts where heresy was reported most powerful and conducting their investigations on the spot.   The inevitable sequel was not long in occurring.

On the night of May 28th–29th, 1242, the Inquisitor Guillem Arnaud and a lay brother called Stephen of St. Tiberi were assassinated by heretics at the castle of Avignonnet, with their notary, several clerks, three other lay brothers, a canon of Toulouse and the prior of the Dominican convent.

The Dominicans of Languedoc promptly appealed to Innocent IV, recounting at length the terrible obstacles which they had encountered and of which the massacre was only the culmination, and asking to be relieved of the perilous duties that had been imposed upon them. The request was summarily refused ; the Inquisitors Bernard of Caux and John of St. Pierre were appointed to replace the martyrs of Avignonnet.   But the Pope expressed his recognition of the risks that were necessarily

---

[1] M. Vidal has noted one or two cases in which the Popes granted special extensions, where good reason existed. (*Bullaire*, pp. 117, 444, 466.) ·

BEZIERS.

run by the Inquisitors and stipulated that in future they should conduct their inquiries in such places as seemed to them most secure. His recommendation was re-affirmed in 1246 by the Council of Narbonne.

In the ordinary run of things the Inquisitor travelled round his district, staying usually at the various Dominican or Franciscan convents. Naturally he spent more time in his official headquarters than in any other one place. But he had an enormous circuit of places to be visited and would usually visit each village and town, where heresy was known to exist, every two or three years. Sometimes his arrival was quite unheralded and the people would be startled by a sudden rumour that the Most Reverend the " Inquisitor hereticæ pravitatis " was in their midst. But more usually his impending arrival would be elaborately announced beforehand; it would be given out in the churches and proclaimed by handbills posted upon the church doors and official notice-boards. When his actual approach was heralded, the faithful proceeded outside the village to meet him on the road, and he then passed into the place in solemn procession and took up his residence in the convent.

In the eyes of the faithful the prestige surrounding the Inquisitorial office was very great. He was venerated and respected as the guardian and champion of the Faith against the spread of heresy in their midst. Nothing was allowed to interfere with the carrying out of his office. When he announced his intention of addressing the people, none of the churches in the place could hold services at the particular time; for his message was for all the faithful. This was specially enjoined in a number of Papal Bulls; and anathemas were fulminated against those false preachers, secret favourers of heresy, who, by promises of indulgences and so on, sought to draw away the people from the official gatherings convoked by the Inquisitor.

The whole organization and routine of the Holy Office was based upon an absolutely ruthless determination to let nothing whatever stand in the way of the successful prosecution of heresy. Not only were the *curés* commanded to keep silence when the Inquisitor spoke; not only were the faithful enjoined, as they were true Catholics, to lend unstinting support to the mission of the Inquisitors. The Holy Office claimed and exercised complete ascendancy over the secular courts. If a criminal, who was actually standing his trial for some secular crime, became suspected of heresy, the magistrate was bound to suspend procedure against him. He was immediately placed under the jurisdiction of the Holy Office and the secular authorities could not touch him. A summons to appear before the Inquisitors took precedence over everything else. Similarly, if a heretic who was undergoing examination by the Inquisition committed a crime against the secular laws, the magistrate could not proceed against him without the express permission of the Inquisitor.

As to the local *curés*, they were pledged to a great variety of duties in connection with the smooth working of the Inquisitor's office. They had to see that the penances prescribed by the Inquisitor were conscientiously carried out; to translate any official correspondence which concerned all the people; to make arrangements for the journeys of those penitents who had been ordered to go upon pilgrimages; to bear witness in the trials for or against their parishioners; to keep up their parochial registers, wherein were inscribed the names of those who were absent from Mass without proper reason on Sunday and who did not communicate at Easter. It may well be imagined that, in a parish where heresy was at all widespread, the conscientious performance of all these duties was a difficult and by no means enviable task. But any laxity incurred heavy censure; and gross neglect might even invite suspicion of heresy.

On the day following his instalment in the district, or at any rate shortly after his arrival, the Inquisitor summoned the faithful to the principal church and preached a solemn sermon upon the duties that lay before him.   All heretics were urged to come and confess their errors; and a period, known as the " time of grace," was named, usually between fifteen and thirty days.   Any heretic who voluntarily confessed his lapse during this period had nothing to fear.   Having abjured his heretical actions and opinions, he was at once re-admitted to the communion of the faithful—of course with a suitable penance.   He appeared before the Inquisitor simply as a penitent seeking absolution for sin.   Those who had only practised heresy in secret, received only the usual private penance in the form of special devotions and other religious exercises.   Those who had openly manifested their heretical beliefs and flouted the authority of the Church were exempt from the heavier penances and were probably sent upon some short pilgrimage, ordered to make special fasts or to perform some other ordinary canonical penance.   But all, as a sign that they were truly repentant, were commanded to give full information concerning all heretics known to them.

Here we have another example of the complete ruthlessness with which the Inquisition invariably worked. We need not search in the records of the Holy Office for any manifestation of fair play or a spirit of sportsmanship; or if we do, we shall search in vain.   Where it was a question of getting hold of the suspected heretics and bringing them before the tribunal, no demand was too stringent, no subterfuge too unscrupulous.   No considerations of sentiment or chivalry could be allowed to stand in the way.   Everything subordinated this primary object of securing the appearance of every heretic in the district before the Inquisitor's tribunal. Once they had got him there, the whole idea was to induce in him a consciousness of guilt and a genuine desire to be reconciled with the Church.   The last thing that they desired was to abandon him to the stake; for that was, as we have seen, an admission that the Holy Office had failed in its mission, as far as he was concerned.

The Inquisitors, of course, never wavered for an instant in their inflexible determination to destroy heresy completely.   But to destroy heresy is not necessarily to exterminate the heretics.   The Inquisitor was a priest and an official of the spiritual power ; his sole concern was with the souls of men and their intimate salvation. He would not have been in the least disturbed by the thought of the terrible sufferings that awaited the heretic whom he abandoned to the stake.   But he also knew that such a man, dying in a state of mortal sin, invited thereby all the torments of eternal punishment.   Anything that could possibly be done to save him from the loss of his soul was clearly a duty from which the Inquisitor might not shrink.

To assist in the performance of its office the Inquisition necessarily employed a fairly large permanent staff of messengers, notaries, personal retainers, jurors, prison officials, doctors, barbers, janitors and so forth.   In parts of Italy and Spain they often employed armed men to make arrests and bring the heretics before their court ; but in France and Languedoc these duties were almost invariably performed by civil officials.   As regards the actual number of assistants retained by each Inquisitor, we learn from a letter written by the Archbishop of Embrun to the Inquisitor at Florence that the Inquisitorial staff is to consist of two notaries, twelve other persons described as " familiars " and four assessors or advisers.   The Inquisitor is instructed " to choose these and no more."   At Pamiers in Languedoc the Inquisitorial prison was staffed by one head gaoler, two warders with their wives, and another person whose duties are not described.

The Keeping of the Records

One of the most striking characteristics of Inquisitorial procedure was the enormous care and labour that were spent upon the accurate keeping of the records.   Everything said in the trials, every detail of every cross-examination was taken down verbatim by the notaries, subsequently copied out on official parchment and filed in proper order.   The archives grew to almost incredible dimensions.   Nor was it a matter of stacking the records away in dusty old cupboards and never referring to them again. They were all elaborately catalogued, special lists were kept of all heretics that had appeared before the tribunal, the files were always kept in easily accessible places and were in constant use. We hear of instances in which, by reference to the records of thirty or forty years previously, it was shown that a certain suspected person was a relapsed heretic—that is to say, that he had appeared previously before the tribunal, had been reconciled to the Church, but had now returned to heretical practices. For instance, in the examination of an old woman who appeared before the Inquisition in 1316, it was found, by referring to the records, that she had confessed to the practice of heresy and been reconciled in 1268 and that therefore she was a relapsed heretic. This is an extreme and almost unparalleled case; but it shows clearly the possibilities of the thing.

The Notaries

The taking down, arrangement and collating of all this enormous mass of information was the task of the notaries, who were by far the most important and responsible of the minor officials of the Holy Office. Until 1561, when Pius IV granted them the permission, the Inquisitors could not nominate notaries. They had to be chosen from amongst the notaries public of the civil courts or from members of religious Orders, who had had experience of the work prior to embracing the monastic life. Failing the possibility of obtaining them thus, the Inquisitor might employ temporarily two priests or laymen. Like all those who had any official connection with the work of the Inquisition, the notaries were required to take an oath of secrecy before assuming their duties. They were present at all cross-examinations and recorded all questions put to the accused together with his answers. Often they were called upon to act as interpreters. And in an emergency they might be employed in connection with the arresting of heretics and issuing of the official summonses.

The Position of the Inquisitor

In all that related to the conduct of the trials the Inquisitor had an absolutely free hand. Anyone who sought in any way to hinder his work was represented as an enemy of the Church and courted the heaviest censures. Thus a prince or nobleman who refused the aid of the secular arm in carrying out the prescribed punishment against relapsed and impenitent heretics, or who hesitated to suppress laws which hindered the smooth operation of the work of the Holy Office, or who refused to insert in the civil statute books the Imperial constitutions against heretics, could be summarily excommunicated. This was no light matter ; it meant that his vassals were released from all oaths of allegiance to his person and that he himself could not enter a church under any pretext. He was cut off from the communion of the faithful. His enemies promptly rose fearlessly against him. Most alarming, perhaps, of all, if he remained excommunicate for a year and a day without seeking reconciliation with the Church he became automatically suspected of heresy.[1]

The Popes, in fact, stuck at nothing which might increase the dignity and prestige of the Inquisitorial office in the eyes of the people. The Inquisitor was invested in all the most imposing regalia of inviolate sacro-sanctity. The plenitude of the spiritual power belonged to him ; to oppose him in any manner was the work of the devil. Here were these heretics declaring that the Pope was Antichrist, that Jesus Christ was neither human nor divine, that marriage was a greater crime than incest, that suicide was the highest of the virtues and a number of other things. Clearly, in the

[1] In 1228 a law was made in Languedoc that persons who thus became suspects might have their property confiscated. This stipulation was reproduced in the peace treaty of 1229 and in the statutes of the Council of Toulouse in the same year. Restrictions were placed upon its enforcement by Philip the Brave in 1271 ; and in 1303 Philip the Fair, declaring that the greater prestige and authority of the Church rendered it unnecessary, formally abrogated it altogether. See Tanon, *op. cit.*, p. 237.

matter of destroying so revolting and blasphemous a philosophy, there could be no half-measures: " he that is not with us is against us." But heresy, as far as the Church was concerned, was first and foremost a sin, which could be confessed to a priest and renounced, and for which the sinner could receive sacramental absolution. A hatred of heresy did not necessarily involve a hatred of heretics. Accordingly the Church, whilst committing herself with inflexible determination to the task of extirpating heresy and whilst insisting upon the absolutely unstinted assistance of the secular powers, nevertheless prescribed that the preliminary duty of deciding what was heresy and who was heretical belonged exclusively to the Inquisition. She admitted no precedent in the development of Inquisitorial procedure. The business in hand was to secure the appearance of all heretics and suspects before the tribunal; to the attainment of that end everything else was subservient.

It is difficult to exaggerate the immense difficulties and responsibilities of the Inquisitor's position. His was not the relatively simple task of discovering the perpetrator of a particular crime, but the far more delicate one of searching into a man's innermost thoughts; and, having done so, of leading him to a salutary change of mind, which would make possible his return to the loving tutelage of Mother Church. The number of defiant heretics, of those who willingly and even eagerly confessed their heretical beliefs and welcomed the crown of martyrdom in the cause of religious liberty, was quite negligible. Only a profound ignorance of historical facts could have suggested the comparison which I have seen made in a serious text-book on the subject, between the mediæval heretics of Languedoc and the early Christian martyrs. The vast majority of the former strove under cross-examination to establish their own orthodoxy by every possible evasion and quibble; just as, prior to arrest, they had striven, by a rigid adherence to the outward observances of the Church and even by regular attendance at Mass, to avert all possible suspicion from their lives.

Rules concerning the Appointment and Deposition of Inquisitors

Although naturally possessing a very wide latitude in the actual conduct of their investigations, the Inquisitors were, nevertheless, strictly bound by the ordinary rules of their Orders and by a number of special statutes. It is, perhaps, unnecessary to point out that only men of exceptionally varied talents and of the highest integrity were even eligible for the Inquisitorial office. Of course mistakes were made in the early days in the appointment of such men as the ruffianly Robert the Bougre, whose exploits we shall touch upon later. But the number of bad and corrupt Inquisitors known to us is extraordinarily small; and it may be confidently asserted that by the end of the thirteenth century the Holy Office had become a thoroughly well-organized tribunal, distinguished almost always by its high regard for justice and by the unsullied honour of its officials.

Still, there is much truth in the statement that the Inquisition was an office which, if staffed by saints, would have been hard put to it to avoid abuses and corruptions. Bernard Gui has left us a very celebrated description of the ideal Inquisitor:

" He should be diligent and fervent in his zeal for religious truth, for the salvation of souls and for the destruction of heresy. He should always be calm in times of trial and difficulty, and never give way to outbursts of anger or temper. He should be a brave man, ready to face death if necessary; but while never running away from danger through cowardice, he should never be foolhardy in rushing into it. He should be unmoved by the entreaties or the bribes of those who appear before his tribunal; still, he must not harden his heart to the point of refusing to delay or mitigate punishment, as circumstances may require from time to time.

" In doubtful cases he should be very careful not to believe too easily what may appear probable, and yet in reality is false; nor, on the other hand, should he stubbornly refuse to believe what may appear improbable, and yet is frequently true. He should zealously discuss and examine every case, so as to be sure to render a just decision. . . .

" Finally let him, like a good judge, preserve in his sentences so rigid an adherence to justice that the true compassion within his heart is manifested even upon his countenance; so that all anger and ill-temper which lead to recrimination and cruelty, may be wholly avoided . . . and let him never be swayed by motives of greed or vindictiveness." [1]

Such human compendia of all the virtues are rare enough at all times. But nearly all Bernard Gui's points had been dealt with in various Papal Bulls and Encyclicals and had been given the force of disciplinary statutes. It was a rule that no one under forty years of age could be an Inquisitor. As precautions against bad temper or peevishness in the Inquisitors, which might result in hasty, ill-considered judgment, it was laid down that everything said in court should be preserved in writing, should be submitted to the local bishop and that no sentence of abandonment to the secular arm should be valid without his ratification. Moreover, all denunciations made to the Inquisitor, as well as all interrogatories and answers of accused and witnesses, had to take place in the presence of at least two other persons.

The Generals of the Orders, as well as the Provincials, possessed the absolute right of suspending an Inquisitor in cases of laxity or incompetence in the performance of his office. When ignorance or some momentary carelessness had been the cause of his lapse, he was merely removed from his post and replaced; and the same applied in cases of ill-health or proved unsuitability of temperament. But if it could be shown that the Inquisitor had failed to carry out his duties through sheer laziness or weakness of will, if he had been guilty of wilful cruelty in his sentences or had been influenced by

[1] *Practica Inquisitionis* (ed. Douais, 1886), pp. 232, 233.

motives of personal hatred, he drew upon himself not only summary deposition, but solemn excommunication from the Pope in person. The same sentence was reserved for any Inquisitor who had allowed himself to be corrupted by bribes, whether in stiffening or mitigating his judgments, or who had in any way taken advantage of his official position to benefit himself. When it was known that he had accepted bribes or extorted fines for his own gain, he could not be released from the state of excommunication until he had personally made full restoration of all such unjust exactions.

When we have added that all the bishops were commanded to give immediate information to the Pope in cases where the superiors did not promptly replace incompetent or over-zealous Inquisitors, and that the duty was incumbent upon all Inquisitors of exercising an unobtrusive watch upon one another's actions and of reporting any shortcomings to the superior, it will be apparent that no effort was spared in ensuring that a high standard of integrity should always be preserved. Unquestionably the Inquisitor possessed powers which made him almost an autocrat in his own court and enabled him, if he was so minded, to proceed in an arbitrary, violent and dishonourable manner. But, on the other hand, the severest penalties were always held over his head to deter him from abusing his authority.

Let us briefly note the case of that unconscionable ruffian, Robert the Bougre. A converted heretic and a member of the Dominican Order, he had been entrusted by Gregory IX in 1233 with the task of combating heresy in the north of France. After conducting investigations at Péronne, Élincourt, Cambrai, Douai and Lille, and sentencing a number of persons to the stake—remarking genially that his mission was not to convert, but to burn— he turned his attention to the Champagne district. At the village of Montwimer he found a large heretical community, presided over by a certain Manichee bishop called Moranis. Wholesale arrests were made; and within less than a week Robert passed judgment upon more than one hundred and eighty of them.   On May 29, 1239, in the presence of a huge concourse, which included the King of Navarre, the Count of Champagne, the Archbishop of Rheims and a great number of ecclesiastical and secular dignitaries, the entire number, with their bishop, were burnt alive.

As was natural, this holocaust caused a great sensation. Complaints were immediately lodged with the Pope and a court of inquiry was held.   It transpired, on investigation, that the complaints of Robert's conduct, so far from being exaggerated, actually fell far short of the whole beastly truth.   Robert was immediately suspended from office and condemned to perpetual imprisonment.[1]

General Integrity of the Inquisitors

This wild outburst of fanaticism was without precedent or repetition in the French kingdom; and it was justly visited by the severest censure.   The traditional idea of the Inquisitor, as a savage, implacable zealot, sinning against every law of God and man, whilst triumphantly claiming that he was doing the work of Christ, is wholly without foundation.   In the ordinary way a man who was known to be hot-tempered and hasty in his judgments of others would never have been chosen for the Inquisitorial office.   It is not the whole truth, but it is much nearer the truth, to represent the average Inquisitor as a patient and even laborious person, terribly conscious of the responsibilities of his position, genuinely anxious to secure not only the spiritual salvation, but also the corporal safety of each heretic, sympathetic in his treatment of those who came before him, formidable only to the defiant and impenitent.   In recent times this point has been well brought out in the trial scene of Mr. Shaw's play, *St. Joan*.

All officials of the Holy Office were strictly forbidden

[1] There is a detailed account of his activities as an Inquisitor in Beuzart, *Les Hérésies pendant le Moyen-Age et la Réforme* (Le Puy, 1912).

to receive gifts of any kind. It was a salutary and necessary precaution. Of course the general upkeep of the tribunal, whose running expenses were, as may be imagined, very considerable, was the affair of the authorities, whether secular or ecclesiastical; and was maintained chiefly by the fines and confiscations which were inflicted upon the heretics. We shall have occasion to examine this point in a later section. But, apart altogether from official expenses, it is clear that the possibilities of petty bribery and corruption were innumerable. We hear of cases where accused or suspected persons approached the relatives or friends of the Inquisitor, with a view to making some amicable arrangement concerning mitigation of penance. It cannot have been at all a usual thing, for the authorities almost always saw to it that neither the Inquisitor nor any of his staff were local men; indeed it was one of the primary purposes of the whole organization that its officers should be entirely removed from the local sympathies, jealousies and prejudices of the districts in which they worked.

Still, we come across such cases as that of Guillem Arnaud Bornh, a notary of the Inquisition at Carcassonne, who admitted that he had received a sum of money and a pair of shoes as a gift from one Arnald Cat, a condemned heretic; and that, in return, he obtained for Cat a dispensation from the penance of wearing crosses.[1] Particularly in Languedoc, where the heresy was so widespread amongst the rich nobility, the temptations to favouritism and to acceptance of personal bribes, which would doubtless have been freely offered, must have been extraordinarily strong.

Moreover, the Inquisitors and their staffs were, as a rule, miserably paid. Members of the Mendicant Orders were, of course, bound by a vow of poverty and neither desired nor expected more than what was sufficient for their simple daily needs. Often enough, however, they did not even receive this much. In 1248 John of

---

[1] Douais, *Documents*, Vol. II. p. 301.

Burgundy invited the assistance of the Holy Office in uprooting heresy in his domains. From the time of their arrival he left them without financial support of any kind; and in 1255 they were forced to ask Pope Alexander IV to recall them. Many years later we find the Archbishop of Embrun keeping the Inquisitor, Pierre Fabri, working in his diocese for two years without paying him a penny; and, although the Inquisitor was invited to attend the Council of Basle in 1432, he was unable, on account of poverty, to make the journey. It would seem that only when the King himself kept the matter in hand did the Inquisitors receive their grants with any regularity.

Taking these factors into consideration, it may safely be asserted that the general integrity of the Holy Office was maintained at an extraordinarily high level—very much higher, certainly, than that of the secular courts either at that time or at most others. It is the opinion of Tanon that—

" If it has been possible to direct against some of them (the Inquisitors) charges of exaction, we must recognize that the Orders, who had assumed the task of suppressing heresy, and those of their members who worked so stead-fastly at that task, were, taken in general, free from all suspicion of avarice and that . . . they conducted their work in a spirit of the most complete disinterestedness." [1]

The " Periti " or " Viri Boni "

In his official capacity the Inquisitor had always the last word in everything relating to the punishment and penancing of those who were summoned before him. Nothing could infringe upon that. He initiated and conducted the trials, and the final decision rested with him alone. But it was laid down by Urban IV in 1264 that he should in all cases submit the evidence to a body of " experts " (*periti*) or " good men " (*boni viri*) and

[1] Tanon, *op. cit.*, p. 206 (author's trans.).

should await their judgment before proceeding to the sentences.[1] Like most other features of Inquisitorial procedure, the introduction of these " experts " was based directly upon the procedure by *inquisitio* in the old Roman law. It was also a development of the episcopal system, in which the bishop, although presiding in heresy trials as the supreme arbiter of faith and morals for the diocese, was invariably assisted by several of his priests, and in which the trials often took place in the presence of kings, noblemen and a number of the common people, all of whom had the right of making known their opinions.

The experts, who were summoned by the Inquisitor, acted more or less in the capacity of jurymen. The primary idea was not to restrict in any way the authority of the Inquisitor, but to prevent hasty and irresponsible decisions, and to provide him at all times with expert professional advice on points of canon and civil law. Bishops and civil lawyers, abbots and canonists appeared regularly on the bench of the *periti*. Often, when the Inquisitor found it impossible to convoke a representative gathering, or when he was worried by some technical point, or some particularly difficult case, he would refer in writing to a famous theologian or jurisconsult, as the case might be. Sometimes he would even refer to one of the law schools or to the great Universities. Thus the Inquisitors at Rouen, during the trial of St. Joan of Arc, submitted a summary of the proceedings to the University of Paris, and asked for advice in the matter.

Having many cases to consider, the experts were often in session for several days. There was no official ruling as to their number, which was left to the discretion of the Inquisitor. But usually there seem to have been at least twenty of them, and sometimes many more.

" At a consultation called by the Inquisition in January

[1] He merely gave the force of canonical authority to what was already an established practice. The first Inquisitors in Languedoc, Guillem Arnaud and Etienne de St. Tiberi, almost always consulted a body of experts before passing judgment. From the first it seems to have been a regular feature of Inquisitorial procedure.

1329 at the Bishop's Palace at Pamiers there were thirty-five present, nine of them were jurisconsults; and at another in September 1329 there were fifty-one present, twenty of whom were civil lawyers." [1]

They were provided with a brief summary of each case, sworn to secrecy and invited to give a decision—" penance at the discretion of the Inquisitor," " this person to be imprisoned or abandoned to the secular arm," and so forth. Generally, but not always, the Inquisitor allowed himself to be guided by their counsels.   Thus a certain Guillaume du Pont, who had been condemned by the experts to the form of imprisonment known as the *murus largus*, had his sentence commuted by the Inquisitor to the *murus strictissimus*, with chains on both hands and feet.   On the other hand, in the case of a priest, G. Traderii, who had falsely accused five persons of heresy, the experts decided that he deserved to be abandoned to the stake; but the Inquisitor changed the sentence to one of imprisonment. It would seem that in the majority of cases when the Inquisitor altered the ruling of the experts, he did so in favour of the accused.

In tending to lessen the enormous personal responsibilities of the Inquisitor, this rough jury system was an unquestionable benefit.   But as a legal safeguard for the accused its value was considerably neutralized by the fact that the names of accused and witnesses were invariably withheld from the experts and that they were provided, not with the full reports of the proceedings in court, but only with a brief summary.

" We can easily see," says Vacandard,[2] " how the *periti* or *boni viri*, who were called upon to decide the guilt or innocence of the accused from evidence considered in the abstract, without any knowledge of prisoners' names or motives, could easily make mistakes. In fact they did not have data enough to enable them to decide a concrete case.   For tribunals are to judge criminals and not crimes, just as physicians treat sick people and not diseases in the abstract.   We know that

---

[1] Vacandard, *op. cit.*, p. 99.   [2] *Op. cit.*, p. 101.

the same disease calls for a different treatment in different individuals; in like manner a crime must be judged with due reference to the mentality of the man who has committed it. The Inquisition did not seem to understand this."

That is a modern way of looking at it. But we must remember that the Inquisitors would never have seen the matter in that light. The Holy Office was not a criminal tribunal; it was more like a sort of glorified confessional. If we are to applaud or criticize the institution of the Committees of Experts, we must do so with a clear realization as to the exact function which the experts were intended to fill. Unquestionably, from the point of view of safeguarding the accused, the thing had many defects. But that was not its primary purpose. It had no power to curb the arbitrary action of the Inquisitor, but only to assist and advise him. It possessed no executive powers of any kind. It was simply an auxiliary, making for greater care and consideration in each individual case, to the penitential mission of the Inquisitor.

CHAPTER VI

The Thought and the Act

HERESY may be defined as voluntary and persistent rejection of truths explicitly defined by the Church; and unless such rejection influences in some degree the conduct of the person concerned, it has no objective existence. Nor, moreover, is mere heretical belief the concern of anyone but the individual. On innumerable occasions the Fathers and Canonists insisted that the Church does not judge a man's thoughts—*ecclesia de internis non judicat*. And even without their assurance on the point we should recognize it as axiomatic. A man is at perfect liberty to make sacrilegious confessions, to receive the Sacraments when he knows himself to be in a state of mortal sin, and, whilst not believing a word of the Catholic Faith, to perform all the obligations of a practising Catholic with ostentatious regularity. The Church has never pretended that a confessor cannot be deceived or that an impious communicant will be stricken by lightning from Heaven. *Ecclesia de internis non judicat.* In such matters she claims no jurisdiction, saying merely that these things will be answered to before the Throne of God alone.

Not that she belittles their sinfulness in any way. The Church teaches, of course, that to abuse in any way the sanctity of the confessional is to sin against the Holy Ghost and that the deliberately impious communicant invites the loss of his soul. But she claims no supernatural power of detecting the sin and no magical machinery for punishing it.

The same is true in the matter of heresy. For it is

only over those of the household of faith and over those who have strayed therefrom that the Church claims any authority. Formal—as distinct from material—heresy is a voluntary repudiation of one or more articles of the Faith; it implies the definite rejection of that which one knows to be true. Clearly, therefore, the infidel who is in good faith is not a formal heretic; and clearly the schismatic is not necessarily a formal heretic.

"The holy and humble men of heart," as Mallock well puts it,[1] "who do not know her or who in good faith reject her, she commits with confidence to God's uncovenanted mercies; and these, she knows, are infinite; but except as revealed to her she can, of necessity, say nothing definite about them. . . . Her anathemas are for none but those who reject her with their eyes open. . . . These are condemned, not for not seeing that the teaching is true, but because, having really seen this, they continue to close their eyes to it. They will not obey when they know that they ought to obey."

But it is clear that the mere holding of heretical opinions is a purely individual matter, of which the outside world need not have any knowledge at all and in which, further, it can have no interest. It was quite one thing for the Church in the Middle Ages to have pledged herself to the extirpation of heresy and for the State to have declared that heresy was a crime. But again we are brought up by the fact that the Church *de internis non iudicat*; she does not judge a man's thoughts. Mere obliquity of belief, unreflected in conduct or speech— supposing such a thing possible—can do no possible harm to anyone except the person concerned. And if mediæval heresy had been of so tenuous and unreal a nature as this, neither Church nor State would have given it a moment's attention.

In fact, of course, it was nothing of the kind. It is a truism to say that in the Middle Ages religion had a far greater importance in the lives of everyone than it has to-day. But you do not obtain a picture of the whole

[1] W. H. Mallock, *Is Life Worth Living?* pp. 217, 218.

by looking at the part under a microscope; and we have to appreciate a radical difference in the very meaning of the word religion. Religion in the Middle Ages, whether orthodox or heretical, had nothing vague about it. It was clearly defined, coherent, fully worked out, logical. It was the chart by which a man plotted the course of his life; it moulded his opinions and his character and influenced his actions. It informed his judgments and supplied him with certain fundamental principles, to which he always appealed. Note that we speak of religion in general, not of orthodox Catholicism in particular. Granted the dualistic principle, the Albigensian heresy was a logically impregnable system of ethics and belief.

The reasons for the organized prosecution of heresy have been discussed at sufficient length in earlier chapters. We are here concerned to note that, although the formal crime consisted merely in the holding of certain opinions, yet the grounds for prosecution were necessarily found, not in the heresy itself, but in its reflections in action and speech. Moreover, as the mediæval mind was, in general, more truly scientific and logical than the modern, less idealistic and conciliatory, so those manifestations were correspondingly more violent and subversive. Heresy could never be innocuous as long as heretics were logical; and it is fortunate, perhaps, that men are seldom guided in their actions by logic alone.

But the fact remains that no opinion is in itself criminal; and that an opinion can only be regarded as subversive because of consequences which actually follow upon its being held. You cannot arrest a man for thinking that the established monarchy is an abomination; although, if you find him loitering near Buckingham Palace with a bomb in his hand, you may justly become suspicious. Supposing, however, that you are animated by a firm persuasion of the Divine Right of Kings and are concerned to uproot all contrary opinions in the matter. Supposing that your determination to do this is a guiding principle, overriding even your natural solicitude for the personal safety of the reigning monarch; and that, in your judgment, the throwing of a bomb is primarily culpable because it is an implicit denial of the Divine Right; then several inferences may be drawn.   Even if you actually see the culprit throw the bomb, even if you find conclusively incriminating evidence upon his person, you cannot legitimately regard him as more than a suspect.   You can prove the *external* case up to the hilt; you can prove that he has been guilty of conduct which suggests that he disbelieves in the Divine Right of Kings.   You can be morally certain that he does so disbelieve.   But as to the *internal* case— the question of the actual disbelief—you have nothing more than suspicion; and, however strong that suspicion may be, you are not justified in calling it proof.

Extending the idea, supposing that you then discovered the existence of a certain society whose shibboleth was a specific denial of the Divine Right; and that you found out that its members were distinguished by certain little " traits " of conduct, as, for instance, that they always held their knives in their left hands and their forks in their right; then, in your concern for the monarchy in general and the reigning monarch in particular, you would view with suspicion any persons whose table manners betrayed this slight eccentricity; and you would suspect such persons in exactly the same manner as, though in a lesser degree than, you would suspect the detected bomb-thrower.   In neither case would you have proof, but only different degrees of suspicion.   You might conceivably make a mistake and arrest one who had a personal grudge against the monarch; just as you would very probably arrest a number of perfectly innocent people, whose only fault was that of being left-handed.

Suspicion of Heresy

This is a rough and, it may be admitted, rather loose analogy to the matter of the prosecution of heresy as it confronted the Inquisitors.   But it brings out a point which is of the highest importance to our understanding of the work of the Holy Office—I mean the clear and absolute distinction between the external act and the internal thought. When a person was denounced to the Inquisitors, it was invariably on the strength of some words or actions of his which suggested that he held heretical beliefs. Thus he might have frequented the houses of persons who were known to be heretics or to have attended heretical places of worship or received heretical sacraments. It might be that something in his ordinary manner of living indicated the possibility of heresy. We hear, for instance, of a certain Peter Garsias who became suspected because his father was believed to be a Manichee, his mother a Waldensian, and because, further, it was said that he had not known his wife for two years. In another case, at the time of the agitation against the Spiritual Franciscans, a witness accused a woman of heresy because she never invoked Christ or our Lady, but always the Holy Spirit. " I am not a heretic," declared one suspect to the Inquisitor, Guillem Pelhisse, " for I have a wife and I live with her and we have a family." [1]

Actually, therefore, all who were summoned before the Inquisitorial bench came before it merely as suspects. A conclusive proof that they had actually been guilty of the words or actions imputed to them did not amount to proof that they were heretics. It is not, therefore, legitimate to assert that the Inquisitors, in their prosecution of heresy, created the special offence which they called suspicion and then proceeded to punish it. In the latter case cited above, for instance, it was not a matter of determining whether the person concerned had been living a celibate life and of condemning him for it. Or, in the case of Peter Garsias, even if it had been conclusively proved that he had been living apart from his wife for a long period, the Church could have had nothing to say about such conduct *per se*. It amounted merely to a

---

[1] " Ego non sum hereticus ; quia uxorem habeo et cum ipsa jaceo et filios habeo." See De Cauzons, Vol. II. p. 158.

confirmation of suspicion. Everybody knew that the Albigenses condemned marriage and taught that a woman with child was possessed with a devil. Therefore when you found a person who was notoriously a lax Catholic acting in such a manner as Garsias, you suspected him of holding these perverted beliefs and of being one of the Albigensian " Perfect." But there was no proof. You had proof of the external act, but not of the internal thought. That could only be obtained by voluntary confession on the part of the accused.

It may be observed in parenthesis that this idea of suspicion came to possess in the secular courts a far more elastic significance than was ever allowed to it by the Holy Office. On December 20, 1402, the Parliament of Paris condemned Jehan Dubos and Ysabelet, his wife, " on suspicion " of having murdered Jehan de Charron, the lady's first husband. Jehan was sentenced to be hanged and drawn, and Ysabelet to be burnt at the stake.

Jews and Infidels

The Inquisition was an ecclesiastical court and a weapon of internal Church discipline ; and it therefore neither claimed nor exercised any jurisdiction over those who were outside the household of faith. It had no concern with the professing infidel or the Jew; and, in theory at any rate, it did not concern itself with schismatics. Nevertheless in its ruthless determination to uproot heresy it was prepared to sweep aside every obstacle that could possibly stand in its way. We have noted that to remain excommunicate for a year and a day was sufficient to incur suspicion of heresy and, hence, to bring oneself within the jurisdiction of the Holy Office. Thus schismatics were virtually included in the ban against heretics and could be cited to appear before the tribunal. A Jew who had been converted to Christianity and had subsequently reverted to Judaism was regarded as heretical. And although the Jews were not interfered with in the ordinary practices of their religion, yet if they committed any aggressive acts of sacrilege or denied beliefs that were common to Judaism and Christianity or omitted to wear the usual distinctive marks upon their dress or insulted Catholics in any way or sought to lead them to apostasy—in any of these cases the Inquisitors proceeded swiftly and summarily against them. The same applied to the treatment of Mohammedans and professing pagans.[1]

" Fautors "

Another class of persons whom the faithful were specifically ordered to denounce to the Inquisitors were " fautors " or defenders of heresy. In this category were included those who received heretics into their houses, protected, fed them and helped them to avoid detection or to escape ; as well as princes, noblemen and secular magistrates who failed to assist the work of the Inquisition to the fullest of their power. Such conduct invited excommunication. And in cases where a town or district had placed any hindrance in the way of the Inquisitors, a solemn interdict would be laid upon it. This was no light matter. It meant that all churches were closed, that no Sacraments save Baptism, Confirmation and Extreme Unction could be administered, and that no other services of any kind could be held without special dispensation—and even then, only behind closed doors and with no lights in the building.

" The interdict was exceedingly formidable because it fell without distinction upon the innocent and guilty, a whole country, a city or a community. Stephen of Bourbon relates that, in consequence of one such measure, a strong castle and its environs, near Valence, became completely deserted." [2]

[1] In 1372 Gregory XI addressed a rescript to the Dominican and Franciscan Inquisitors, ordering the prosecution of persons who had apostatized to Islam and of converted Moslems who had returned to Mohammedanism (Vidal, *Bullaire*, p. 391).

[2] Tanon, *op. cit.*, p. 213.

Sorcerers

As far as the treatment of sorcerers was concerned, there was some difference of opinion; and until nearly the end of the fifteenth century the Popes made no definite ruling in the matter. Sorcery was not very prevalent during the Middle Ages and did not become widespread until late in the fifteenth century and during the sixteenth. The Council of Valence in 1248 did not treat them as heretics and asserted further that the task of dealing with them belonged exclusively to the bishop. In cases of obstinacy and impenitence they should be sentenced to a term of imprisonment at the bishop's discretion. Bernard Gui said that sorcerers were no concern of the Holy Office; and in almost all recorded cases where they were brought before his tribunal he simply passed them on to the episcopal courts.[1]

Eymeric, on the other hand, makes a clear distinction between those whom he terms " simple " and " heretical " sorcerers.[2] Amongst the former he counts those who dabble in palmistry, astrology, fortune-telling and other innocuous hobbies of a similar nature; and with them the Inquisition and the ecclesiastical power in general has nothing to do. But when it was a question of worshipping demons, baptizing images, using holy oils for improper purposes, indulging in any of the numerous forms of black magic, or using in connection with sorcery any article that had been blessed, then there was immediate suspicion of heresy and the Inquisition was bound to take notice.[3]

Up to nearly the end of the fourteenth century sorcery was recognized as being exclusively the concern of the Church. The secular power had nothing to do with its suppression or toleration and there was no question of abandonment to the secular arm in extreme cases. But

[1] *Practica Inquisitionis*, pp. 156 ff.
[2] A very similar distinction had been made by Pope Alexander IV as early as 1260. See Vidal, *Bullaire*, p. xlviii.
[3] *Directorium* (Venice, 1607), pp. 335-6.

by about 1390, in spite of several attempts by the Popes
to keep the whole matter within the ambit of ordinary
ecclesiastical discipline, we find that in more than one
district heresy has been officially recognized as a crime
by the secular Courts, and that the judgment of sorcerers
has been taken out of the hands of the bishops and
Inquisitors.   M. Tanon notes that—

" We have several important examples in the criminal
Register of Le Chatelet from 1390 to 1393 published
by M. Duplès-Agier.   And we see, moreover, that the
unfortunate persons accused of sorcery gained nothing
by the change of jurisdiction ; for whilst the Inquisitors
or the bishops could have condemned them only to
imprisonment . . . they were now invariably punished
by death and burnt by the provost of Paris." [1]

Other Heretical Offences

The Inquisition never set itself up as a judge of
ordinary moral offences and obliquities of conduct.   The
pursuit of heresy was the beginning and end of all its
activities.   Yet heresy covered a multitude of sins and
led to all sorts of perversions of the Christian moral code—
witness the Albigensian teachings regarding marriage,
the eating of flesh meat, obedience to constitutional
authority and military service.   Accordingly, certain
perfectly general offences, which had no apparent connection with heretical belief, might, on examination,
prove to be the outcome of perverted moral teaching and,
hence, of heresy.   Thus the Inquisitors had no immediate
concern with the practice of usury.   But if a usurer
declared that he did not regard usury as sinful, then he
could be regarded as suspected of heresy.   Alexander IV,
it is true, declares that no examinations of cases of usury
should be heard before the Inquisitors, and that the matter
concerned the bishops only.   But several of the later
Popes laid it down explicitly that anyone who presumed

---

[1] *Op. cit.*, p. 250 (author's trans.).

to say that usury was not a sin was to be treated as a heretic.

Sexual irregularities and offences such as bigamy were, of course, entirely outside the province of the Holy Office. But here again, if it were known that such actions had been committed in deliberate defiance of the Church's teaching or in the express belief that they were not sinful, then there was suspicion of heresy and the examination of the case lay with the Inquisitor. In Italy, for instance, a priest who had taken a mistress was condemned by the Holy Office, not because of his breach of ecclesiastical discipline, but because he asserted that the mere act of putting on the priestly vestments released him from the state of sin. Priestly misdemeanours of this kind did not, of course, escape censure and punishment. But unless there was suspicion of heretical belief behind the action, the Inquisitors had no concern with it.

Much energy and solicitude were expended by the Holy Office in the seeking out and destruction of heretical books, of unauthorized translations of the Scriptures and, in general, of all propaganda contrary to the Faith. The fact that so few of the heretical books of worship, ritual and instruction have survived to the present day has frequently prompted the suggestion that the mediæval heretics have been grossly misrepresented by historians. It is only another instance, we are told, of the devil being painted black because God has written all the books. We know, of course, that by far the greater proportion of the surviving evidence is the work of persons who were bitterly hostile to them, and who regarded their presence upon earth as a pollution. From the point of view of the modern historian it is unfortunate that the labours of the Inquisitors in the matter were so extraordinarily successful. We hear of a certain rich and cultured nobleman, the Marquis of Montferrand, who was an ardent bibliophile and had made a large collection of Catharan literature. During his last illness he was visited by the Dominicans, whom he informed of his hobby, assuring them that he read these books simply from interest and, indeed, that to manifest his contempt for the teachings contained therein, he always stood upon the box, in which the books were kept, when he was dressing himself. But the Inquisitors were taking no chances; the volumes were taken out and burnt in his presence.

In 1319 at Toulouse Bernard Gui made a clean sweep of a great mass of Jewish literature that he had collected. Two cartloads of books—the majority, it seems, were copies of the Talmud—were dragged through the streets, accompanied by a public herald, officials of the ducal court and a great number of citizens, and solemnly burnt. It would be easy to cite similar instances.

Denunciation of Heretics to the Inquisitor

We shall now resume our discussion of the actual course of events after the arrival of the Inquisitor in an heretical district. The solemn sermon, the " *Edit de foi,*" has been preached and the time of grace has been named. The faithful are commanded, as they are loyal members of the Church, to give full information to the Inquisitor concerning all heretics known to them. The heretics are urged to confess their errors and, approaching the Inquisitor as penitents to a father confessor, to seek reconciliation with the Church.

Following upon this pronouncement, the Inquisitor would be kept very fully occupied. On the one hand he usually received a great number of voluntary confessions. Bernard Gui stated that the " time of grace " was a most salutary and valuable institution and that many persons were reconciled thereby. These heretics had nothing to fear; they came before the Inquisitor in a spirit of repentance and submission—whether feigned or genuine —and their acknowledgment of guilt was simply in the nature of sacramental confession. In cases of " secret " heresy—that is, in which the penitent had merely toyed with heresy in a spirit of curiosity and had in no way compromised himself by speech or action—he received only the usual canonical penances. In the more serious cases he would be ordered to make a short pilgrimage and would probably be saddled with a comprehensive routine of fasting and ecclesiastical observance. Under no circumstances could he be sentenced to imprisonment —still less to abandonment to the secular arm. The Inquisition was primarily a penitential office and not a penal tribunal, and the heretic who voluntarily confessed was simply an ordinary penitent.

In the meantime there poured in upon the Inquisitor a number of denunciations and allegations against various persons supposed to be heretics. This man had frequently visited the house of a notorious " perfected " heretic or had been seen coming away from one of their meetings. Another had made repeated and explicit statement of heretical doctrines. A third had suddenly started to lead a life of extreme asceticism ; and so on. It is difficult to repress a shudder when we consider that the Inquisitors accepted and even encouraged the denunci- ation of suspects by their closest relatives, that wives would sometimes denounce their husbands, sons their fathers and mothers their own children. For it was an invariable condition of reconciliation with the Church that the penitents should give full information concerning all their former associates. The whole machinery of the thing was ruthless and unscrupulous, entirely regardless of any considerations of chivalry or sentiment. Certainly it was not a time for half-measures. No loophole could possibly be left through which an obdurate and impenitent heretic might escape summons. Certainly the Inquisi- tors knew their job better than we, six centuries from the scene of action, can profess to know it ; and we may presume that the methods employed were indeed necessary to the successful carrying through of the business in hand. " The tribunal," says Mr. Turberville, " gave every facility for the escape of the prisoner from all the possible unhappy consequences of his defamation, down *one* avenue—confession, penance, reinstatement." [1] Beyond and apart from that it was absolutely inflexible.

[1] *Mediæval Heresy and the Inquisition*, p. 199.

Witnesses

It accepted, for instance, the testimony of persons who would not have been allowed to give evidence in the secular courts. Criminals, heretics, excommunicates and notorious evil livers could appear as witnesses. There seems to have been no definite ruling as to age limits; but we hear of one case, certainly exceptional, where a child of ten, living at Montségur, gave evidence against six members of his own family and several others. As regards the evidence of heretics against one another, Frederick II had declared that they could not testify in the courts; and at first the Inquisition accepted this ruling. But in 1261 Alexander IV abrogated the restriction and the testimony of heretics became fully recognized.

No heretic could be arrested unless concurrent and corroborative evidence had been given against him by at least two witnesses. A single denunciation by itself had no force whatever. The Inquisitor Guy Foulques, writing quite unofficially, advised that this number should be regarded as a minimum; and that when the accused was a person of good reputation and had not previously been suspected of heresy, the evidence of two witnesses should not be regarded as sufficient. Eymeric expressed the same opinion. But it would seem that, in the ordinary run of things, the minimum which had been declared necessary was accepted as being also sufficient.

False Witnesses

The removal of the *pœna talionis* for a false accusation, together with the concentration of all juridical authority in the hands of a single man, the Inquisitor, necessarily laid the Inquisition open to the impositions of false witnesses. The method of trial was simply a form of duel between the accused and the Inquisitor; a clean sweep had been made of all the usual legal paraphernalia which, distasteful to the Inquisitors on account of their cumbrousness, would necessarily have acted as powerful safeguards against perjury and calumny.   Eymeric noted the evils and corruptions that might arise therefrom, but declared that such conspiracies could almost invariably be detected by careful scrutiny of the evidence and examination of witnesses.   It is to the credit of the Holy Office that from the first they treated the false witness with the utmost possible severity.   Since the secular power could provide no safeguard in the matter, they were thrown back on the employment of their own penal machinery, which was purely penitential in its aim and concerned only the repentant and reconciled heretic. For the false witness they had no mercy, reserving for him the most rigid form of imprisonment, often for life. In Languedoc alone, between December 1328 and September 1329, Lea has noted the condemnation of sixteen false witnesses to this punishment.   A year or two later the Inquisitor of Carcassonne tracked down a deeply-rooted conspiracy to ruin an innocent man and, forcing five perjurers to confess, sentenced them to perpetual imprisonment.   Finally, in 1518 Leo X, in a rescript to the Spanish Inquisition, authorized the abandonment of false witnesses to the secular arm, which was to treat them in the same manner as relapsed heretics.

The Summons

The denunciations made to the Holy Office were, as soon as received, co-ordinated and transcribed by the notaries, and then submitted to the Inquisitor for examination.   If it was decided that there were sufficient grounds for proceeding against the person concerned, a warrant was despatched to him, ordering his appearance before the Inquisitor on a specified date.   This warning was conveyed to him either by the parish priest or, more usually, by one of the minor officials of the Inquisition ; and it was accompanied always by a full written statement

THE HIGH CITY OF CARCASSONNE.

of the evidence held by the Inquisitor against him.   In the meantime, if it was judged that further interrogation of the witnesses was desirable, they were summoned before the Inquisitor and all further evidence that might be forthcoming was carefully recorded.

Finally came the formal order of arrest; and from that time onwards until his release the accused heretic was completely in the hands of the Holy Office.   If there was reason to fear that escape might be attempted, the warrant for arrest was issued simultaneously with the preliminary mandate and the copy of the evidence; which meant, of course, that the unfortunate suspect received no warning of any kind and had no opportunity for serious and accurate study of the case against him. In the infrequent cases where the accused did not put in an appearance on the specified date, the Inquisitorial summons was published on three consecutive Sundays in the cathedral church of the diocese and the parish church.   Handbills were placed on the official notice-boards outside the churches and copies of the summons were sent to the last house at which the suspect was known to have lived.   If, at the end of the period, nothing had been heard of him, he became an excommunicate and a proscribed man; he could not be sheltered or fed by anyone under pain of anathema—he was an outcast upon the face of the earth.   I need hardly say that this rule was not applied in cases of illness or where any good reason was submitted to account for his non-appearance.

Suppression of the Names of Witnesses

Neither in the written summary of the evidence against him nor at any time during his trial were the names of those who had borne witness against him revealed to the accuser.   Sometimes the Inquisitor would show him the full list of all who had given information, without specifying those who were concerned in his own case. But more often a complete secrecy was preserved; and Bernard Gui recommended that, when there was any possibility of danger to the witnesses, the most that should be conceded was the showing of the whole list. The practice was given the force of canon law by Pope Boniface VIII, who, however, added a stipulation that the names of witnesses might be revealed if the Inquisitors judged that there was no danger in so doing.[1]

The accused, therefore, was, as a rule, completely in the dark as to who had lodged information against him; and, except in special cases, was confronted by no accuser in court. The proceedings simply took the form of an interrogation conducted by the Inquisitor, every word of which was sedulously recorded by the notaries. It is clear that such methods transgress against the first principles of legal justice as we understand the term. We have only to picture the Inquisitor, suave, patient, conscientious, yet inflexibly stern, confronted, say, by some unfortunate old peasant, half dead with fright, overwhelmed by the solemnity of his surroundings and perplexed by the relentless fire of questions and sugges-tions—we have only, I say, to picture such a scene as this to realize that the scales were heavily weighted against the accused, however kindly might be his judge and however vague the evidence against him.

But it is quite gratuitous to assert, as has often been done, that the method was adopted with the express intention of depriving the suspects of a fair trial. As a matter of fact there were several weighty reasons which, on purely utilitarian grounds, justified it completely. The primary purpose, of course, was to safeguard the witnesses. We come across numerous instances in which, either on suspicion or when the names of informers had leaked out, the Cathari killed those who had denounced their brethren to the Inquisition: and it is not, perhaps, an exaggeration to say that in the early days when the heresy was still powerful and widespread, the effect of promiscuously making public the names of witnesses would have been to paralyze the work of the

[1] See Eymeric, *Directorium* (Rome ed., 1585), p. 445, and Bernard Gui, *Practica*, pp. 189-90.

Holy Office and to make assassination the almost inevitable fate of the denouncer. Even as it was, such acts of violence were by no means exceptional. We hear of a certain Arnold Dominici, who had denounced seven heretics to the Inquisitors, being murdered in his bed by the " Believers " of the sect, who conveniently forgot their rigid teachings concerning the inalienable sanctity of human life. At Narbonne in 1234 the arrest of a citizen called Raymond d'Argens led to a regular massacre of informers.

Further, as we have already noted more than once, the Inquisition was a penitential office and not a penal tribunal; and those who appeared before its officers were in the position of sinners rather than criminals. All that was sought was an acknowledgment of the sin of heresy and a genuine profession of repentance; and it must be remembered that during the " time of grace " all heretics had had full opportunity of making that acknowledgment. Moreover, it is certain that in the vast majority of cases that came before the Inquisition, the evidence was of so unequivocal a character as to make it a moral certainty that the accused was a heretic, whether he admitted it or not. That is to say, there was usually little difficulty in proving the *external* act, in showing that he had actually behaved in such a manner as to justify the strong suspicion that he was a heretic.

The Trial

The suspect would first be asked whether he had any mortal enemies; and if in reply he gave the names of any who had witnessed against him, the whole case received a damaging blow. Indeed, this was practically the only way in which he could conclusively invalidate testimony against him; and the Inquisitors always made a point of asking whether he had recently quarrelled with any of his neighbours or relations. For the purpose of proving the facts of such a quarrel he was allowed to summon witnesses in his support.

The accused also had the power, though it seems seldom to have been employed, of appealing above the Inquisitor to higher authority. Lea has noted a case where an Italian gentleman, a devout Catholic, was arrested on suspicion of having sheltered heretics, and summoned before the tribunal. He promptly appealed to Rome; and the Pope, after examination of the circumstances, quashed the whole indictment. More striking is the case of a nobleman, Jean de Parthenay, who was accused of heresy by the Dominican Inquisitor in Paris and arrested by the order of King Charles the Fair. Asserting that the Inquisitor was incompetent and unfit to exercise his office, the accused refused to stand his trial and appealed to the Pope. He was summoned to Rome and, after a lengthy palaver, was dismissed without a stain upon his character. One may be pretty certain that this kind of thing was only possible for persons of wealth and position—and, it may be added, for persons whose orthodoxy was unassailable. No heretic, however affluent and influential, would have dared to take the risk.

During the actual course of the proceedings against him, the treatment of the accused depended entirely upon the Inquisitor. Between the interrogations he might be free to come and go as he chose. Sometimes he was detained in one of the monasteries or allowed to go back to his ordinary avocations, on condition of his finding sponsors who would guarantee his appearance before the Inquisitor at the proper time. In the more serious cases he might be imprisoned.

Clearly the whole idea in the mind of the Inquisitor was to get the accused to confess. It was not simply a matter of satisfying himself whether the person who stood before him was or was not a heretic. That would have been comparatively easy. He was not in the position of the judge in an ordinary criminal case, whose concern is to determine simply the guilt or innocence of the accused, and to whom the confession or denial of guilt by the accused is an altogether unimportant consideration. The Inquisitor had to go beyond this. Even when the external act of heresy had been proved by an iron chain of evidence, even when he and everybody else was morally certain that the accused was a determined heretic, the most delicate and the most vitally important part of his work lay before him. In his capacity as an Inquisitor he could do nothing without a confession of the internal thought; and if such a confession were not forthcoming and if, further, the evidence against the accused was regarded as conclusive, he had then no alternative but to admit the failure of his office by abandoning him to the secular arm as an obstinate and defiant heretic.

It is often said that the Inquisition never acquitted anybody; and it is certainly true that very few persons left the Inquisitor's tribunal without a stain upon their characters. Penance of some kind, however trifling, was almost always imposed. But it is not quite legitimate to use the word "acquitted" in this connection. As we have said before, the Holy Office imposed penances and not punishments; and the Inquisitors always spoke of their ministrations in this way. Moreover, this fact was fully appreciated by the heretics themselves. They were penitents and not condemned criminals, and we find frequent requests "not for justice, but for mercy." [1] There is no question of condemnation or acquittal in the confessional; the sin has been acknowledged and penance necessarily accompanies the granting of absolution.

Only when the evidence against the accused was definitely proved perjurous or calumnious were the Inquisitors prepared to grant a formal declaration of innocence. For the rest, the various Inquisitorial handbooks insisted strenuously that the greatest care should be taken in instituting proceedings against anyone. The strictest secrecy was to be observed in the examinations of witnesses and the subsequent co-ordinating of their evidence; lest, as Pegna said, the reputation and honour of any man might be injured. Consequently, if the Inquisitor judged that the case against a particular person

[1] M. de Cauzons (Vol. II. p. 209 note) gives several specific instances of such appeals.

was insufficient to justify arrest, nobody knew anything about it.   The evidence was simply set aside and, as far as any official procedure was concerned, the accused heard nothing at all.   Further, the Inquisition was at perfect liberty to suspend proceedings at any point of the trial. If it was judged that the accused had cleared himself or had explained away the evidence against him, the whole matter was dropped and he was, of course, set at liberty. These two points explain why, if the trial went its full course, a sentence of acquittal was extremely rare.

The Interrogations

All the features of Inquisitorial procedure which strike us as most revolting and cruel were inspired by this single-minded determination to secure confession.   Confession was sought by every imaginable means, by elaborate and long-winded cross-examinations, by efforts to entrap the prisoner into some compromising admission, and often by lengthy adjournments of the inquiry, whilst the accused was imprisoned with full leisure to think matters over.   We hear of an extreme instance of the latter means, when a person summoned before the tribunal in 1301 was finally penanced in 1319.   Lea has an amusing and extraordinary story of a certain Italian Inquisitor, who kept a suspected heretic without food and then reduced him to a state of hopeless intoxication by giving him a bottle of wine.   It appears that some sort of confession was immediately obtained.   We hear nothing of the sentence subsequently passed upon the unfortunate man ; but he lives in history as probably the only person who ever got drunk at the expense of the Holy Office.

In the general run of things the interrogation was apt to assume the form of a spirited tussle of wits between the Inquisitor and the accused.   On the one hand, the Inquisitors had no hesitation in resorting to all kinds of tricks and subterfuges in order to catch the suspect off his guard and obtain damaging admissions; and so

great was their skill and subtlety in such methods that
the famous Franciscan, Bernard Delicieux, remarked, in
an oft-quoted phrase, that, if St. Peter and St. Paul had
been brought before the tribunal as suspects, they would
have been unable to clear themselves completely.[1] Thus
the Inquisitor, pretending to be satisfied on a particular
point, would pass on to another, and then suddenly swoop
back to the first with a leading question ; or he would
make a great show of consulting written evidence and put
his next question in a note of feigned surprise, as though
he had found some contradiction between his documents
and the statements of the accused ; sometimes he would
threaten, sometimes he would plead, sometimes he would
be genial and conciliatory. And whilst it must be
admitted that most of his expedients were sufficiently
innocent and even transparent, it is obvious that they were
quite unworthy of the high dignity of a judge's office and
that they were grossly unfair to the accused.

As may naturally be supposed, the great majority of
the suspects exerted every nerve, not so much to disprove
the evidence that had been lodged against them, but to
repudiate the suspicion that they were actually heretics.
We have noted earlier that the number of defiant heretics,
of those who voluntarily and steadfastly proclaimed
their heretical beliefs before the Inquisitor, was quite
negligible. The majority, by every possible evasion
and equivocation, sought primarily to avoid committing
themselves to any statement of heretical doctrine and to
convince the Inquisitor that the actions for which they
had been convicted were merely trifling indiscretions
which could easily be explained away. Eymeric observed
that usually the Cathari or Albigenses were the most
tractable heretics and that they usually made confession
without much difficulty. But the other sects—and
Bernard Gui agrees with him here—were much more
slippery and resourceful. The Waldensian, for instance,
" presents himself for interrogation with an air of
assurance. When he is asked if he knows why he has

[1] *Liber Sententiarum* (ed. Limborch), p. 269.

been arrested, he replies sweetly and with a smile, ' Lord, I wish indeed that you would tell me the reason.'   Asked about his belief, he replies that he believes all that a good Christian ought to believe.   If he is asked whom he regards as a good Christian, he says that a good Christian is one who believes whatever Holy Church teaches.   If one wants to know what is Holy Church, he answers that it is what you consider as such.   If he is told that Holy Church is that of which the Pope is sovereign, he replies that he also believes it, meaning that he believes that such is the belief of the judge.   On other questions, such as transubstantiation, he avoids replying by exclaiming, ' How could I believe otherwise ? '   Or perhaps he will turn the question back at his judge.   ' And you, my Lord, surely you believe this ? '   And if the judge affirms his belief and if he is obliged to stick to it, it is always with the mental reservation that that belief is not his, but that of the judge.   If, piercing finally through his equivocations, the judge gets him into a corner, he assumes an appearance of great humility, declaring that, if they want to twist some meaning out of everything that he says, he will not know how to answer, for he is a simple and unlettered man, and that it is not fair to try to trap him in his words.   But in order to avoid taking an oath or in order to introduce into the formula of the oath something which will alter its character, the Waldensian will put forth all his resources." [1]

Antecedent Imprisonment

If during the simple interrogation the Inquisitor found it impossible to secure the desired confession, it was deemed that stronger measures were necessary. " If he (the accused) has been *convicted* by witnesses," says the Inquisitor, David of Augsburg, " let no mercy be shown him, lest he should be delivered over to death ; let him be given only a little food, since fear may then

[1] Tanon, *op. cit.*, pp. 355, 356 (author's trans.).   See also Bernard Gui's *Practica Inquisitionis*, pp. 253, 254.

humble him." In 1325 the Inquisitor of Carcassonne imprisons a man " until he shall make fuller confession of the truth." Note that in both these instances there is an absolute presumption of guilt; the external case is regarded as being proved beyond question. All that is sought, therefore, is a confession of guilt,[1] for without it the Inquisition has no alternative but to abandon the heretic to the secular arm. Consequently, against the obstinate heretic the most ferocious methods were employed in a spirit of quite genuine altruism—a sort of wild, nightmarish altruism which is the age-long hallmark of religious fanaticism.

" Such a man," says Eymeric, " shall be shut up in prison, strictly confined and in chains. None except the warders shall enter his cell . . . the bishop and Inquisitor . . . shall frequently summon him and instruct him in the truth of the Catholic faith and the falsity of those articles to which, in the obstinacy of his mind, he still clings. . . . But if he shows no willingness to be converted, there is no need for haste . . .; for the pains and privations of imprisonment often bring about a change of mind. . . . And . . . the bishop and Inquisitor . . . shall try to bring him back by certain alleviations, placing him in a less unpleasant prison . . . and shall promise that mercy awaits him if he be converted from his errors." [2]

The Use of Torture

As a last resort, to be employed only in the gravest cases, yet constituting unquestionably the blackest stain upon the record of the Holy Office, was the employment of torture. Under Roman law it had been laid down that

[1] It is important to realize that a confession of guilt does not mean merely an admission that the charges made were true. It implies a renunciation of error and a firm purpose of amendment—a confession that heresy is culpable and execrable. It is quite separate and distinct from the simple acknowledgment that one is a heretic.

[2] Quoted by De Cauzons, *op. cit.*, Vol. II. p. 185.

torture might be employed against a slave, but not against a freedman or citizen; and it is the opinion of M. Tanon that the use of torture had never been wholly discontinued throughout the Dark and early Middle Ages.   But with the revival of Roman law throughout Europe in the twelfth and thirteenth centuries, and with the contemporary lapsing of the ordeal as a means of deciding disputed questions, torture began again to creep into the sphere of recognized legal practice.   Lea finds it mentioned " in the Veronese Code of 1228 and the Sicilian Constitutions of Frederick II in 1231," but thinks that " in both of these the references to it show how sparingly and hesitatingly it was employed." [1]   M. de Cauzons cites evidence which seems to show that, at the beginning of the thirteenth century, torture was not unknown in the secular courts at Paris.   At any rate from about 1230 onwards the references become more frequent and more uncompromising in secular administration.   In 1252 Pope Innocent IV formally sanctioned its introduction into Inquisitorial practice.   In the celebrated Bull " *Ad Extirpanda*," which was to be renewed and confirmed by Alexander IV in 1259 and by Clement IV in 1265, it was enjoined that—

" Moreover, the *podesta*, captain, consuls, ruler or such persons as are in authority are ordered to compel all captured heretics to make full confession of their errors and to denounce such other heretics as are known to them; with the restriction that such compulsion should not involve injury to limb or danger of death; just as thieves and robbers are forced to confess their crimes and to denounce their accomplices.   For those heretics are true thieves, murderers of souls and robbers of the Sacraments of God." [2]

The restriction that such torture as was imposed should not " imperil life " nor " injure limb " was unknown in the secular courts, where the judge was free to indulge

---

[1] Lea, *op. cit.*, Vol. I. p. 421.

[2] The text of this Bull is given in the *Practica*, pp. 310 ff.   Note the reference to the recognized use of torture in the secular courts.

in any refinements of cruelty that might occur to him. On the other hand, under civil law neither soldiers, knights, doctors nor noblemen could be submitted to torture; the Holy Office made no such reservation. They could torture anybody, irrespective of age, sex or social position. As in so many other matters, everything was left to the discretion of the individual Inquisitor; although Clement V in 1311 prescribed that the permission of the local bishop must always be sought in each individual case before torture could be employed by the Inquisitors.

As to the restriction that the torture should be such as not to " injure limb," it was a meaningless mockery. When a suspected heretic had been extended upon the rack or bounced from floor to ceiling by the *strappado*, to console oneself by the reflection that no bones had been broken argues an almost incredible obliquity of mind. In fact the Inquisitors got round every restriction placed upon their use of torture by a series of the most blatant equivocations that could possibly be imagined. At first, for instance, they were forbidden by the canons of the Church to be present during the torturing of a prisoner; and the torturer himself was always a civil officer. The tribunals, however, complained so strenuously about the restriction and urged so forcibly that their work was greatly complicated thereby, that in 1260 Alexander IV authorized the Inquisitors to grant one another all the necessary dispensations from " irregularity " that might be incurred by presence in the torture-chamber. The permission was re-affirmed by Urban IV in 1262, and clearly amounted to an explicit authorization to the Inquisitor to assist at the questionings under torture.

" Torture was not to be employed until the judge had been convinced that gentle means were of no avail. Even in the torture-chamber, whilst the prisoner was being stripped of his garments and was being bound, the Inquisitor kept urging him to confess his guilt. On his refusal the *vexatio* began with slight tortures. If these proved ineffectual, others were applied with gradually

increasing severity.   At the very beginning the victim
was shown all the various instruments of torture, in order
that the mere sight of them might terrify him into
yielding." [1]

It was also a rule that no prisoner might be tortured
more than once and that the torture was not to last more
than half an hour.   The point was, however, evaded by
another palpable equivocation.   For when a second
torturing took place, it was described as a " continuation"
and not a " repetition " of the first.   Bernard Delicieux
was put to the torture three times, and—an exceptional
and unparalleled case—some Waldensian sorcerers of
Arras were tortured twice a day for a week.

" Usually," writes Lea,[2] " the procedure appears to
have been that the torture was continued until the accused
signified his readiness to confess, when he was unbound
and carried into another room, where his confession was
made.   If, however, the confession was extracted under
torture, it was read over subsequently to the prisoner and
he was asked whether it were true.   In any case the
record was carefully made that the confession was ' free
and spontaneous,' without the pressure of ' force or
fear.' "

If one were to place exclusive reliance upon the official
records of the Inquisition, one would find it easily arguable
that torture was practically unknown.   The register of
Bernard Gui, who was Inquisitor of Toulouse for sixteen
years and who was called upon to examine more than six
hundred heretics, shows only a single instance in which
torture was used.   Even here there is a contradiction ;
the accused retracted certain admissions that he had made,
on the ground that they had been wrung from him by
torture ; but the transcriber expressly contradicts him,
asserting that the confession had been made quite
voluntarily.   Bernard of Caux's register shows one case
in which a heretic made confession under threat of torture.
In the records of the Carcassonne tribunal from 1250 to
1258 there is no mention of torture at all.   Torture

---

[1] Vacandard, *op. cit.*, p. 111.   [2] Vol. I. p. 427.

seems almost never to have been employed by the Inquisition in Germany, where the usual methods of forcing confession in obstinate cases were by starvation and by repeated cross-examinations, the intervals being spent by the accused in prison.   In the register of Geoffrey d'Ablis, whose excesses as an Inquisitor drew upon him the censures of Pope Clement V, torture is mentioned more often.   But what is recorded is not its employment, but its non-employment.   That is to say, we find a number of explicit statements that the confession in point was made freely and without constraint. Still, as Lea remarks—

"There are numerous instances in which the information wrung from convicts who had no hope of escape could scarce have been procured in any other manner. Bernard Gui . . . has too emphatically expressed his sense of the utility of torture on both principals and witnesses for us to doubt his readiness in its employment."

That the references to its employment are so rare in the abundant records of the Inquisition need not surprise us.   The forced confession had no legal significance; and we have noted that the official confession was not made in the torture-chamber, but after the completion of torture.   Thus, by a quibble, it was recorded as having been entirely free and spontaneous.   In a word, the purpose of the torture was not to force a confession, but to bring the accused to such a chastened and salutary frame of mind that he would confess afterwards !   It is true, of course, that torture was only resorted to in the last extremity and when all other means had failed. Nor were all the Inquisitors convinced of its utility. Eymeric declared that it was a useless and misleading way of obtaining confessions.   It is difficult to summarize the discussion as to the extent of the use with any finality.   One can only say that, on the one hand, the almost complete silence of the records cannot be regarded as proving anything, and that, on the other, its employment was reserved only for the most obstinate cases.

The Instruments of Torture

In general it would seem that the Inquisition employed the same methods of torture as the secular courts; principally the water torture, the rack and the *strappado*. A particularly revolting variation of the former was occasionally practised in Spain. A damp cloth was placed upon the tongue and a small trickle of running water allowed to fall upon it. Then, by the natural actions of breathing and swallowing, the cloth was drawn down into the throat, producing an agonizing sensation of suffocation : when it was drawn out again, it was often found to be saturated with blood.

The rack, it is perhaps unnecessary to explain, was a square or triangular frame on which the prisoner was stretched and bound by wrists and ankles. The ropes passed round windlasses which could be operated and turned by the torturer, producing dislocation of joints and horrible muscular injuries.

The *strappado* was probably the most usually employed instrument of torture. It consisted simply of a rope passing over a pulley fixed to the ceiling. The hands of the accused were tied behind his back. Then by the rope attached to his wrists he was raised to the ceiling and allowed to fall with a jerk, thus dislocating the shoulder-joints. The torturers would sometimes add to the general gaiety of the proceedings by attaching heavy weights to the feet of the prisoner.

The transparent brutalities of the whole business are too obvious to need comment. Even if the whole position of the mediæval canonists be admitted, even if it be conceded that heresy was a worse crime than treason and that the Inquisition was far more cautious and hesitating in its use of torture than the secular courts, even if it be recognized, as was unquestionably the case, that heresy was as much a social as a religious menace—even granting all these things, the employment of torture by the Inquisition was a crime which merits the perpetual obloquy of posterity. Nothing but some ingrained obliquity of vision can blind the historian to this fact. It has been suggested that torture was regarded as a sort of substitute for the ordeal; and we have noted that the reappearance on any considerable scale of the use of torture in the secular courts was almost exactly contemporaneous with a series of Papal enactments which declared trials by ordeal illegal. Yet we are inclined to doubt that the secular and ecclesiastical tribunals regarded the two things as being in any way analogous. It seems to us that the most that can be said is that, in adopting the use of torture, the Holy Office was consciously following, with certain theoretical restrictions, the precedent of the secular courts and the Roman law; that the Inquisitors recognized their difficulties better than we can expect to recognize them to-day; and that, in deciding that their task was beyond their powers, unless they were allowed to employ torture in obstinate cases, they probably decided rightly.

Granted the validity of these points, we may surely dismiss the idea that torture was employed with the object of benefiting the victim's soul. The supposition that a confession of orthodoxy, extracted after a lengthy session in the torture-chamber, should be capable of improving in any way his chances of ultimate salvation—such a supposition, I say, is so repulsive and grotesque that one can scarcely bear even to contemplate it. I cannot believe that the Inquisitors ever regarded the use of torture in this light; nor, indeed, is there any evidence to suggest that they did so. The idea of the thing was much more mundane and practical. Torture was employed with the primary object of extracting information. We have noted that one of the conditions of reconciliation with the Church was that full information should be furnished concerning all heretics known to the penitent; and it was in this connection that torture might be employed in obstinate cases or when it was believed that important evidence was being held back. The whole point about most of the mediæval heresies was that they were societies and not mere schools of

thought.   For this reason—it is the old *cliché* over again—
the interests of Church and State were identical.   It was
not a matter of combating the erroneous theology of a
few isolated eccentrics, but of breaking up a highly
organized secret society whose triumph would have
involved the destruction of civilization.

This does not imply a justification of the use of torture,
which remains, as we observed above, an indelible stain
upon the record of the Holy Office.   But it is as well
that we should try to appreciate the issues at stake and
to understand why the employment of torture came to be
sanctioned in an ecclesiastical tribunal.   It is an
unpleasant subject, and we turn from it with relief.

CHAPTER VII

THE MAJOR PENALTIES

THE lengthy and tortuous course of the trial has been run. Probably it is a long time—a matter of weeks, months or even in extreme cases years—since the accused made his first appearance before the Inquisitor. At any rate the conclusion has been reached. It remains to decide upon the sentence. The Inquisitor communicates with the secular magistrates and with the local ecclesiastical courts in order to verify any doubtful points in the evidence collected. He makes inquiries concerning the family history of the accused, his education, his friends and so forth—anything which might shed light upon the probability or otherwise of his having lapsed into heresy. All this supplementary information has been carefully recorded by the notaries and added to the *dossier* of the accused. The most important points have been summarized in a written *précis*, and submitted to the assembly of experts. Finally, their judgment has been received by the Inquisitor, who, after a last consideration of the case, pronounces the Inquisitorial " fiat."

When the sentence is one of abandonment to the secular arm or of perpetual imprisonment, the further necessity remains of submitting the whole process to the bishop and of obtaining his official endorsement. In case of serious disagreement between the bishop and the Inquisitor, the matter must be referred to the Holy See.

The Holy Office then issues a formal summons, ordering the accused to attend on a certain day at such-and-such a place, that he may hear the decision arrived at. He furnishes an affidavit, guaranteeing his compliance.[1]

[1] See Douais, *Documents*, Vol. II. pp. 117 ff., where many examples of these formularies are given.

The " Sermo Generalis " or " Auto-da-fé "

It is not, perhaps, an exaggeration to say that a great many people know only one word of Spanish, and that word is *auto-da-fé*. The thing is regarded as a sort of public holiday, with much feasting and merrymaking ; the great spectacular attraction being the ceremonial burning of large numbers of heretics. In view of this curious misconception it may be well to discuss briefly the real nature of the ceremony.

The *Sermo Generalis* or *Auto-da-fé* comprised, as its name implied, the preaching of a sermon and the making of a solemn act of faith by all who were present. It did not necessarily involve the condemnation or punishment of heretics, still less the infliction of the death penalty upon the impenitent. During his long term of office at Toulouse, Bernard Gui presided over eighteen *autos-da-fé*; yet at seven of these his most severe sentences were to terms of imprisonment. Between 1318 and 1324 the Inquisition at Pamiers held nine *autos-da-fé*; but during that period only five heretics were abandoned to the stake. At the *auto* convened on November 28, 1319, Bernard Gui made only one anti-heretical judgment, ordering the burning of a great collection of Jewish literature that had come into his hands. At the *auto* of July 14, 1321, he condemned one heretic to banishment. On June 29, 1321, the only measure relating to heresy was the removal of the interdict laid upon the village of Cordes. An *auto-da-fé* was primarily a solemn and ceremonial assertion of Inquisitorial authority, intended to confirm the faithful and to stimulate their zeal. Any important event, such as the installation of a new Inquisitor in the district, might be accompanied by one of these functions.

From an early date, however, it became the recognized practice to add to the impressiveness of the *auto-da-fé* by the formal promulgation of judgment against all heretics who had appeared before the tribunal and been convicted since the last ceremony of the kind. Most of the sentences of Bernard of Caux were passed at the General Sermons and, as far as we know, all of Bernard Gui's. Generally the thing took place in a church.   But we hear of the holding of an *auto-da-fé* in 1247 just outside the gates of Toulouse, and in 1248 at the *Hôtel de ville*.   The Inquisition of Pamiers, with that lack of any sense of humour that was so characteristic of Inquisitorial methods in the Middle Ages, made use of the cemetery.   Sometimes the *auto* took place in the bishop's palace, sometimes in a monastery, sometimes in one of the public squares. Bernard Gui's " sermons " were always held in St. Stephen's church at Toulouse.

There was no general rule as to the day on which an *auto-da-fé* should be held.   But usually, in order to facilitate the presence of as large a number of people as possible, a Sunday or a general holiday was chosen.   On the other hand, the great feast-days of the Church, such as Christmas, Easter and Pentecost, as well as the Sundays in Advent and Lent, were avoided, since it was considered undesirable to interfere with the offices of the Church and the religious exercises of the faithful.

The proceedings were opened quite early in the morning.   In the church or public place in which the ceremony was to be held, two large wooden stages had been erected. Entering the building in solemn procession, preceded by a herald and accompanied by an armed guard, the Inquisitor and his personal staff, the bishops, clergy, representatives of royalty, nobility and the civil magistrates took their places upon the central daïs.   Upon the other were grouped the heretics who were to hear the judgment of the Holy Office in their respective cases. The whole building was packed from end to end by the people, who always assembled in huge numbers.   On one occasion, at Arras in 1420, the proceedings were interrupted by the sudden collapse of the stage upon which the body of dignitaries were seated—an incident which, whatever the others thought about it, must have afforded immense enjoyment to the heretics in the dock.

The opening ceremony was the Inquisitor's sermon,

usually a short disquisition on some primary article of the Faith, touching upon the perversity of the heretics in general and the special obliquity of the beliefs which they upheld; and concluding with words of general exhortation and admonition. The Inquisitor then pronounced the Papal indulgence of forty days, which was granted to all present. This was followed by the making of the solemn Act of Faith—the *auto-da-fé*—on the part of the royal personages or their representatives, the noblemen, the seneschals, bailiffs, magistrates and other secular officials. These persons made profession of loyalty to the Church and the Faith, binding themselves to pursue the heretics and to support the mission of the Holy Office. The Inquisitor terminated these preliminary ceremonies by pronouncing a sweeping "anathema" against all who sought to oppose the Inquisition.

Now came the turn of the heretics. It seems to have been the general rule that the various penances and judgments were made known to the persons concerned several days prior to the public announcement at the *auto-da-fé*. The point cannot be decided definitely, but as M. de Cauzons remarks—

"Particularly in the *autos-da-fé* where there were a comparatively large number of convicts, the thing seems very probable, as a means of avoiding disturbances, tears and perhaps protests." [1]

First of all the Inquisitor or his representative pronounced the pardons or commutations of sentence. Thus, at the *auto* held on September 30, 1319, Bernard Gui released fifty-seven persons from prison and absolved twenty from the penalty of wearing the crosses.[2] On July 3 and 4, 1322, he released one from prison and eleven from the obligation to wear crosses. Following upon this, all those heretics who had made confession to the Inquisitor and professed a desire for reconciliation

---

[1] De Cauzons, *op. cit.*, Vol. II. p. 279.

[2] This penance will be discussed in Chapter VIII. We may here note that it consisted in the wearing of strips of cloth in the form of a cross upon the breast, thus branding the person as an ex-heretic.

with the Church knelt down in turn and, with their hands upon the Gospels or the altar, took the solemn oath of abjuration.   The penitential psalms were recited and then the bishop if he was present, or the Inquisitor if he was not, pronounced absolution.   Finally, commencing with the more trifling cases, penanced to short pilgrimages and various religious exercises, and passing in order of guilt to the impenitent and relapsed, who were to be abandoned to the stake, a notary read out a full list of the sentences.   The reading was made first in Latin and then in the vernacular, describing in summary the offences of each person and announcing the judgment of the Inquisition.   Last of all came any orders concerning the destruction of houses.   Those condemned to imprisonment were marched off by the sergeants-at-arms ;   the relapsed and impenitent (if there were any) were handed over immediately to the secular authorities.

I need hardly add that the above description is a purely general one and does not imply that sentences of every kind were pronounced at every *auto-da-fé*. We have seen that at seven out of his eighteen *autos*, Bernard Gui abandoned nobody to the secular arm. At only three of them did he order the demolition of houses ; and at eight he condemned no one to imprisonment.   The whole thing, naturally, depended upon circumstances.

Bernard Gui

For several reasons it is worth while to speak more fully of Bernard Gui.   Born in 1261, he made his profession in the Dominican Order at Limoges when he was nineteen.   In turn he became Prior of the Dominican houses at Albi, Carcassonne, Castres and Limoges.   For more than sixteen years he occupied the post of chief Inquisitor at Toulouse ; and when he was relieved of this charge, he was appointed Archbishop of Tuy in Galicia in recognition of his notable services.   In many respects he must be accounted one of the most remarkable men of his time. In an age of prolific writers he was amongst the most prolific of them all; and his works include *An Abridged Chronicle of the Emperors* (a general history from the Incarnation to his own time), *A Chronicle of the Kings of France*, *A Treatise on the Saints of the Limousin*, *A Treatise on the History of the Abbey of St. Augustine at Limoges*, *The Mirror of the Saints*, *Lives of the Saints*, *An Historical Treatise on the Dominican Order*, *A Treatise on the Mass*, and a *Summary of Christian Doctrine*. Finally, there is his most famous work, the *Practica Inquisitionis*, in which he gathered up the fruits of his long experience as an official of the Holy Office, outlining with a wealth of illustration and with much careful advice the whole duty and functions of the Inquisitor.

It is not, perhaps, an exaggeration to say that Bernard Gui was the man who launched its death-blow upon the Albigensian heresy. Throughout the struggle Languedoc remained the chief battleground; and throughout the struggle Toulouse remained the greatest heretical stronghold and the hub of the whole movement. Further, it was during the early years of the fourteenth century that the crisis and culmination of the conflict against Albigensianism was reached. When Bernard Gui assumed office in 1307 the situation was supremely critical. There had been strong heretical demonstrations, bolstered up by political propaganda against the French King, in Albi and Carcassonne. Philip the Fair had failed to deal effectively with the trouble. The Franciscan Friar, Bernard Delicieux, agitating violently against the Papacy and the Holy Office, was at the height of his prestige; and huge numbers of heretics, driven out of Languedoc by the earlier strictness of the Inquisition, were pouring back into the country from Italy.

During his term of office, which lasted from 1307 to 1323, Bernard Gui convened eighteen *autos-da-fé* and pronounced 930 sentences—an average of rather more than five a month. Of the effects of this iron inflexibility we may judge by noting the subsequent activities of the Inquisition in Languedoc. Between 1326 and 1330 we hear of the holding of *autos-da-fé* at Narbonne, Pamiers, Beziers and Carcassonne. There was one at Carcassonne in 1357, at Toulouse in 1374, and finally at Carcassonne in 1383. That is all; and it is a sufficient commentary upon the work of Bernard Gui. No Inquisitor was more zealous, efficient and implacable in his action against the heretics. Under his direction the Inquisition, in the plenitude of its power and the full enjoyment of its innumerable privileges, operated with the easy smoothness of a machine. Its public cere-monies were conducted with grim and tremendous solemnity. Based upon the experience of nearly a century, its procedure displayed at once the patient thoroughness of the mill-wheel and the elastic adapta-bility of the hungry octopus. Before the hot blast of Bernard Gui's zeal the Albigensian heresy rocked in its tracks and withered away.

It is therefore of the highest significance that, in the Inquisitorial records of the Toulousain tribunals, we possess the full count of Bernard Gui's 930 sentences from 1307 to 1323. The summary is as follows :—

Released from obligation to wear crosses	132
To pilgrimages, without wearing crosses	9
Released from prison	139
Sentenced to wearing crosses	143
Imprisoned	307
Dead persons, who would have been imprisoned	17
Abandoned to the secular arm and burnt	42
Dead persons, who would have been abandoned	3
Bones exhumed and burnt	69
Fugitives, declared excommunicate	40
To be exposed in the stocks or pillory	2
Priests to be degraded	2
Exiled	1
Houses to be demolished	22
Condemnation and burning of the Talmud (two cart-loads)	1
Removal of interdict	1
Total	930 [1]

[1] Douais, *Documents*, Vol. I. p. 205. Dom Brial, in his preface to the

It will be seen that by far the most frequent sentence was imprisonment; and that of the 307 heretics so committed, 139 were released before the expiration of their prescribed terms.   According to M. Langlois, 19 out of the whole number were condemned to the " murus strictus," which involved solitary confinement in chains.[1] It is also interesting to note that 17 out of the 42 persons abandoned to the secular arm were condemned at the *auto-da-fé* held on April 5, 1310; during his last eleven years in office Bernard passed judgment in 715 cases, abandoning 19 impenitent and relaxed heretics to the stake.   Out of the whole number of 930 sentences, 89 concerned persons already dead, 40 fugitives were condemned " in absentia," and there were two condemnations for false witness.

Particularly important is the relative preponderance of the various penalties.   Subtracting the 271 grants of pardon and commutation of sentence, we have 659 condemnations.   Of this number 307 were sentenced to terms of imprisonment and 143 to the wearing of the crosses. Clearly, under Bernard Gui's régime, these were by far the most common penances.   Before passing to a more detailed consideration of the different punishments, it will be well to re-affirm what we have already said—that Bernard Gui's activities show the mediæval Inquisition at the summit of its efficiency and operating with its most relentless thoroughness.   Its efficiency is demonstrated by the exceedingly small number of failures—that is, abandonments to the secular arm.   Of its thoroughness the enormous number of sentences, as well as the subsequent course of events in Languedoc, provide sufficient evidence.

---

early edition of Vol. XXI of the *Recueil des Historiens des Gaules*, says that Bernard Gui burnt 637 heretics.   This is a mistake; the figure 637 represents the total number of individuals who appeared before Bernard's tribunal.   The same error, copied from Dom Brial, is made by M. Molinier, *L'Inquisition dans le midi de la France*, p. 207.   The actual number burnt is 42.

[1] Ch. V. Langlois, *L'Inquisition d'après les travaux récents.*

The Stake

The formula with which the relapsed or impenitent heretic was handed over to the secular power stated that—
" We dismiss you from our ecclesiastical forum and abandon you to the secular arm. But we strongly beseech the secular court to mitigate its sentence in such a way as to avoid bloodshed or danger of death."

It is a little difficult to see why such a form of words was used. In the early days, of course, before the formal authorization by Innocent IV of the capital punishment for heresy, the thing had some real significance. But later it was obviously nothing more than an empty phrase, retained, presumably, by long force of custom. If the secular authorities had shown the smallest inclination to take it literally, they would have been swiftly called to book by the ecclesiastical power. Indeed, it was laid down by more than one canonist that failure on the part of the State to enforce the full penalty within five days of condemnation by the Holy Office should render the officials concerned liable to censure. Theoretically the Inquisitors had no share in the infliction of the death penalty. But they knew as well as everybody else that abandonment to the secular arm meant certain death at the stake; and when, many years later, the famous Dominican Inquisitor, Sprenger, spoke frankly in his *Malleus Maleficarum* of " those whom we cause to be burnt," he was expressing an idea that must have been a commonplace to the majority of mediæval Inquisitors. It was absurd of De Maistre to declare that " all that is terrible and cruel about this tribunal, especially the death penalty, was due to the State. . . . All the clemency, on the contrary, must be ascribed to the Church." Such a summary is a gross exaggeration of the actual facts.

On the other hand, it is clear that the mediæval Inquisition was very far from being the holy holocaust that certain controversialists have sedulously represented it to have been. Bernard of Caux was Inquisitor of Toulouse from 1244 to 1248, and the portion of his

register relating to impenitent heretics has not been preserved.[1]   But upon relapsed heretics he pronounced no
more severe penalty than imprisonment.   Between 1318
and 1324 the Inquisition at Pamiers conducted nine
autos-da-fé, condemning sixty-four heretics in all, of
whom five were abandoned to the secular arm.   Thus in
Bernard Gui's cases forty-two out of six hundred and
thirty-five, or about one in every fifteen, and at the hands
of the Pamiers tribunal about one in every thirteen,

EXECUTION OF AN HERETIC.
A pencil sketch made by a notary of Count Alphonse of Poitiers in the
margin of a proposed edict against heresy. The date is somewhere
between 1249 and 1254.

suffered the extreme punishment.   M. Langlois estimates that, during the worst days of the later Spanish
Inquisition—with which, in the present study, we are not
concerned—one heretic out of every ten was burnt.
Lea does not attempt any general summary concerning
the mediæval Inquisition proper, but he observes that
" the stake consumed comparatively few victims."
Gibbon, discussing a portion of Bernard Gui's register,
remarks with a rather unnecessary offensiveness of phrase,

[1] This, at least, is the more likely hypothesis. It seems extremely
improbable that Bernard of Caux was never confronted by any
impenitent heretics; that is to say, it seems extremely improbable that
the records are, in fact, complete.

that "since one must not calumniate even Satan or the Holy Office, I will observe that, of a list of criminals which fills nineteen folio pages, only fifteen men and four women were abandoned to the secular arm." [1]

Certainly, as Vacandard points out, those heretics who managed to avoid being tried by the Inquisition had no reason to congratulate themselves. In 1244 the Count of Toulouse undertook the destruction of several fortresses in Languedoc, particularly the château of Montségur, which was known to be a great heretical stronghold. The place was besieged and finally captured; and two hundred Albigensian "Perfect" were burnt on the spot without trial.[2] In 1248 Raymond VII of Toulouse arrested eighty heretics at Berlaiges. They confessed in his presence and, without being given an opportunity of recanting, were all burnt at the stake. This summary violence contrasts strongly with the exactly contemporary methods of Bernard of Caux. On January 31, 1257, Renaud de Chartres, Inquisitor of Toulouse, wrote to Alphonse, Count of Toulouse and Poitiers, and brother of St. Louis, complaining strongly of the conduct of the secular authorities. A number of relapsed heretics, whom Renaud had sentenced to imprisonment, had been seized by the magistrates and burnt.[3] Such complaints are by no means isolated; in the thirteenth century the secular arm, as a rule, needed no encouragement in the vigorous prosecution of heresy. And, so far as the burning of heretics was concerned, the Inquisition was a damping factor rather than a driving force. Unquestionably Vacandard is right when he says that—

"Taking all in all, the Inquisition in its operation denoted a real progress in the treatment of criminals; for it not only put an end to the vengeance of the mob, but it

---

[1] *Decline and Fall of the Roman Empire*, Vol. VI. p. 135, note (World's Classics Ed.).

[2] The most accessible contemporary account is that of Guy de Puy-Laurens, "Historia Albigensium," cap. xlvi in Bouquet, *Recueil des Historiens des Gaules*, Tom. XX. p. 770. See also Molinier, *op. cit.*, p. 24; De Cauzons, Vol. II. p. 331.

[3] Douais, *Documents*, Vol. I. p. 157; Tanon, *op. cit.*, p. 472.

diminished considerably the number of those condemned to death." [1]

The Impenitent Heretic

From the time of Frederick II's law for Lombardy the stake was the recognized legal punishment for the impenitent heretic. Under the Inquisition there was never any question about that. The impenitent or obstinate heretic was the heretic *par excellence*, acknowledging his adherence to heresy and resisting every effort on the part of the Inquisitors to obtain his abjuration. He had been cajoled, exhorted, threatened, probably imprisoned and even tortured with the idea of obtaining, not an admission that he was a heretic, but a confession of the guilt of heresy. And if he perished at the stake, he perished, in the truest sense of the word, as a martyr to his cause. For the avenue of escape, of certain escape from death, was open to him up to the very last moments. He was accompanied to the scaffold by representatives of the Holy Office, who were strictly forbidden to take the line of encouraging him to meet death bravely or of offering spiritual consolation of any kind. On the contrary, their duty was not to cease from beseeching him to repent before it was too late; and the slightest sign of softening on his part was sufficient to remove all possibility of his being burnt. We even hear of one case at Barcelona, in which the condemned man had been bound to the stake and the faggots had been lighted and had begun to scorch him. With the flames actually licking round his feet, he cried out and professed renunciation of heresy. He was at once unbound.

It may be added that the number of impenitent heretics was extraordinarily small. In the huge majority of cases, the fear of death, together with the strenuous efforts of the Inquisitors, was sufficient to procure abjuration. Out of the forty-two persons abandoned to the secular arm by Bernard Gui, only nine were impenitents; the others were relapsed heretics.

[1] Vacandard, *op. cit.*, p. 143.

We have already discussed, or rather hinted in a vague and tentative fashion at, the reasons why burning was considered an appropriate punishment for heresy. It seems certain that in the eyes of these men there was a deeply symbolical idea attaching to the consuming of the body by fire; and it is quite clear that burning was not chosen on account of its particular painfulness. Frequently the victims were strangled before being burnt. Moreover, we have to note the comparatively large number of sentences against persons already dead. It has been plausibly argued that this violent hatred which pursued the heretic even in his grave, was dictated solely by what Lea calls the stimulant of pillage—that is, the desire to secure the confiscation of property which necessarily accompanied condemnation for heresy. We shall have more to say on this point later. But it may be observed here that the Inquisitors were not content merely to execrate the memory of the dead. They ordered the exhumation of his remains. They ordered that the remains should be burnt with the greatest ceremony and solemnity. It was unthinkable, they would have said, that consecrated ground should be polluted by the bones of a heretic, that his body should be allowed to rest in a place which had been specially hallowed to receive the bodies of the faithful and to which he had, as it were, obtained entry by false pretences.

The Relapsed Heretic

Concerning the impenitent heretic there was never any difference of opinion. As soon as the secular legislative powers had decided that heresy was a crime deserving the capital sentence, wilful persistence in heresy could lead only to the stake. But with relapsed heretics—that is, those who, after reconciliation with the Church, returned to heretical practices ("*ut canes ad vomitum*," as Pope Gregory XI tersely expressed it)—this was not, at first, the case. The Councils of Tarragona in 1242 and of Beziers in 1246 ruled that relapsed heretics, if they made profession of repentance, should only be imprisoned. Amongst the sentences of Bernard of Caux, whose zeal earned him the nickname of the " Hammer " of heretics, we come across sixty cases of relapse, none of whom were abandoned to the secular arm. In the Inquisitorial records of Carcassonne is recorded the examination of a relapsed heretic, who had " adored " the Albigensian " Perfect " and had laid aside the crosses imposed upon him by an earlier sentence. He was condemned to wear the double crosses and to make public penance in all the churches in the town.

As a typical example of Inquisitorial procedure in this earlier period we may briefly note the case of Alaman de Roaix. He was, perhaps, the most active member of a family whose name appears with great frequency in the records of the Languedocian tribunals. They were all rich and influential heretics, and seem to have thrown themselves with the greatest zest into the dual enterprise of fostering the Albigensian heresy and stirring up agitations against the Church.

Suspected of being an heretical bishop, Alaman had been condemned in 1229 by the Papal legate, Romano ; and, professing abjuration of his errors, had been reconciled to the Church under the penance of making a pilgrimage to the Holy Land. This pilgrimage he had made no attempt to carry out. In 1237 the first Inquisitors of Toulouse, Guillem Arnaud and Etienne de St. Tiberi, made a second investigation of his case ; and after examination and inquiry, charged him with active propagation of heresy. He was known to have made his house a regular heretical headquarters, to have instigated assaults upon Catholic clergy and to have successfully appropriated ecclesiastical dues. The Inquisitors condemned him *in absentia* and he became a proscribed man. Yet when, in 1248, he again professed abjuration of his heresy and sought reconciliation with the Church, Bernard of Caux did not abandon him to the stake. He was sentenced to perpetual imprisonment.

" We enjoin further," proceeds the writ of condemnation, " that he shall provide Pons, who used to live with Raymond Scriptor, with food and clothing as long as the said Pons shall live, by an annual payment of fifty solidi. Further, he shall make reparation to the Hospitallers of St. John for what he has stolen from them, and to all others whom he had cursed and injured." [1]

The year 1258 is pinned down by M. de Cauzons as marking the end of this period of comparative leniency towards the relapsed heretic. Up to that time we know of no single instance in which relapse was punished by the stake; from that time onwards it seems to have been the general rule that it should be so punished. We have already noted that, out of the forty-two persons abandoned by Bernard Gui to the secular arm, thirty-three were relapsed heretics. St. Thomas Aquinas said that relapsed and impenitent heretics should be treated with equal severity. In one point, at any rate, their position was more hopeless than that of the impenitent; since, when once the sentence of abandonment had been passed, their fate was absolutely sealed. They could not escape death by repenting at the last moment; and the only privilege accorded to them, and denied to the impenitent, was that of receiving the last Sacraments, if they so desired.

The position of the relapsed heretic is therefore interesting because it is unique. To him the Inquisitor was a judge and not a prospective father-confessor; to the Inquisitor he was a criminal and not a prospective penitent. Had he not deliberately rejected the loving chastisement of Mother Church and turned again to wallow in the filth of heresy? Was not his earlier return to the Faith a manifest fraud and an imposition upon the clemency of the Church? It was, indeed, almost a sacrilege—a proof in itself of impenitence. Moreover, it was plainly absurd that one who had taken advantage of the leniency of the Inquisition and flouted its authority should be treated in the same manner as one who,

[1] Douais, *Documents*, Vol. II. pp. 69–72 (author's trans.).

however tardily, had made sincere abjuration of heresy.
The fact that the Holy Office had power to inflict lifelong
imprisonment as a penance pointed logically to the death
penalty for relapse.

The Church, the Secular Arm and the Stake

In everything relating to the execution the secular
magistrate acted simply as an instrument of the Church.
The heretic abandoned by the Inquisition appeared before
him as a condemned criminal, convicted already of a crime
for which death was the legal punishment.   There was
no question, therefore, of any second trial by the secular
power ; nor was it even deemed necessary that the
magistrate should know anything about the case.   The
word had been spoken by the Inquisitor, and all that
remained to be done was to arrange for the execution.
After the trial of St. Joan of Arc the civil magistrates
were not even consulted.   The stake had been prepared
beforehand, and, as soon as the Inquisitor had pronounced
judgment, the soldiers led her off to execution.   Sometimes the condemned persons were placed for several
days in the secular prisons.   For it was always desired
that the final terrible ceremony should take place in the
presence of as many people as possible, so that their
hearts might be filled with a salutary fear and that the
awful gravity of the sin of heresy might be impressed
upon them anew.

In all this the Church was an active participator.   It
is quite absurd to suppose that the secular magistrates
acted as an independent power, pronouncing and
executing a sentence of their own in which the Inquisitor
had no concern.   The line of argument adopted by
certain modern apologists, who have attempted to maintain that the Church could and did have no share in the
infliction of the death penalty, would have been quite
incomprehensible to the mediæval Inquisitors.

" It is a strange obtuseness," remarks Mr. Turberville,[1] " that does not see that the whole attitude of the Inquisition to the heretic points logically, and indeed inevitably, to death as the fate of the obdurate. The tribunal had been created, and it existed, to the end that heresy might be exterminated. To have failed to secure that those who to the last resisted all its most strenuous efforts to obtain confession and reconciliation must expect a worse fate than those who proved compliant, would have stultified its very existence. . . . Once granted the point of view that heresy is a more heinous offence than coining—to use St. Thomas' analogy—or than treason, to use a commoner and more forcible comparison, and the penalty of death for heresy appears not shocking and horrible, but something eminently just and proper. . . . It is modern humanitarianism, not Inquisitorial authorities, that seeks to disclaim moral responsibility for the stake."

Imprisonment

Upon the repentant heretic—that is, upon all whom he did not abandon to the secular arm—the Inquisitor himself passed judgment in the form of penance. The most usual penances were imprisonment, the wearing of crosses and the performing of pilgrimages. They were not regarded as punishments, but rather as measures of salutary discipline designed to restore the spiritual health of the penitent; and, in theory, the Inquisitor was simply in the position of a father-confessor imposing the loving chastisement of the Church upon her erring children.

The idea of imprisonment as a punishment for crime is purely monastic in origin and was unknown under Roman law. The Rule of St. Benedict enjoined the strict seclusion of delinquents as a regular measure of monastic discipline; and the penalty, which was at first imposed only upon monks and clerics, was later extended to the laity and finally became established in all secular

---

[1] *Mediæval Heresy and the Inquisition*, pp. 221 ff.

legislation. As forming part of the recognized discipline of the Church, it was, of course, adopted by the Holy Office.

" Imprisonment according to the theory of the Inquisition," says Lea, " was not a punishment, but a means by which the penitent could obtain, on the bread of tribulation and the water of affliction, pardon from God for his sins, whilst at the same time he was closely supervised to see that he persevered in the right path, and was segregated from the rest of the flock, thus removing all danger of infection." [1]

The procedure of the tribunals in the various districts varied considerably; but as a general rule it would seem that a term of imprisonment was by far the most common penance imposed upon repentant heretics. Bernard Gui's sentences show that he condemned 307 heretics to prison, or nearly half of the whole number brought before his tribunal. From the register of Bernard of Caux it may be gathered that the proportion was even higher than this; but there is no single instance of abandonment to the secular arm. Between 1318 and 1324 the Inquisition of Pamiers passed judgment upon ninety-eight heretics, of whom two were acquitted, whilst there is no mention of the penance inflicted upon twenty-one others. The most common sentence was imprisonment.

On the other hand, the register of the notary of Carcassonne shows that, during the years 1249–55, 278 sentences were passed. But by far the most common penalty was enforced service in the Holy Land; and there are very few cases of imprisonments.

The practice of mitigating and commuting sentences of imprisonment seems to have been frequently exercised. It has been noted that, of the 307 persons condemned to prison by Bernard Gui, 139 were set at liberty by special mandates. In 1328 twenty-three prisoners at Carcassonne were released by a single sentence, with the substitution of other slight penances. Of thirteen heretics sentenced to imprisonment by the Pamiers

[1] *Op. cit.*, Vol. I. p. 484.

tribunal on March 8, 1322, eight were set at liberty on July 4 of that year. On January 16, 1329, fourteen were released from prison and forty-two from the obligation to wear crosses. Moreover, as a general rule, the Inquisitors showed themselves perfectly ready to relax the full strictness of incarceration when it was a matter of providing for one's family, or caring for sick and aged relatives. Thus on May 6, 1246, Bernard of Caux sentenced a certain Raymond Sabbatier, a relapsed heretic, to perpetual imprisonment; but added that, since the culprit's father was a good Catholic, and old and poor, the son may remain with him and support him as long as he lives, meanwhile wearing a black garment and crosses with two transverse bars.[1] A number of instances could be cited in which prisoners who had fallen ill were allowed to go to their homes, so as to obtain proper attendance and to get back their health and strength under more wholesome conditions. Thus on October 28, 1251, a woman of Coufoullens is granted permission " to leave the prison into which she has been committed for the crime of heresy, until she shall have recovered from her illness; at the end of that time she must, without any summons, return to the prison to perform the penance imposed upon her for the said crime."[2] On another occasion an imprisoned heretic, a mason, received leave of absence for two years in order to carry out some constructional work at the monastery of Rieunette.[3]

In 1229 the Council of Toulouse had decreed that repentant heretics should be imprisoned " in such a way that they could not corrupt others "; adding that, in cases where property had been confiscated, the bishop was to provide for the needs of the prisoners out of such property. The Council of Narbonne went further, prescribing that, irrespective of age, sex or condition, all heretics who did not voluntarily give themselves up

[1] Douais, *Documents*, Vol. II. pp. 8–10; De Cauzons, Vol. II. p. 371; Lea, Vol. I. p. 486.
[2] Molinier, p. 445.
[3] Douais, *Documents*, Vol. I. p. 280.

during the time of grace should be imprisoned for life. This was in 1244, two years after the massacre of the Inquisitors and clergy at Avignonnet. But it would seem that, even in these early years, when the strength of the heresy was greatest, the statute was never applied in its full ruthlessness. Even the Council of Narbonne itself introduced qualifying clauses ; remarking, as though in recognition of unpalatable facts, that the Inquisitors should not condemn everybody to perpetual imprisonment, since there was not sufficient bricks and mortar to build prisons for them.

Under the fully developed Inquisitorial routine perpetual imprisonment was usually reserved for those who had committed perjury or whose confessions had been manifestly due to fear of death. On the other hand, the number of determinate sentences known to us is exceedingly small. Two sentences of Bernard of Caux, for ten and fifteen years respectively, are preserved ; and in another case he imprisons a man " for as long as the Church deems fitting." In the huge majority of cases the sentence is for life. Still, there is reason to believe that the term " perpetual imprisonment " was little more than a stock phrase, retained through long force of custom, although meaning very little in practice. We have noted, in other connections, the manner in which the Inquisitors adhered to the use of terms and phrases which had long become obsolete and even meaningless. So it was with the elastic formula, " *animadversio debita* "— the appropriate punishment ; and so it was with the absurd sentence of abandonment to the secular arm. At any rate, in the matter of imprisonment, we have to note an enormous number of releases from prison ; nearly half of Bernard Gui's sentences to perpetual imprisonment were commuted. It would seem that, provided he behaved himself and gave the authorities no reason to doubt the sincerity of his conversion, the prisoner had every chance of being released fairly soon.

The " Murus Largus "

There were two forms of imprisonment—the milder or *murus largus* and the harsher known as the *murus strictus*. The *murus largus* was the ordinary sentence. Unless otherwise stated, a condemnation to, imprisonment meant the *murus largus*: if the confinement was to be in the *murus strictus*, that fact was specially noted in the sentence. Bernard Gui condemned nineteen persons out of 307 to the *murus strictus*.

The large proportion of the sentences, then, were to the lighter and less severe form of imprisonment, the *murus largus*. In the ordinary way the prisoners were allowed a considerable degree of freedom within the precincts of the building. It seems certain that they lived a more or less communal life, taking their meals together and seeing one another regularly. The routine of the prisons, in fact, was planned upon monastic lines. Eymeric, writing as of a regular practice, stipulated that Catholic friends might be allowed to visit the prisoners. Husband and wife were permitted to live together, if either or both were imprisoned. Contributions of food, money, wine, clothing and so on might be received from outside ; and, according to Lea, " among the documents are such frequent references to this that it may be regarded as an established custom."

The state of affairs in the Inquisitorial prison at Carcassonne is strikingly demonstrated in a pronouncement made in 1282 by the Inquisitor, Jean Galand. He was a savage, fanatical person ; and his conduct as an Inquisitor had already excited a number of complaints, and had drawn upon him the censures of the Pope and of Philip the Fair. In 1282, alarmed by a great outburst of heretical activity in Albi and the neighbourhood, he drew up a series of regulations for the stricter enforcement of discipline in the prison at Carcassonne. Imprisoned heretics are forbidden to leave the prison without the express permission of the Inquisitor. The gaoler and his wife are to discontinue their practice of eating with the prisoners and of playing games with them. In future no games of any kind are to take place. Under no pretext whatever is money to be accepted from the prisoners; and there is to be no tampering with letters and parcels sent to them from their friends and relations outside. It is a curious and interesting commentary on the conduct of prison routine under a gaoler, who was evidently an easy-going person and sufficiently dishonest into the bargain.

The " Murus Strictus "

For the false witness, for delinquent priests and members of religious Orders, and for any whose conduct seemed to merit special severity, the form of imprisonment was the *murus strictus*. It was a most fearsome penalty. The prisoner was thrust into the darkest and most pestilential of dungeons, sometimes underground. The confinement was solitary, and the diet of bread and water. Occasionally he was chained and manacled. The only persons who were allowed to visit him were the bishop and the Inquisitor. But in 1351, on the representations of the Vicar-General of Toulouse, King John II prescribed that twice a month the prisoners should have opportunity for recreation and converse with their friends.

" I have met with one case," says Lea,[1] " in 1328, of aggravated false witness, condemned to the *murus strictissimus*, with chains on both hands and feet. . . . In the case of Jeanne, widow of B. de la Tour, a nun of Lespinasse, in 1246, who had committed acts of both Catharan and Waldensian heresy and had prevaricated in her confession, the sentence was confinement in a separate cell in her own convent, where no one was to enter or to see her, her food being pushed in through an opening left for the purpose—in fact the living tomb known as the *in pace*."

[1] *Op. cit.*, Vol. I. pp. 486 ff. The sentence is given in Douais, Vol. II. p. 31. Bernard of Caux was the Inquisitor who decreed it.

General Condition of the Prisons

The Inquisition had its own prisons at Carcassonne and Toulouse. It is not certain whether they had one at Beziers: at Pamiers the bishop placed the *prison des Allemans* at their disposal. It would seem that, in general, the Inquisitorial prisons were quite as bad as the secular—dirty, ill-ventilated and sometimes altogether unfit for human habitation. Curiously enough, this was not the case in Spain, where they seem to have been far better equipped and managed than either the ecclesiastical or secular prisons. But in Languedoc and Italy there was little or no distinction. The rations were never plentiful and the food was never of the best; whilst in the *murus strictus* the horrors of solitude and the deadening weight of the chains were added to the privations and discomforts of the less severe confinement. Death, under these conditions, became an end devoutly to be wished. Indeed, in the *murus strictus* it was really little more than a question as to which would give out first, the mind or the body. We hear, in 1273, of a prisoner who " had struck himself and wounded himself in the head, desiring death and seeking to kill himself."

It must be conceded, however, that this kind of thing was exceedingly distasteful even to the most hardened Inquisitor. The last thing that the Holy Office desired was to kill off all its penitents by the rigours of imprisonment. " Care should be taken," said one authority with a truly staggering obliquity of mind, " lest the discipline of the prisons should be so severe as to cause the death of delinquents . . . for in that case the judges who had decreed the sentence would incur irregularity." So that, even if the Inquisitor were a monster of cruelty, he could not contemplate the death of a prisoner with any complacency. Even if we accept the controversialists' picture of the average Inquisitor and present him as a being dead to every appeal of justice and common decency, we must admit that it was in his own interest to run his prison properly.

A number of much-needed reforms were introduced into the Inquisitorial prison system by Pope Clement V. The successful agitations of Bernard Delicieux had roused a storm of hostility against the ecclesiastical authorities in Languedoc; and the Inquisitors had countered by a campaign of ferocious activity against heresy. In 1306 the chapters of two religious houses wrote to the Pope, urging him to interpose in the matter; whilst the consuls of Albi and Cordes made formal complaints of the conduct of the Inquisitors and of Bernard de Castanet, Bishop of Albi. It was stated that numbers of innocent persons had been arrested and imprisoned, that torture had been employed without restraint and that the condition of the prisons was utterly unspeakable; several persons had been so weakened by the lack of proper food and the severity of their tortures that they had died.

The Pope promptly appointed a commission led by Cardinals Taillefer de la Chapelle and Berengar Frédol, to proceed to Languedoc, for the purpose of making full investigation. They were empowered to summon the bishop and Inquisitors before them, to visit the prisons, to suspend the trials that were running at the time, to take steps to ensure the immediate rectification of the trouble and to submit a full report of their findings and actions to Rome. The legates, after examination, discharged a number of gaolers, ordered that no prisoners should be confined in irons and that those who had been placed in underground cells should be immediately removed. All were to have opportunity for regular exercise in the precincts of the building and the use of the subterranean dungeons was to be discontinued. It may be noted that it was not until 1550 that the latter measure was introduced into civil legislation in France.

The results of the Papal inquiry issued in the important Bull, "Multorum Querela," which was promulgated from the Council of Vienne in 1311. It enjoined the strictest co-operation between the officials of the Holy Office and the local bishops in everything relating to the prosecution of heresy. The Inquisitor could not abandon anyone to the secular arm, nor condemn to the *murus strictus* nor put any accused person to the torture without the express agreement of the bishop. The prisons were to be visited regularly. The bishop was to appoint one warder and the Inquisitor the other ; and each was to have his own keys. All things considered, it was a fairly drastic reform and an effective clipping of the wings of the Inquisitor. Bernard Gui grumbled frequently about these new regulations, declaring that the work of the Holy Office was considerably hampered and that the Holy See had shown little of its customary wisdom in ordaining them. In a sense, the former opinion was true. The Clementine reforms, as they are known in history, effected a real curtailment of the almost complete freedom which, hitherto, had been granted to the Inquisitor in the conduct of his office. But there can be no question as to their wisdom. If all the Inquisitors had been capable and upright men like Bernard Gui, little fault could have been found with the old régime. Such men could safely be trusted to act always with the strictest regard for justice and with every genuine desire to be merciful. Yet it was not always so. There had been flagrant abuses, and it was necessary to render their repetition impossible. That was the aim of the Clementine reforms. The physician, whether he liked it or not, whether he considered it desirable or futile, was henceforth bound to obtain a " second opinion."

A Note on the Idea of Imprisonment

It is clear, I think, that in the Middle Ages imprisonment was not regarded in quite the same manner as in our own time. It was a comparatively new thing, monastic in origin and primarily penitential in purpose. Thus if a prisoner attempted to escape from the Inquisitorial gaols, his escapade was treated, not as a defiance of authority, but as a wilful rejection of the loving chastisement of the Church—an act of rebellious ingratitude ! To us such an idea seems ludicrous and

fantastic.   But that imprisonment was so regarded alike
by judge and penitent is shown, in some degree, by the
fact that prisoners so seldom attempted to break gaol.
It is inconceivable that this should have been due to the
intense vigilance of the warders or to the massive strength
of the prison buildings.   Many of the warders were
corruptible;   the prisoners in the *murus largus* were
together for the greater part of the time and had limitless
opportunities for making plans of escape.   Yet it was very
rarely attempted.

Further, we have to reckon with the influence of
established monasticism.   When members of religious
Orders were convicted of heresy, they were usually
sentenced to the *murus strictissimus*—solitary confinement
in chains and upon a diet of bread and water.   This was
the fate of a Carthusian monk of the monastery at
Beaulieu in the diocese of Carcassonne.   He was condemned as a Spiritual Franciscan and was ordered to be
shut up in a cell of his monastery for the rest of his life.
Now it is true that the priesthood are, as it were, bound
by a stricter discipline, and that formal heresy in a religious
is an even greater sin than in an ordinary layman.   Thus
it is natural that the punishment should be correspondingly more severe.   But after all, what would the *murus
largus* have meant to a monk?   How could such a man
be imprisoned, when imprisonment was a first condition of his life?   What was a man's profession in one
of the great enclosed Orders but a voluntary self-con-
demnation to lifelong imprisonment?   It is true that he
did not regard it in that light; and it is true that the lofty
ideals of the monastic vocation were not for the ordinary
layman.   Still, there was that atmosphere surrounding
the idea of seclusion.   In our own age imprisonment is
regarded primarily as the loss of personal liberty, the
shutting out of all that makes life worth living; and the
instinct which so regards it is a thoroughly sound and
natural one.   But in the Middle Ages there was another
side to the matter.   Many of the monastic Orders, whose
members were notoriously jolly and cheerful people, lived

under a rule far stricter than that of the *murus largus* ; and did so simply as a means to an end. The seclusion and restraint, therefore, were essentially purposeful. Imprisonment was negative, in that it involved deprivation of ordinary liberties ; but it was also positive, in that it provided an aid to spiritual convalescence.

Yet, when all is said and done, the record of the Inquisitorial prisons is a sufficiently discreditable one. Certainly the huge majority were condemned only to the fairly easy routine of the *murus largus* : whilst of those false witnesses and others who were sentenced to the *murus strictus*, we may perhaps say that they generally deserved all they got. Certainly there are very many cases of prisoners being released for good behaviour ; so that it is at least arguable that none but the really hard cases failed to have their sentences commuted. But between the ideal and the actual there was a wide gulf. It is characteristic of the men of the Middle Ages that in all their enterprises they aimed so high and consequently had a greater distance to fall. The theory of imprisonment as propounded by the Inquisition, with its genuinely lofty ideals of penance and spiritual regeneration, contrasts only too strongly with what Henry Osborn Taylor calls " the spotted actuality."

CHAPTER VIII

The Wearing of Crosses

IT has been pointed out that, in theory, there was no difference between the penalties inflicted by the Inquisition and the penances imposed by an ordinary confessor. Even imprisonment had long played a part in the penitential discipline of the Church; and throughout the Middle Ages the bishops could imprison people in exactly the same manner and with exactly the same purpose as could the Inquisitors. In practice the only penance imposed exclusively by the Inquisition was the wearing of crosses.

This form of penance seems to have been introduced by St. Dominic. At any rate, the first explicit mention of the imposition of crosses as a penance occurs in the formula by which the Saint reconciles the ex-heretic Pons Roger with the Church.[1] The penitent is ordered to undertake a great variety of fasts and religious exercises; and, in addition, to wear upon his tunic two small crosses, stitched one on either side of the breast. It is difficult to believe that St. Dominic regarded the crosses as a mark of degradation. If he had done so, if his idea had been to brand the penitent with a mark of his former infamy, a cross was surely the last symbol that he would have chosen for the purpose. At that time the only people who wore crosses upon their dress were the Crusaders and the Military Orders. The cross was the sign of Christ; the sign of honour, not of dishonour. Clearly, in St. Dominic's vision, the cross was to be worn by the reconciled heretic as a badge of triumph, reminding

[1] Cf. *supra*, Chapter IV.

192

him, on the one hand, of the perils from which he had been delivered, and proclaiming to the faithful, on the other, that the lost sheep had returned to the fold.

But there are few St. Dominics in history. And in the eyes of Church and State, united in their fervent hatred of heresy, the significance of the crosses underwent a rapid change. When they are first mentioned in the records of the Holy Office, it is clear that they are regarded by everybody as marks of degradation. Bernard Gui ranks the wearing of crosses with imprisonment, as belonging to the category of *pœnitentiæ confusibiles*—the humiliating penances; and it has been noted that he imposed the obligation to wear them in 143 cases. Moreover, a study of the Inquisitorial records shows clearly that the wearing of crosses was generally looked upon as being, with the obvious exception of imprisonment, the most severe penance that the Inquisition could impose. The gravest offences were expiated in this manner. The most arduous pilgrimage was regarded as a less severe penalty. Thus on October 5, 1251, the Inquisitor of Carcassonne released a number of persons from the obligation to wear crosses and penanced them to set out at once upon several of the recognized pilgrimages; " and let those instructed to proceed overseas (*i.e.* to the Holy Land) leave by the first available ship." [1]

St. Dominic had prescribed that Pons Roger should have two " little crosses "—*cruces parvulæ*—sewn upon his tunic. In 1229 the Council of Toulouse formally recognized the practice of marking converted heretics in this manner, decreeing that the crosses should not be the same colour as the clothing and that they should be worn, as St. Dominic had said, upon either side of the breast. It stands to reason, therefore, that they cannot have been very large. But in 1243 the Council of Narbonne made several alterations and standardizations as to size. Clearly by this time the crosses were regarded as a brand of infamy and nothing more. The assembly ruled that in future the crosses should be worn back and front,

[1] Douais, *Documents*, Vol. II. p. 159; Molinier, p. 404.

the one centrally upon the breast and the other between the shoulder-blades. The crosses were to be stitched upon the outer garment and were to be yellow in colour. The vertical arm was to be two and a half palms in length, the transverse arm two palms; and both were to be three fingers in breadth. Further, a " perfected " heretic, who for any reason was not sentenced to imprisonment, was to wear three crosses—the third being placed upon the cap in the case of a man, and upon the veil if the culprit was a woman. This was decreed in 1246 by the Council of Beziers, which prescribed also that those heretics who had deliberately lied to or concealed the truth from the Inquisitors should wear special crosses with two transverse bars.

The idea of thus branding those whom they had occasion to condemn was developed by the Inquisitors in a number of different directions. The false witness wore strips of red cloth representing tongues. Those who had practised black magic or any occult rites which involved profanation of sacred things wore yellow discs representing the Sacred Host. Sorcerers, idolaters and devil worshippers were decorated with grotesque figures like the gargoyles on the cathedrals. All this kind of thing, it would seem, was intimately bound up with the mediæval passion for heraldry and symbolic display. It was an age of uniforms, emblems and, if one may use the term, of hallmarks. There were the uniforms of the various monastic Orders; the coats-of-arms of the knights; the lions of St. Mark were as familiar in the Mediterranean as had been the eagles of Imperial Rome. At certain periods during the Middle Ages the Jews were constrained to wear a circlet of yellow cloth upon the breast. At the time of the Black Death the travelling bands of Flagellants, or Brethren of the Cross, marching in procession with tapers and banners carried before them, wore scarlet crosses on breast, back and upon the cap as insignia of their Order. In the seventeenth century the Tsar Peter the Great ordered the members of certain schismatical sects to wear a kind of red scapular. In our own time we may note such emblems as the Fiery

Cross of the Ku-Klux-Klan and the broad-arrow costume of the convict, some assumed voluntarily and others imposed by law. Many writers have commented upon the interesting resuscitation of heraldry during the War, as manifested by the Divisional and Brigade signs of the British Army.

At first sight, then, it would seem that the wearing of the yellow crosses prescribed by the Inquisition was sufficiently easy penance. But, as we have already observed, this was by no means the case. In the eyes of the people the yellow cross was a sign of infamy; and the person who wore it was a plague-spot who, unbeknown to them, had been living in their midst. He had been found out and justly branded. Of course he had abjured and was now nominally as good a Catholic as anybody. But the taint of heresy was upon him. The Church in her mercy had granted him absolution; but was it possible for the leopard to change his spots? Heresy, as we have said several times before, was an assault upon society as well as an assault upon the authority of the Church.

The consequence was that the wearers of the Inquisitorial crosses frequently found themselves completely ostracized. A bargeman who had been re-arrested for not wearing his crosses declared that he had laid them aside ten years previously, since he had been unable to make a living. Under similar circumstances a woman, Raymonde Mainfère, summoned before the Carcassonne tribunal on October 2, 1252, said that her mistress would not allow her to go about with the crosses upon her dress. Labourers could not obtain employment. Fathers who had been branded could not find suitors for their daughters; and, *a fortiori*, girls who wore crosses could not get husbands. Bernard Gui, who released 139 persons from the penalty, discusses the circumstances under which permission to lay aside the crosses might legitimately be given. In cases of old age, illness, or when it was a question of providing for a family or marrying one's daughters, or "for any other reason which seems good to us," he considered that dispensation should be granted. The Inquisitors recognized very clearly the grave social stigma attaching to the yellow crosses of the Holy Office.

Still, this kind of thing was not quite the purpose of the crosses. And it is to the credit of the ecclesiastical authorities that they attempted again and again to preserve the condemned persons from molestation, derision and boycott. The Council of Beziers made explicit rulings in the matter; the Inquisitors frequently sought the assistance of the secular magistrates in enforcing the statutes. There is a pleasant dash of humour in the action of the Archbishop of Narbonne, who in 1329 threatened to impose crosses upon all those who molested or interfered with the persons condemned to wear the crosses.

The frequency with which the penalty was imposed seems to have varied greatly throughout the period of Inquisitorial activity. It was not often employed by Bernard of Caux; and in the voluminous records of the Inquisition at Carcassonne between 1250 and 1258 there are not more than twenty or thirty references to it. Bernard Gui seems to have inflicted it more frequently than anybody else; and the full count of his sentences shows that he imposed the crosses upon nearly a quarter of the whole number brought before him. But from about the middle of the fourteenth century onwards there are very few mentions. M. Tanon has noted, as late as 1451, a case in which a certain Jean Acarin was condemned to wear the crosses for four years and to be imprisoned for three; and he observes that " the crosses imposed upon him (Acarin) were the traditional ones, with the same dimensions, the same shape and the same manner of wearing them." [1] But by this time the French Inquisition had fallen into almost complete desuetude. It played only a secondary part in the trial and condemnation of St. Joan of Arc. During the second half of the fifteenth century there was only one execution for heresy in Paris; and the Inquisition had no concern with it. It seems that on June 3, 1491, Jean Langlois, a priest, assailed a brother priest who was celebrating Mass

[1] Op. cit., p. 498.

in Notre Dame Cathedral, threw him to the ground, upset the Chalice and trampled the consecrated elements underfoot. He was arrested; and, after violently and repeatedly denying the Real Presence, was delivered over to the secular arm and burnt on June 21, 1491.[1]

Pilgrimages

Imprisonment and the crosses were bracketed together by the Inquisition as humiliating penances; that is to say, they were regarded as measures of chastening discipline, whose purpose was to arouse feelings of remorse for past misdeeds and aspirations towards a true humility of mind. I have suggested earlier that the manner in which the Holy Office was organized seems to have been based upon the presumption that all the Inquisitors were Saints. One might go further and say that, in its dealings with malefactors, the Holy Office tended to act upon the presumption that all penitents were would-be Saints. It imprisoned them so that they might have opportunity, upon the bread of tribulation and the water of affliction, to work out their spiritual salvation. It branded them with crosses so that, with downcast eyes and chastened mien, they might be ever mindful of the perils from which, by the mercy of the Church, they had been preserved. And these two exceedingly arduous penalties, said the Inquisitorial hand-books, were not punishments, but humiliating penances.

It was otherwise with pilgrimages, which were not regarded as being in any way humiliating. The performance of pilgrimages was looked upon throughout the Middle Ages as an essentially pious act, by which many spiritual benefits might be obtained. Everybody went on pilgrimages from time to time, sometimes to the distant shores of the Holy Land, more often to the innumerable little local shrines such as, in England, to our Lady of Walsingham or to St. Thomas of Canterbury.

---

[1] The event is referred to in *The Ship of Fools*. See the new translation by Fr. Aurelius Pompen, O.F.M., pp. 157, 158.

Thus we find William Newland of London, who died in 1425, desiring in his will that—

"a man be founden to go to Rome and to Jerusalem, and to have ther-of for his costes and labour L marc; another for to go fro the Swerd in Fletstrete vu-to Caunterbury, barefot, Xs; and another to seynt Iames in Galis." [1]

It is interesting also to note that in the Middle Ages persons were often ordered to go upon pilgrimage by the secular magistrates—a curious detail, as M. de Cauzons remarks, which emphasizes once again the intimate inter-association of the religious and civil aspects of society. The performance of pilgrimages was one of the chief duties and even one of the chief delights of our mediæval ancestors. Like all forms of ecclesiastical observances it could, of course, be imposed as a penance. By this I mean that the fact that one might be ordered to make a pilgrimage as a penance does not imply that pilgrimages were regarded as burdensome obligations, of which one would willingly have been rid. An ordinary penance might well consist in the hearing of so many Masses or the recitation of so many prayers. Such pious actions will be joyous and pleasant to the faithful, though they may well be tedious to anyone else. What more jolly crowd ever marched the roads than Chaucer's Canterbury Pilgrims?

The performance of pilgrimages was therefore regarded by the Inquisition as one of the lightest of penances. Indeed pilgrimages were seldom prescribed, save as sentences supplementary to the wearing of crosses, or as commutations from an earlier and more severe sentence. In the summary of Inquisitorial sentences made by Limborch there are 127 cases of commutation from imprisonment to pilgrimage with crosses; and 131 commutations from the wearing of crosses to pilgrimage. The few instances in which pilgrimage was ordered as a first sentence show that the most trifling offences were expiated in this manner. Thus the Inquisitor Peter

[1] E. L. Guildford, *Travellers and Travelling in the Middle Ages*, p. 23.

Cella imposed a pilgrimage to St. James of Compostella
upon a person whose only delinquency was that he had
seen some Waldensian heretics on a ship and had entered
into conversation with them, although he had withdrawn
as soon as he heard them professing heretical doctrines.

The Inquisitors distinguished categorically between the
major pilgrimages, the minor pilgrimages and the *passagium transmarinum*—the journey to the Holy Land.
The major and minor pilgrimages naturally varied from
district to district.   For Languedoc the major were to
Rome, St. James of Compostella, St. Thomas of Canterbury and the Three Kings of Cologne.   The minor were
more numerous and included St. Gilles, Rocamadour,
St. Antonius of Vienne, Our Lady of the Tables at
Montpellier, Our Lady of Paris, St. Severinus at Bor-
deaux, St. Dominic of Bologna, Narbonne, Castres, St.
Martial of Limoges and Pamiers.   To all of these shrines
came a constant stream of pilgrims at all times of the
year, though naturally there were greater crowds upon
the particular feast-days and commemorations.

The persons concerned received from the Inquisitors
a document detailing the various places which they were
to visit and any religious exercises or other penances that
they were to perform.   The script, which was in Latin,
served them throughout the journey as a safe-conduct
and as a sort of passport.   A translation was provided by
the parish priest, who was also charged to give advice
concerning the route to be followed and any other useful
information that might be in his possession.   The
pilgrims were ordered to bring back from each shrine to
be visited a written statement from one of the resident
priests, declaring that the pilgrimage had been duly
performed and the prescribed penances carried out.
Thus on November 30, 1250, permission is given by the
Inquisitor of Carcassonne to Peter Pelha—

" to lay aside the crosses imposed upon him for the
crime of heresy, until he returns from France, where he
desires to go ; and after his return he shall, within eight
days, present himself before the Lord Bishop of

Carcassonne; . . . and he must show him a written statement concerning the pilgrimages which he has made." [1]

The major pilgrimages seem to have been imposed with comparative frequency during the early years of the Inquisition. Peter Cella dispatched most of those whom he sent upon pilgrimage to St. James of Compostella and St. Thomas of Canterbury. But Bernard of Caux very rarely enjoined this form of penance; and Bernard Gui imposed only the minor pilgrimages. Very often the condemned person would be ordered to make, perhaps, one of the major and three or four of the minor pilgrimages.

More frequently, particularly in the later period, the penance took the form of a series of visits to the principal churches in the immediate neighbourhood, at each of which the culprit received the penitential discipline of the rod. He presented himself at the church, barefooted and bearing in his hand the rods with which he was to be beaten. Between the readings of the Epistle and the Gospel he advanced to the altar, handed the rods to the officiating priest; and then, stripped to the waist, he knelt down and received the salutary chastisement. Clearly the whole thing was intended to be in the nature of a public humiliation rather than of a painful ordeal. The penitent was not held or constrained in any way. He was perfectly free to cry out, to protest or, as perhaps seems a more natural action, to burst out laughing. We have already seen Count Raymond VI of Toulouse submitting to this penance in all its most humiliating details. It was introduced into Inquisitorial practice by the Councils of Tarragona and Narbonne, and thenceforth figured fairly often in the sentences of the Inquisition. Bernard Gui punished by corporal punishment those who had deliberately hindered the work of the Holy Office.

The actual ceremony must surely have formed a most diverting, though incongruous, interlude to the celebration of the Mass. We shall have gone a long way

[1] Douais, *Documents*, Vol. II. p. 135 (author's trans.).

towards understanding the Middle Ages when we can understand how this public castigation could be conducted in perfect solemnity, how it could be regarded alike by priest, penitent and people as a fitting intrusion upon the most sacred office of the Church.

Until the loss of Jerusalem in 1304, the most formidable and dangerous as well as the most meritorious pilgrimage was to the Holy Land as a Crusader. As enjoined upon reconciled heretics as a penance it was known as the *passagium transmarinum*; and as forming an admirable method of recruiting the crusading forces and consolidating the Latin Kingdom of Jerusalem it was adopted with great frequency both by the first Inquisitors and by the secular powers. Twelve inhabitants of Albi were condemned to it by a single sentence. In 1237 the seneschal of the King of France dispatched several citizens of Narbonne to go and fight the infidel, some in Spain and others in the Holy Land; they were convicted for having been actively implicated in demonstrations against the Dominican Friars at Narbonne.

But the danger of shipping off to the Holy Land great boat-loads of ex-heretics, whose conversion to the Faith might well be only transitory, was too obvious to be overlooked for long. In 1244 the Council of Narbonne, confirming a recent Papal brief, ordered that these enforced pilgrimages should be suspended. It was feared that, by thus congregating these ex-heretics, the Holy Land might easily become a regular heretical stronghold. But apparently this apprehension was soon recognized to be groundless. At any rate the Council of Beziers in 1246 removed all previous restrictions in the matter. In 1247 Innocent IV authorized the commutation of sentences of imprisonment and the crosses to that of service in the Holy Land. Resulting from these pronouncements, the Inquisitorial records of Carcassonne from 1250 to 1258 show that the *passagium transmarinum* was inflicted in large numbers of cases. But from about 1260 onwards the practice became less and less frequent; and after the fall of Jerusalem it seems to have lapsed almost completely. Bernard Gui made one condemnation only of enforced service as a Crusader; and in his *Practica* he does not mention it as a penance.

" What is rather strange," says M. de Cauzons,[1] " is the admission that a pilgrim who could not perform his pilgrimage was not thereby absolved from his obligation. He had to find a substitute; and, if the pilgrimage was to the Holy Land, the substitute had to be a man-at-arms. Naturally this substitution was dependent upon the agreement of the Inquisitor. In case of death before departure, the heirs of the dead person, although not obliged to go in his stead, were bound, nevertheless, to pay a certain sum in compensation for the unperformed journey."

It may well be imagined that the order to go crusading in the Holy Land was a most arduous and unpleasant penance. It was quite a different matter for those who made the journey voluntarily with every assistance of the Church. They chose their own time and, before their departure, naturally made full arrangements as to the welfare of their families and the upkeep of their business during their absence. But the position of the ex-heretic who had been ordered away at a few weeks' notice was obviously far more serious. His sentence usually prescribed residence in Palestine for several years. The time of his sailing, as well as the port of embarkation, were minutely regulated. It amounted practically to a sentence of exile; and it is by no means surprising that, in the Carcassonne register, we find frequent instances where those condemned to the pilgrimages failed to perform them and failed to send a substitute, and compounded for their failure by paying a sum of money.

The sentences varied between one and eight years; and there seem to have been two principal times for sailing, in March and August.

" It has been decreed," reads a typical condemnation made on November 5, 1253, " under a forfeit of fifty pounds and in virtue of an oath duly taken, that Ber. des Martys, Ber. Armen the elder and P. Dalbars of Alzonne shall proceed upon the overseas passage in the month of March. Let them be in readiness, either at Aigues

[1] *Op. cit.*, Vol. II. p. 298 (author's trans.).

MAIN GATE OF THE HOUSE OF THE INQUISITION
AT TOULOUSE.

[The figures on either side of the Crucifix are
St. Peter Martyr (left) and St. Dominic (right).
The coats of arms are those of the Dominican Order
(left) and of the French Crown (right)].

Mortes or Marseilles, for the purpose of embarking upon their voyage." [1]

It must be remembered, of course, that the actual journey entailed little or no expense to the pilgrim himself. He could always obtain the fullest hospitality at the various convents and monasteries that lay upon his route. He could stable his horses without charge, and in most of the monasteries could remain for two days without making any payment. Clearly the European pilgrimages, which involved absence from home for, at the most, a few months, cannot be regarded as severe penalties. The pilgrim was always upon well-beaten tracks and was performing what was everywhere looked upon as a pious and worthy exercise. M. Molinier speaks in harrowing fashion about " the pitiless jeers of foreign populations," " seeking misery upon the great highways of Europe," and so forth, as though the inconveniences and dangers of mediæval pilgrimages were penalties specially invented by the Inquisition.[2] The truth is that the pilgrim had to put up with many things which we should to-day regard as hardships ; and that the reconciled heretic fared no better and no worse than the ordinary wayfarer.

Procedure against the Dead

In the twenty-third chapter of the Second Book of the Kings it is related that Josiah, having overthrown the altars of Baal and cast out the idolatrous priests, " spied the sepulchres that were in the mount " ; and he " sent and took the bones out of the sepulchres and burnt them upon the altar." [3] It was the traditional manner of expressing formal execration of the memory of the dead ; and we find references to similar action in the plays of Sophocles and Æschylus, in the chronicles of Josephus and in the Theodosian Code. The denial of the ordinary rights of burial was regarded long before the

---

[1] Douais, *Documents*, Vol. II. p. 210; Molinier, p. 408.

[2] It is, of course, ridiculous to talk about " foreign populations " in this context. [3] 2 Kings xxiii. 16.

Christian era as an appropriate punishment for the dead whose wickedness had remained undiscovered during their lifetimes. It was reserved for the most atrocious criminals, and signified the repudiation by society of their memory, the disowning of their bodies. In 1022, when heretics were first burnt at Orleans by King Robert the Pious,[1] it was discovered that a canon of the Church, who had died three years previously, had been tainted with heresy. His body was solemnly exhumed and cast out of the cemetery. In 1209 the body of the heretic Amaury de Bènes was disinterred and his remains cast to the dogs.

Perhaps it is not altogether surprising that the mediæval Church, with her concentrated hatred of heresy, should have adopted the practice of thus branding the dead with infamy. Heresy was a curse and pollution, which was not obliterated even by death. Clearly it was intolerable that the consecrated burial-ground—the family tomb, as it were, of all the faithful—should harbour the remains of one whose very presence upon earth had been a blasphemy. To this family tomb he had gained entry solely by successful deception. Let him by all means be suitably and peacefully buried in some other place. Let all things be done decently and in order. But how could he be allowed to occupy in death a place reserved for those whom in his life he had contemned and repudiated ?

Such seems to have been the general attitude from the Patristic period until well into the Middle Ages. But with the reappearance of organized heresy in Europe and with the corresponding growth of a fiercely anti-heretical temper in all ranks of society, the malediction of the dead began to assume a more comprehensive form. By the time that the Inquisition appeared upon the scene there were plenty of precedents for the practice, not only of casting the remains of the sinner out of conse-crated ground, but of refusing the right of re-burial. The reason for the new development is sufficiently clear and is, indeed, explicitly stated in a number of cases. It

[2] Cf. *supra*, Chapter II.

was feared that the disciples of the dead heretic would gain possession of his remains and venerate them as holy relics. In this way, of course, the sect might well take on a fresh lease of life; and a superstition, which had been almost completely forgotten, might revive with renewed vigour. Thus, after the death of Arnold of Brescia, it was ordered that his body should be burnt and his ashes cast into the Tiber, " lest the people should gather them up and honour them as the ashes of a martyr."

The Holy Office, with its voluminous records and its elaborate system of cross-references upon the careers of all who appeared before it, was admirably suited to the energetic prosecution of the memory of the dead. A chance remark by a son or a grandson might be followed up, compared with the carefully preserved records of half a century previous, and might reveal the strong suspicion that the dead person had been a heretic. The body of a certain Arnaud Pungilupos, who died in 1260, was exhumed and burnt in 1301. Ermessinde de Foix and her father, Arnaud de Castelbon, were condemned thirty years after their death. In 1330 condemnation was passed upon the memory of Bernard Arnaud Embrin, who had been dead for no less than seventy-five years. In 1319 the Inquisition at Carcassonne commenced proceedings against the memory of Castel Faure, a Franciscan Friar. It was alleged that upon his death-bed in 1278 he had been received into the sect of the Albigenses. A sentence of guilt was given; and the exhumation of his remains was immediately ordered. Those who had been deputed to disinter the bones found, however, that it was impossible to recognize them from those of other persons in the immediate vicinity. There was suspicion that the Friars, jealous of the honour of their dead brother, had in some way manipulated the confusion of the bones. The whole matter was referred to the Pope. An investigation was made and the charge was finally dismissed as groundless.

The trials of dead persons were conducted in exactly the same manner as those of the living. The evidence was collated and discussed, witnesses were interrogated and the summary of the proceedings was submitted to the body of experts in the ordinary way. M. Tanon had noted, in the posthumous trial of thirteen citizens of Carcassonne, a summary of expenses which " mentions the salaries of the Inquisitorial jurymen who issued the summonses, of the notaries who heard the witnesses for twelve days, and finally of two barristers who had been deputed by the Inquisitor to defend the dead persons." [1]

The sentence was promulgated in the usual way— either at a " Sermo Generalis " or at any rate in the presence of the heirs of the deceased and of all who had been concerned in the trial. The exhumation and trans- lation of the remains were conducted with the greatest solemnity and circumstance, the bones being taken through the streets upon a wagon, accompanied by great crowds of people and by a public herald, who proclaimed the name of the execrated person and the sins of which he had been found guilty. The actual ceremony of cremation was, of course, carried out by the secular power. The Holy Office were concerned only in the passing of sentence and in the removal of the bones from consecrated ground. For the rest, it was simply a matter of abandonment to the secular arm. Indeed the Council of Arles, which met in 1234 and ruled explicitly in the matter, used exactly the same formula as that employed in case of impenitence : " if their bodies or their bones can be distinguished from the others, they shall be exhumed and *delivered over to the secular judge.*"

Like that of most other Inquisitorial penalties, the frequency of proceedings against the dead seems to have varied according to time and place. Bernard Gui passed judgment upon eighty-nine dead persons and ordered the exhumation of the remains in sixty-nine cases. It may well be imagined that, when the Holy Office had got into its full stride and had accumulated an enormous mass of documentary evidence extending

[1] *Op. cit.*, p. 410 (author's trans.).

far back into the past, the possibility of discovering a dead man's heresy was greatly increased. On the other hand, the developed efficiency of Inquisitorial methods made it correspondingly more difficult for a heretic, however cautious and self-effacing, to escape detection; so that there were likely to be very few persons who, although they were really heretics, died in peaceful communion with the Church. Thus Bernard Gui's numerous sentences against the dead may be taken to indicate two things: first, the meticulous and comprehensive exactitude of the records, enabling the Inquisitor to inform himself in a moment about a person who had been in his tomb for anything up to fifty years; and second, the inefficiency of Bernard Gui's predecessors in allowing such a person to escape detection during his lifetime. Out of Bernard's eighty-nine sentences against the dead, forty-six were pronounced at the *auto-da-fé* held on April 23, 1312—less than five years after his assumption of office.

It has been urged by some that, in thus committing to the flames the mortal remains of those whom she had anathematized, the Church was concerned in some way to anticipate the Last Judgment and to prevent the resurrection of the body. The idea is too childish to be discussed. The real considerations, attested in innumerable documents, were twofold. In the first place, the body was disinterred and cast out of consecrated ground because the Church held, and holds, the highest view of the sanctity of the Christian burial-ground. Secondly, the remains were dispersed or disposed of in some manner, lest they should be procured by the heretics and venerated as holy relics. Throughout the ages the burning of a man's mortal remains has been associated with execration and disgrace. The sentiment survives to the present day in the disfavour with which the Church looks upon cremation. She has never pronounced against the practice; but she is slow to break with an age-long tradition of our race. That is all.

Demolition of Houses

Another very old practice, which may be traced far back into the mists of antiquity, is that of destroying the very dwelling-places and possessions of enemies and criminals: so that the memory of their actions should be wholly blotted out and disowned. It was a symbolic expression of the belief that everything which the execrated person had touched and possessed, the very chair that he had sat upon, the very walls that had protected him, had been indelibly stained and tainted by his touch. Everything that could awaken a memory of his character or his actions was a pollution upon earth and should be utterly destroyed. Thus Abimelech, after capturing the city of Shechem, massacred the population, razed the city to the ground and sowed salt upon the ruins. Thus the Romans, not content to wipe Carthage from the face of the earth with fire and sword, gave the site of the mighty capital over to the plough, so that no man might even know the place where it had stood. In like manner the Code of Justinian prescribed the demolition of heretical places of worship; and thus, probably, with the revival of Roman law in the eleventh and twelfth centuries, the idea passed naturally into the Middle Ages.

At any rate the first specific example in Europe of the order to destroy the houses of heretics occurs in the Assizes of Clarendon of 1166. Herein is the clear recognition that heretics are natural enemies of society and that their very presence is a curse and a pollution. After prescribing the civic ban upon "that sect of renegades who were excommunicated and branded at Oxford," the Statute adds that "if anyone shall receive them, he himself shall be at the mercy of the lord King; and the house in which they have been shall be carried without the town and burnt."[1] In 1184 the Emperor Frederick Barbarossa promulgated anti-heretical decrees,

[1] Cf. *supra*, Chapter II.

condemning heretics to loss of all civil rights, to confiscation of property and banishment: this involved inability to fill any public office as well as the destruction of their houses. In 1207 Innocent III confirmed these enactments in his letter to the magistrates at Viterbo, enjoining that all houses where heretics were known to have lived should be razed to the ground, and that no one should ever presume to build upon the same site. From that time onwards the destruction of heretical houses was recognized by secular and ecclesiastical authorities as an integral prescription of the anti-heretical laws.

It may be noted, however, that heretics were not the only persons whose memory was execrated in this summary manner. In 1187 Philip Augustus, ratifying the statutes of the city of Tournai, ordered that the houses of murderers should be demolished, and St. Louis IX made a similar enactment concerning highwaymen and brigands.

In theory the position of the Inquisitors was clear and unmistakable. Whenever they condemned a heretic, they were empowered to prescribe the destruction of his house. Innocent IV ordered the demolition, not only of every house in which heretics had lived, but of all the neighbouring houses which belonged to the same proprietor. But it was clear from the first that the carrying out of such a wholesale programme of destruction was quite impracticable. In Languedoc and Northern Italy a literal obedience to the Papal instructions would have involved the disappearance of whole villages; and we are not surprised to find Alexander IV introducing certain qualifying clauses. Even so, the theoretical position remained sufficiently inflexible. Every house in which heretics or favourers of heresy had lived, as well as every building which had been used for heretical worship, was to be demolished, and the site was not to be built upon. Only the stones might be used for some pious purpose, such as the construction of a church or hospital.

In Italy it seems to have been generally approved that the execrated plot of land might be built upon or put under cultivation after a lapse of forty years. But in France the Inquisitorial malediction was regarded as permanent, and could only be lifted by Papal authority. On March 22, 1374 Pope Gregory XI granted permission to Bernard Versavin, secretary to the Duke of Anjou, to build upon a piece of waste land which the latter had recently acquired and which had been anathematized some years previously by the Inquisition.[1]

Yet in spite of a long array of precedents and prescriptions, the Holy Office very rarely ordered the demolition of houses. Whether the Inquisitors found it impossible to get their sentences carried out or whether they desired to heighten the effect of the penalty by prescribing it only in extreme cases, cannot be decided. Bernard Gui ordered the demolition of twenty-two houses during his term of office; and in every case the building condemned was one in which the most flagrant acts of heresy, such as the ceremony of " heretication," had been frequently performed. A striking commentary upon the effects of these sentences is provided by a letter written to Pope Clement VI by the Inquisitor Aymon de Caumont of Carcassonne. Apparently there existed in one of the most fashionable quarters of the town an open space upon which two heretical houses had previously stood. As a result of the demolition of the houses and the execration of the ground, the place had become so littered up with rubbish of all descriptions as to constitute a serious menace to the public health. The Inquisitor goes on to say that his attention has been drawn to the matter by the authorities and he asks the Pope what is to be done about it. Clement replies that the place should be thoroughly cleaned up and then fenced off from the public.[2]

The destruction of buildings by the orders of the Inquisition is deserving only of passing mention. It

---

[1] The letter is reproduced in Vidal, *Bullaire*, p. 404.

[2] Vidal, pp. 295, 296.

was never practised as a regular thing; it is not mentioned in Bernard of Caux's sentences nor in the Carcassonne register from 1250 to 1258; and after the middle of the fourteenth century it seems to have been almost completely discontinued. Not until the Reformation did the spirit of savage destructiveness rise in all its fury, alike amongst Catholics and Protestants. At the beginning of the sixteenth century the Augustinian canons of Antwerp were convicted of Lutheranism; the priory was promptly razed to the ground. In 1559 a royal proclamation in France ordered the demolition of all Protestant meeting-places. Henry VIII in England, not content to break up the monastic communities, smashed their dwellings to the ground and destroyed the accumulated treasures of centuries; so that to-day a few gaunt ruins are all that remain of some of the grandest architectural monuments that have ever graced our country-sides.

Confiscation of Property

In summarizing the work of the Inquisition, Lea has observed that "persecution, as a steady and continuous policy, rested, after all, upon confiscation"; and although the statement needs qualification, it unquestionably contains a large element of truth. Certainly mediæval heresy was something more than mere disagreement with the dogmatic definitions of the Church; and heresy may be more fitly looked upon as a crime for which the recognized punishment, under civil law, was death and confiscation of property.

From the Theodosian Code onwards all anti-heretical legislation insisted that lapse into heresy involved unconditional surrender of property. The sequence was quite automatic. As soon as a man wavered in the faith, he became *ipso facto* incapable in the eyes of the law of holding property. Heresy implied loss of citizenship; and the property of the heretic was confiscated in exactly the same manner and on exactly the same principle as was the property of the murderer or traitor. The only difference was that, if the heirs of the condemned heretic had not themselves fallen into heresy, they could succeed to his estate; in the other cases the forfeiture was absolute and unconditional.

Accordingly, when Gregory IX formally established the Monastic Inquisition, heresy was recognized by the secular laws of all the European States as a crime punishable by death and by confiscation of property. And in theory anyone who had momentarily lapsed into heresy was liable to the latter penalty. Whether he repented and was reconciled to the Church had nothing to do with the question; the mere act of heresy, like the act of treason, involved loss of all civic rights and the consequent inability to possess property. The attitude of the State, therefore, was quite unaffected by any judgment on the part of the Inquisitor, or by any salutary change of mind on the part of the accused. The fact of heresy was the thing that mattered; and heresy, as Innocent III and Frederick II had pointed out, was a greater crime than treason.

In practice, however, the full rigour of the law was never enforced; chiefly, it may be suggested, because in the early years it would have been impracticable. Suffice it to say that throughout the thirteenth century the property of a heretic could not be touched by the fiscal authorities until the ecclesiastical judge had passed sentence. In Italy the Inquisitors themselves pronounced explicitly as to whether or not confiscation was to be made. But in France and Spain the Holy Office took no official cognizance of the matter and the confiscation was automatically carried out by the State. It was agreed that all those who confessed to the Inquisitors during the time of grace should be exempt from the penalty. For the rest, the generally accepted position, prescribed by the Councils of Albi and Beziers and upheld by Bernard Gui in his *Practica*, seems to have been that property was forfeited by all relapsed and impenitent heretics who were abandoned to the stake, by all who were sentenced to perpetual imprisonment and by all fugitives condemned *in absentia*. The commission sent to Languedoc by Alphonse of Poitiers in 1253 added a fourth category, ordering confiscation of property from those condemned to wear the double crosses. But, according to M. de Cauzons, " this last prescription does not seem to have become operative." [1]

Confiscation was applied only to the actual personal possessions of the condemned heretic. The property and dowry of the wife of a heretic was inalienable, provided that she herself had not fallen into error; and there are several examples in the records of the restitution of dowries which had been unjustly confiscated by the royal officers.

In France the whole of the confiscated property went to the State, except when the culprit was a priest. That is to say, the State could never confiscate the property of the Church. But the personal effects of a priest, anything which belonged to him privately and apart from his office in the Church, were claimed by the State. In the French kingdom proper all confiscated property belonged to the King; in Languedoc, to the Counts of Toulouse and Foix in their respective domains. The right to confiscations carried with it the obligation to defray the expenses of the Inquisition.

In other countries a variety of different methods were adopted. The bull " *Ad extirpanda* " of Innocent IV prescribed that the proceeds from all forfeited property was to be divided into three parts, one-third to go to the urban authorities, one-third to the officials of the Holy Office and one-third " to be put in some safe place that shall be known to the bishop and inquisitors, to be spent as may seem good to them for the benefit of the Faith and the extirpation of heresy."

" The authorities," says Tanon, " were never in agreement as to the rights of the matter. Eymeric applies the first decretals. He assigns the proceeds of the confiscations from laymen to the temporal lords, and those from priests to the churches; the bishops have nothing and take no part in confiscations except when,

[1] De Cauzons, Vol. II. p. 321, note. Also Tanon, p. 527.

as temporal lords, they own an estate. Other authors apply half the confiscations to the exchequer of the Roman Curia and the other half to the needs of the Holy Office. Zanchini says that, in his time, this was the practice in Italy and that the tripartite division prescribed by Innocent IV was not observed. Pegna admits, on the contrary, that this tripartite division should be the rule not only in the lands of the Church, but, in the absence of particular statutes, in all countries ; the first decretals he regards as old and obsolete. But he interprets the prescriptions of Innocent IV in the very general sense that the temporal lords or secular author- ities are not entitled to their share unless they give every assistance to the Inquisitors and pay all their expenses ; if they fail, their share shall be taken from them and assigned to the needs of the Inquisition. He concludes that in Spain, where the Inquisition has become the concern of the King, the latter is entitled to the whole proceeds of the confiscations. But he gives his opinion only with the greatest reserve, observing that, since so many doctors have set themselves to investigate the question, one cannot yet be certain which rule should be observed." [1]

Clearly, then, it is impossible to generalize concerning the manner in which confiscation was carried out or the way in which the forfeited possessions were distributed. In France and Spain the initiative in the matter rested exclusively with the secular authorities, who alone bene- fited directly. In Italy the Holy Office, besides pro- nouncing the actual sentence of confiscation, received a share of the spoils, and was consequently not dependent upon the secular power for the payment of its expenses. At any rate it is evident, from the immense amount of argumentation and discussion as to the most suitable and equitable procedure, that the proceeds of property confiscated from heretics must have been fairly con- siderable. We have direct evidence on the point in the record of confiscations made by the orders of Count Alphonse of Poitiers in the diocese of Toulouse. In

---

[1] Tanon, p. 534 (author's trans.).

1255 the receipts from this source amounted to 541 pounds. From May 6, 1255, to February 2, 1256, the receipts were 820 pounds and the expenses 832 pounds. The account presented on May 22, 1259, shows that 244 pounds had been received; and the expenses are tabulated as follows :

To capture and execution of heretics	. .	60s. 11d.
Paid to the Inquisitors .	. . . .	£11 5s. 6d.
To maintenance of prisoners .	. . .	£17 17s. — [1]

That the practice of confiscating the property of condemned heretics was productive of many acts of extortion, rapacity and corruption will be doubted by no one who has any knowledge either of human nature or of the historical documents. We have plenty of evidence on the point in the report of the Commission appointed by St. Louis to investigate the conduct of the fiscal officers throughout the kingdom. Many unjust seizures were alleged to have been made; and the commissioners found that the numerous complaints were fully justified. A typical instance was that of Pons Geoffrey of Roquebrun, who had been arrested on suspicion of heresy by the Inquisition and subsequently acquitted; the bailiff had disregarded the sentence and confiscated his property. Examples of similar depredations could be multiplied.

It should be remembered, of course, that heresy was by no means the only offence that was punishable by confiscation. Only a small proportion of the revenue so collected was derived from the property of heretics. This point also is illustrated in the report of St. Louis' commission. In the northern kingdom confiscations for heresy are scarcely mentioned; and even in Languedoc they are by no means preponderant. Still, the fact remains that the secular princes had a direct interest in the number of condemnations for heresy. Particularly when the heretics were numerous and—which was more important—wealthy, it was to their own most obvious advantage to support the Inquisition to the fullest of their powers. "In our days," remarked

[1] Douais, *Documents*, Vol. I. pp. 215, 216.

Eymeric gloomily, " there are no more rich heretics, so that princes, not seeing much money in prospect, will not put themselves to any expense ; it is a pity that so salutary an institution as ours should be so uncertain of its future."

Complaints of this kind were frequent ; and we need not waste time in pious recriminations of the avarice of the rulers. After all, granted the universally recognized analogy between heresy and treason, the confiscation of heretical property was a just and obvious penalty, backed by the formidable precedent of the Roman law. And it was perfectly natural that the secular princes should look for some return for the money spent upon the upkeep of the Holy Office. Certainly they stood to make money out of the suppression of heresy, just as, under a system of fines, any authority stands to make money out of the punishment of crime. But it would be a gross over-statement to say that they prosecuted the heretics and supported the Inquisition simply and solely from motives of greed. We come across many instances of petty extortions on the part of local agents ; plenty of corruptions carried on behind the backs of the Inquisitors and often in complete disregard of their sentences. But the proceeds of property confiscated from heretics formed but a small fraction of the royal and baronial revenues ; and it can hardly be supposed that condemnations for heresy seriously affected the exchequers one way or the other.

The point was that heresy was a crime, for which confiscation of property was the legal punishment ; and the Holy Office was a tribunal whose special task was the detection of heresy. It was a tribunal, moreover, which had to be supported out of the public funds. If, therefore, the Inquisitors showed signs of apathy or inefficiency, or if they acted with undue leniency, the princes had some reason for regarding them as useless parasites. Thus, early in the 1250's—it is impossible to fix the exact date—the seneschal of Rouergue, Jean d'Arcis, writes to Count Alphonse of Poitiers, complaining that the Bishop of Rodez makes a practice of deliberately mitigating his sentences so as to save the heretics from having their property confiscated.[1] A year or two later the Inquisitor, Renaud of Chartres, complains to the Count of the flagrant injustices perpetrated by the royal officers against condemned heretics.[2]

The Expenses of the Inquisition

Except in Italy, the Inquisitors never pronounced sentences of confiscation and, indeed, had no concern in the matter at all. They stood neither to gain nor lose by the number of confiscations made. All that they claimed or received from the State exchequer was the payment of the running expenses of the Holy Office. Occasionally the princes, in moments of pious generosity, made donations to their convents or churches or to some good cause recommended by the Church. The Dominican church at Albi was built by Bernard de Castanet, bishop of that city, who shared with the French King the proceeds of confiscations made in his diocese. Count Alphonse of Poitiers gave liberally to hospitals and convents ; nor was any secret made of the fact that the dispositions were drawn from confiscations carried out by his orders. But such generosity was necessarily opportunistic. In 1268 the Count, evidently vexed by a lean period, complained of the enormous expenses of the Inquisition at Toulouse, and recommended that, by way of cutting down expenditure, the Inquisitors should go and live at the castle at Lavaur.

The task of maintaining the Holy Office, including the upkeep of the prisons, the payment of all salaries and of all expenses connected with the arrests, trials and executions, rested with the secular princes. But the Inquisitors occasionally inflicted pecuniary penalties in the form of fines. Thus one might be fined for having failed to perform a pilgrimage ; or the fine might be imposed in commutation of some other form of penance ; or, in cases of old age or sickness, one might compound

[1] De Cauzons, Vol. II. p. 331 note ; Molinier, p. 25.
[2] Cf. *supra*, Chapter VII.

for inability to carry out the prescribed penance by the payment of a sum of money. The disposition of funds so collected was decided by the Inquisitors; and it is clear that the whole system introduced grave possibilities of avarice and corruption. At first, indeed, it was felt to be repugnant that the Friars, bound as they were by a vow of poverty, should have any direct dealings with money or should have the power of enriching their Office by exactions. A provincial chapter of the Dominicans in 1242 and the Council of Narbonne in 1244 sought to forbid the practice altogether. Innocent IV in 1245 ruled that fines should be utilized only in connection with the maintenance of the prisons. But in 1249 he found it necessary to denounce the Languedocian Inquisitors for excessive severity in the extortion of fines; and in 1251 he decided that fines should never be imposed in cases where any other form of penance could be prescribed.

In this pontifical pronouncement, as M. de Cauzons observes, there was at once the recommendation to avoid abuses and the authorization to exact fines. It must be admitted that, provided that the money was duly allocated to some pious work such as the building of churches, hospitals or bridges, or to the payment of necessary expenses, the penalty was a perfectly just and suitable one. But abuses were inevitable. In 1311 the Council of Vienne reiterated the instructions of Innocent IV; and it is certain that Clement VI's injunctions against unjust and excessive extortions were called forth by specific complaints against the officials of the Holy Office.

CHAPTER IX

WE have discussed in broad outline what the Inquisitors did. It remains to consider briefly when and where they did it. It will be convenient to treat of the activities of the Holy Office under the headings of the countries in which it operated; and of these the most important are France, Italy, Spain and Germany. In Northern France, Languedoc, Spain and Germany it was staffed usually by the Dominican Order. In the Papal States, Southern Italy, South-eastern France, Hungary and the Balkans, most of the Inquisitors were Franciscans. There was no hard-and-fast ruling in the matter. Several of the early Inquisitors in Spain were Franciscans; whilst in the cities of Northern Italy the majority were Dominicans. But one may generalize with a fair degree of accuracy by regarding the districts north and west of the Rhone as the province of the Dominicans, whilst the territory east and south of that line belonged to the Franciscans.

I. *The Inquisition in France*

The first Inquisitors in Languedoc took up their residence at Toulouse in 1233. Their names were Guillem Arnaud and Peter Cella, the friend of St. Dominic. Associated with them were three other Dominicans, Arnaud Cathalan and Guillem Pelhisse at Albi, and François Ferrier at Narbonne. It may be doubted whether at this time the heretics formed the majority of the population; but at any rate it is certain that they were a compact, highly organized and wealthy body, possessing much influence in the high places of secular administration and animated by a fierce hatred of the clergy and the Preaching Friars. The Inquisitors, however, were undaunted; they set to work upon their invidious mission in the most uncompromising fashion. The first executions took place at Toulouse towards the end of 1233. Several heretical ringleaders were condemned and delivered over to the prefect of the city; and in spite of popular demonstrations and riots, they were burnt at the stake. In the same year three Dominicans, who had gone to preach at the village of Cordes, were thrown down a well by a mob of heretics. Early in 1234 the Inquisitors passed a sentence of condemnation upon a sick woman of Toulouse, who was actually carried to the place of execution upon her bed. After the horrible ceremony of burning had been completed, the bishop and the Friars returned to the convent, rendering thanks to God and to St. Dominic for the good work that had been performed. The madness of fanaticism was at its height.

In the following year Peter Cella was transferred to Carcassonne and Arnaud remained in Toulouse as the sole Inquisitor. With a fierce courage that may well have been born of despair, he proceeded at once to order the arrest of twelve prominent citizens upon a charge of heresy. This time the civil authorities refused to co-operate and the summons was completely disregarded. Guillem Arnaud himself was seized upon by the mob, dragged and pushed through the streets amidst curses and imprecations, and driven from the city. An official order was issued that no one was to have any dealings with the bishop or the Friars. The former, unable even to purchase the necessaries of life, was forced to leave the city, whilst the Friars barricaded themselves in their convent and prepared for siege.

Meanwhile the fearless Arnaud proceeded to Carcassonne and sent a letter to his brethren at Toulouse, ordering that four of them should immediately go forth and arrest the heretics whom he had accused. The inevitable outcome was an ugly street riot, from which the

four Friars were lucky to escape with their lives.   On the
following day, November 5, 1235, the consuls of Toulouse
proceeded to the Dominican priory and demanded that
the Friars should immediately leave the city.   On
receiving a blunt refusal, they summoned up a detach-
ment of soldiery, who set upon the Friars one after
another and forcibly ejected them into the street.   Led by
their prior bearing the cross, the little company of monks
then passed along the streets to the gates of the city,
chanting the penitential psalms, and took up a temporary
residence at Bracqueville in a house belonging to the
cathedral chapter of Toulouse.

At Albi and Narbonne the first Inquisitors fared no
better than at Toulouse.   In 1234 Arnaud Cathalan
abandoned two prominent heretics of Albi to the secular
arm, imposed pilgrimages to the Holy Land upon twelve
others and ordered the exhumation of several corpses.   He
was seized by an infuriated mob, who announced their
intention of throwing him into the river Tarn.   Street
fighting broke out between the heretics and Catholics,
and the Inquisitor was with difficulty rescued.   At
Narbonne the secular magistrates refused all assistance
to the Inquisitor, François Ferrier.   He seems, however,
to have proceeded vigorously against the heretics and to
have imprisoned a considerable number.   In 1234 the
Dominican convent was invaded by a mob of heretics
and sacked.   In the following year the exploit was
repeated and a great collection of records and documents
were destroyed by the rioters.

At the invitation of Count Raymond, the Dominicans
returned to Toulouse in 1237.   The country was still in
an extremely unsettled condition, and, mainly, it would
seem, for political reasons, the pursuit of heretics was not
resumed on any large scale until 1241.   In that year the
Inquisitors, greatly emboldened, started to journey
round the country-sides, visiting the districts that were
known to be particularly heretical and demanding the
denunciation of all suspects.   Between Advent 1241 and
Easter 1242, Peter Cella seems to have reconciled no

fewer than 724 heretics, penancing almost all of them to pilgrimages. There were a few burnings and a number of fugitives were condemned *in absentia*.

On the night of May 28–29, 1242, occurred the massacre of Avignonnet, when Guillem Arnaud, Stephen of S. Tiberi, three lay brothers, a canon of Toulouse and the Dominican prior, together with the notary and several clerks, were assassinated by an armed gang of heretics. The expedition seems to have been planned by one Peter Roger de Mirepoix without the knowledge of Count Raymond; and the band of assassins was recruited from the great heretical stronghold of Montségur which belonged to Peter Roger. The latter angrily reproached his henchmen for not having brought him the skull of Guillem Arnaud, which he had wished to use as a drinking-cup.

Overwhelmed by this disaster, which was but the culmination of the innumerable difficulties that they had encountered, the Dominicans appealed to Pope Innocent IV, asking to be relieved of the mission that had been entrusted to them. The request was promptly refused; and in November 1243 Bernard of Caux and Jean de St. Pierre were appointed to replace the martyred Inquisitors. But a fearful vengeance awaited the heretics. In March 1244 a powerful armed force, raised and equipped by the Archbishop of Narbonne, the Bishop of Albi, the seneschal of Carcassonne and a number of Catholic noblemen, proceeded to the attack upon Montségur. After a short siege the great fortress was taken by storm; and 200 heretics were burnt on the spot without trial.[1]

It was an important turning-point. From this time onwards the co-operation of the secular authorities with the Inquisitors was assured; and indeed it is scarcely an exaggeration to regard Bernard of Caux and Jean de St. Pierre as the first real Inquisitors in Languedoc. Prior to the holocaust at Montségur the war against

[1] Concerning this series of events see Vaissette, *Histoire Générale de Languedoc*, Tome VI. pp. 738–70; Tanon, pp. 55–65; *Lives of the Brethren of the Order of Preachers* (Orchard Classics), pp. 213 ff.; *Historia Albigensium* in Bouquet, Tom. XX., etc.

heresy had been a war to the knife; and it was a mere mockery to pretend that it could be fought with spiritual weapons. Montségur had been simply a brigand stronghold, from which innumerable strings could be pulled all over the country. Its capture marked, for the time being, the end of the heresy both as a serious political factor and as a centralized conspiracy against the Church.

At any rate it is with Bernard of Caux that the Holy Office really gets into its stride; and for nearly fifty years its work was carried forward with quiet perseverance. Of its methods and conduct during this period we have already spoken at sufficient length. In 1285 the heretics made an unsuccessful attempt to gain possession of the Inquisitorial house at Carcassonne and to destroy the records; and it was clear that further troubles were brewing. The heresy, so far from showing signs of vanishing, seemed to be gaining ground on all hands. The Inquisitors stiffened up their methods correspondingly; and in 1290 the consuls of Carcassonne complained strongly to Philip IV concerning the injustices and cruelties of the two Inquisitors, Nicolas of Abbeville and Fulk of St. Georges. "It was," as Mgr. Douais remarks, "the first warning of the revolt which, under Bernard Delicieux and the *fraticelli* of Narbonne twelve years later, was to imperil the unity of France." [1]

The King, whose actions in such matters seem to have depended always upon the varying fortunes of his quarrel with the Pope, replied in rather half-hearted fashion with a vague denunciation of the Inquisitorial excesses and an appeal for moderation in the future. His instructions were apparently disregarded; for in 1301 loud complaints were raised by the citizens of Toulouse against the conduct of Fulk. This Inquisitor was accused of having imprisoned innocent persons and of having made many unjust exactions. This time the King acted more effectively. A royal commission was despatched to Languedoc, and the case against the Inquisition was taken up by the celebrated Franciscan Friar, Bernard Delicieux,

[1] Douais, *Documents*, Vol. I. p. 189.

who openly set himself at the head of the malcontents. Philip, who happened at the time to be almost at daggers drawn with Boniface VIII, decided that the complaints had been fully justified and took the unheard-of step of removing the two Inquisitors from the further exercise of their office.

Encouraged by his successes, Delicieux started upon a systematic crusade against the Holy Office. As a result of his eloquent agitations, the Inquisitorial prisons at Carcassonne were entered by a mob and the prisoners set at liberty. At Albi the populace became so inflamed that the Dominicans dared not show themselves in the streets or even in the churches. Their convent was assaulted and a great mass of documents and records were destroyed. The riots spread from place to place and soon the whole country was in an uproar. It was here that Bernard Delicieux overstepped the mark and prepared the way for his own downfall. In 1304 he became involved in a political intrigue amongst the citizens of Carcassonne to set up a separate monarchy and to restore the lost independence of Languedoc. Philip, stimulated into alarmed activity, acted with promptness and vigour. The consul of Carcassonne was suspended from office and the city was fined 60,000 *livres*. At the urgent request of the King, Clement V ordered the arrest of Bernard; the rebellion collapsed and the Inquisitors resumed their interrupted activities.[1]

In 1305 the citizens of Albi, Carcassonne and Cordes raised fresh complaints against the conduct of the Holy Office, and the charges were formally submitted to the Pope. The result was the Papal Commission headed by Cardinals Taillefer de la Chapelle and Berengar Frédol,[2] who made a thorough examination of the circumstances and introduced several drastic reforms. Less than two years later began the term of office of the great Bernard Gui. For nearly sixteen years this Inquisitor presided over the tribunal of the Holy Office at

---

[1] Douais, *Documents*, Vol. I. pp. 192–202; Tanon, pp. 66–70; Vidal, *Bullaire*, pp. 4–6.   [2] Cf. *supra*, Chapter VII.

Toulouse, passing nearly a thousand sentences relating to heresy and judging more than six hundred individual heretics. So effective was his administration that, when he retired from office in 1323, the work of the Inquisition in France was virtually completed. The Albigensian heresy—that virulent poison—had been eradicated. In Languedoc the Inquisition was intermittently active until 1330. From then onwards it practically disappears as a permanent tribunal. There were occasional trials of individual heretics, an *auto-da-fé* at Carcassonne in 1357, another at Toulouse in 1374, and a third at Carcassonne in 1383. But the heresy which had brought the Inquisition into being was, long before this, a thing of the past.

In the lurid series of events which led up to the suppression of the Knights Templars in 1311, the French Inquisition played an active and notorious part. The first arrests were made on October 13, 1307. The knights were charged with the most abominable crimes; and it was alleged that heresy was rampant in the Order. The Inquisitor of Paris proceeded immediately to the investigation of individual cases. Of 138 knights examined at Paris only four denied their guilt. Torture was freely employed in extracting information. In Paris thirty-six died from the effects of torture; at Sens twenty-five succumbed; and elsewhere the mortality was considerable. Before the pontifical commission, held in November 1309, a Templar called Jean de Cormèle declared that he had lost four teeth during his first trial On the same occasion Ponsard de Gisi testified that—

"Three months before my confession my hands were tied behind my back so tightly that the blood spurted from beneath my nails. . . . If you put me to such tortures again, I will deny everything that I now say, I will say anything you like. I am ready to submit to any punishment, provided only that it is short."

The arrests had been made without the knowledge of the Pope; and Philip the Fair had only ensured the co-operation of the Holy Office by mendaciously claiming that, in ordering the arrests and trials, he was acting under Papal instructions. On October 27, Clement V, hearing of what had happened, wrote to the King, vigorously censuring his actions and demanding an explanation of this " outrageous insult to ourselves and the Roman Church." Philip manœuvred successfully to allay the angry suspicions of the Pope; and it was not until February 1308 that Clement, thoroughly informed in the matter, suspended the powers of the bishops and Inquisitors throughout the kingdom and reserved to himself the whole future investigation of the case. In July of the same year these powers were restored, but the trials were not resumed until November 1309, and in the subsequent investigations the Holy Office, as such, played no effective part.[1]

Before considering the dealings of the Church with the Waldensian heretics and the Spiritual Franciscans, it will be convenient to turn our attention to the other countries in which the Inquisition operated, and to bring the story up to date all along the line.

II. *The Inquisition in Spain*

As far as concerns the present study, the history of the Inquisition in Spain is a brief and comparatively uneventful one. Throughout the Middle Ages the heterogeneous culture of the Spanish peninsula, with its many Saracen and Jewish affinities, remained almost completely undisturbed; and it was not until 1480, with the accession of Ferdinand and Isabella, that the task of crushing out the foreign elements was seriously undertaken. During the next half-century the Spanish Inquisition, reconstituted on a primarily monarchical basis, played a notorious and bloody part in cementing the national unity of Spain—a unity of which religious uniformity was regarded as being the necessary foundation.

[1] Bouquet, *Recueil des Historiens des Gaules*, Tom. XXI. *passim* ; G. Mollat, *Les Papes d'Avignon* (Paris 1924), pp. 240–44; Lavocat, *Procès des Frères et de l'Ordre du Temple*, pp. 141–6; Lea, Vol. III. pp. 258–63, etc.

With these later developments, however, we are not here concerned. During the mediæval period proper the Inquisition was permanently established only in the kingdom of Aragon. There were no Inquisitors in Castile or Leon until after the middle of the fifteenth century.[1] The first Inquisitor in Portugal seems to have been a Franciscan Friar called Rodriguez de Cintra, confessor of King John I. He was appointed to his office in November 1394. But neither he nor any of his rather nebulous successors seem to have found much scope for the exercise of their duties.

Into Aragon the Holy Office was introduced largely through the efforts of the great canonist, St. Raymond of Pennaforte. In 1238 Gregory IX formally entrusted the prosecution of heresy to the Mendicant Orders in that country; and in 1242 the Council of Tarragona drew up a long series of rules and regulations to be observed by the Inquisitors. In the same year the Inquisitor, Pons d'Espira, was poisoned by heretics. In 1269 a considerable sensation was caused by a sentence of exhumation passed by the Inquisitors of Barcelona against the defunct Viscount of Castelbon and his sister, Ermessinde de Foix. In 1277 Peter of Cadireta, one of the Inquisitors who had decreed the sentence, was stoned to death. These are about the only events of interest during the thirteenth century, and it is sufficiently clear that heresy and the Inquisition were of almost negligible significance in the affairs of the country. Most of the heretics in Aragon at this time were probably refugees from Languedoc. In 1317 we find the Archbishop of Compostella writing to Bernard Gui and asking what should be done with the Languedocian heretics who had recently settled in his diocese : " for, up to the present, the proper manner of dealing with them is unknown in these parts." [2]

During the fourteenth century the pursuit of heresy seems to have been almost as local and spasmodic as

[1] The Inquisitor of Provence, Bernard Dupuy, seems to have paid a flying visit to Castile in 1359; see Vidal, *Bullaire*, p. 340.
[2] *Practica Inquisitionis*, p. 353.

during the thirteenth. Somebody was burnt in July 1325. In 1334 a certain Friar Bonato, condemned as an obdurate heretic, suffered the extreme punishment. In 1357 the famous Inquisitor, Nicolas Eymeric, commuted a sentence of imprisonment to one of abandonment to the secular arm, on the ground that the abjuration of the accused person had been perjurous and insincere. Certainly during Eymeric's time the Inquisition in Aragon was in a very precarious condition. We have already noted, in another context, the laments of this Inquisitor concerning its poverty and the lack of effective support from the secular authorities. " The fact that so little came into its exchequer from confiscations," remarks Mr. Turberville, " and that so ardent and active an Inquisitor should apparently have accomplished so little, seems mainly to prove that heresy was not a serious menace in Aragon at this time." [1] It proves at any rate that, menace or no menace, nobody was very seriously concerned to stamp out heresy and that the secular princes did not regard heresy as being a menace of any kind. Yet only a few years later Aragon was in an uproar. In 1390 and 1391, fearful anti-Jewish riots and massacres took place at Seville, Burgos, Toledo, Barcelona and elsewhere. Huge numbers of Jews saved their lives by professing conversion to the Church. It was the beginning of the great movement which was to issue, nearly a century later, in the union of the thrones of Aragon and Castile, and the expulsion of the Jews from Spain.[2]

III. *The Inquisition in Italy*

To a greater extent, perhaps, than in any other country the fortunes and activities of the Inquisition in Italy were inextricably mixed up in politics. Not until after the middle of the thirteenth century was the long-drawn-out struggle between the Guelph and Ghibelline parties

---

[1] *Mediæval Heresy and the Inquisition*, p. 173.
[2] Llorente, *Histoire Critique de l'Inquisition d'Espagne*, Vol. I. pp. 73–94; Langlois, *op. cit.*, pp. 99–102; Vacandard, pp. 166 ff.; Turberville, pp. 171 ff.; Lecky, *Rise and Influence of Rationalism*, Vol. II. p. 278, etc.; Lea, Vol. II. pp. 162–80.

brought to any sort of conclusion; and it was not until the year 1266, when the Ghibelline forces were heavily defeated by Charles of Anjou at the battle of Benevento, that the organization of the Holy Office as a permanent tribunal for combating heresy was really completed.

The first Inquisitor in Italy was the Dominican Friar Alberic, who was appointed Inquisitor of Lombardy by Pope Gregory IX in 1232. In the following year Rolando of Cremona, also a Dominican, took up his residence at Piacenza and commenced a series of fiery sermons against heresy. The immediate result was an ugly riot, in which one monk was killed, and Rolando and several of his comrades wounded. Quite undeterred by his experience, the Inquisitor moved to Milan, where he came in for more rough treatment at the hands of a powerful heretical nobleman called Lantelmo. A month later we hear of his ordering the confiscation of the property of two wealthy Florentine merchants.

During these early years, up to the death of Frederick II in 1250, the history of Inquisitorial activity in Italy is so hopelessly mixed up in political controversies and so completely secondary to the swaying struggle between Empire and Papacy, that it is impossible to weave it into a connected narrative. It is certain that heresy was rampant all over the north of Italy and particularly in Lombardy. There was no attempt at concealment, and the heretical hierarchy was in some cities as prominent and powerful as the orthodox. But there was no simple dividing line between orthodox and heretics, nor even between Guelph and Ghibelline. In general the Guelphic factions stood for the Papacy and for orthodoxy. Yet Milan, everywhere recognised as the greatest heretical centre in the country, was intensely and traditionally a Guelph city. Hence arose alliances and counter-alliances, intrigues and counter-intrigues, conflicting claims and ambitions of Pope, Emperor, secular nobility, bishops and popular factions, which precluded all possibility of ordered action against heresy. Nevertheless the apparently hopeless task of uniting the orthodox against the heretics was vigorously attempted. The

Dominican Friar, Giovanni Schio, worked with tireless energy in Northern Italy and in Bologna ; and, under the existing circumstances, it is no disparagement of his work to say that his successes were primarily diplomatic.   But the most redoubtable champion of the Faith during these early years was the Inquisitor, St. Peter of Verona, better known as St. Peter Martyr.

Entering the Dominican Order in 1221, he threw himself with tremendous energy into the work of preaching against heresy in the cities of Northern Italy.   We hear of him at Ravenna, Mantua, Venice, Milan, Florence and other places.   In 1233 he was sent to Milan with the task of stirring the municipal authorities to proper zeal against the innumerable heretics in the place ; and he seems to have remained there for nearly ten years.   There is no trace of ordered Inquisitorial activity during this period, and it is stretching a point to describe Peter as an Inquisitor.   Doubtless his sermons and denunciations played a considerable part in rousing popular feeling against the heretics.   But anti-heretical action in Milan at this time was hopelessly mixed up in politics ; and there was certainly no settled and effective co-operation of the secular and spiritual authorities.   Nor is there any evidence to suggest that Peter ever assumed the office of an ecclesiastical judge.

In 1244 we find him at Florence.   The city was at that time convulsed by the ever-recurring struggle between the Guelph and Ghibelline parties ; and the Inquisitor, Ruggieri Calcagni, who had been proceeding vigorously against the heretical nobility, was in the thick of the combat.   Immediately after his arrival, Peter found it necessary to organize a kind of armed guard, whom he called the " Company of the Faith," for the protection of the Dominicans.   Riots and street fighting followed the first attempts to molest the heretics ; both sides rallied their forces ; pitched battles were fought in the streets ; and finally in two bloody conflicts the Guelphs gained an overwhelming victory.   Thus was destroyed in Florence the power of the Ghibellines and heretics.   In recognition of his services, Ruggieri was raised to the

ST. PETER MARTYR.

episcopate in 1245 and St. Peter Martyr succeeded him as chief Inquisitor. From that year may be dated the establishment of the Florentine Inquisition; and when, apparently in 1261, Peter was transferred to Cremona, he could claim that the Holy Office was firmly organized and that the temporal power of the heresy was broken.

We have no records of his doings at Cremona or at Milan, to which he was later transferred. On Low Sunday 1252, after spending Easter in his priory at Como, he set out to return to Milan. Near the village of Barlassina he and his solitary companion were attacked by a gang of heretics and assassinated. So perished a very redoubtable defender of the Faith, whose zeal was never tainted by fanaticism and whom the Church honoured by canonization within a year of his death. Not the least striking sequel to the murder was the repentance of two of the conspirators, one of whom entered the Dominican Order, whilst the other lived and died in the odour of sanctity, and is now numbered amongst the Church's Saints.

Meanwhile the Emperor Frederick II had died (in 1250), and as a consequence the cause of the Papacy and the Guelphs had received a considerable fillip. In 1256 the long-planned crusade against the great Ghibelline tyrant, Ezzelin da Romano, was organized; and an immense force set out from Venice under the leadership of the Archbishop-elect of Ravenna. Padua, which was Ezzelin's chief stronghold, was captured by assault and sacked from end to end. During the next two years there was no more heavy fighting. But in 1258 Ezzelin, by a powerful counter-stroke, regained possession of Brescia and promptly turned his eye towards Milan. Treachery amongst his allies within the city alone prevented his conquest of it. His army was encountered on the march and heavily defeated; and he himself was slain upon the field of battle. The March of Treviso passed into the hands of the Guelphs; and a great stretch of country into which, hitherto, no Inquisitor had dared to enter was thrown open to the salutary operations of the Holy Office.

Eight years later the last political obstacle to its free action throughout the Italian peninsula was removed. At the battle of Benevento, Charles of Anjou triumphed completely over the united Ghibelline forces. The Kingdom of Sicily passed under his dominion and into full loyalty to the Papal policy. The victory at Benevento is warmly celebrated, in a famous passage, by Jean de Meun, who describes the various stages of the combat in terms of a game of chess.[1]

In Sicily and the Kingdom of Naples the action of the Inquisition was exceedingly spasmodic and of very little significance. Under a number of wise restrictions it was established in Venice in 1289. In spite of her continuous contact with the Eastern peoples, the great maritime republic seems to have remained very free from heretical influences and to have enjoyed, moreover, a certain security of the public order which was conspicuous by its absence in the turbulent city-states on the mainland. In 1267 a visitor to Venice testified, " How full of prowess are her people and how all are perfect in the faith of Jesus and to Holy Church obedient; for within that noble Venice neither heretic, nor usurer, nor murderer, nor thief dares to dwell." Two centuries later, St. Bernardino of Siena continually held up the Venetian Republic as an example to the faction-ridden States of Northern Italy, declaring that what most deeply impressed him during his sojourn in Venice was not the fleets and gondolas, and the wealth and prosperity of her citizens, but the unbroken concord and peace that reigned there. It may be assumed, both from the records and from such testimony as the above, that the post of Inquisitor at Venice was practically a sinecure. Six heretics were put to death during the whole period of Inquisitorial activity in Venice; and it is interesting to note that they were not burnt, but either drowned or hanged.

The breaking up of the various Ghibelline alliances struck a heavy blow at the cause of heresy; for it rendered possible the effective co-operation of the secular and ecclesiastical arms in the task of extermination. From

[1] *Romance of the Rose*, 7013 ff. (Temple Classics ed., Vol. II. p. 237).

about 1270 onwards the Inquisition is found pursuing
the heretics with systematic thoroughness all over Northern Italy and in the Papal States.   There were occasional
set-backs, as at Parma in 1279, when the execution of a
relapsed heretic led to the outbreak of riots.   The
Dominican convent was sacked, the Inquisitorial registers
were destroyed and one of the Friars was killed.   The
Papal Legate promptly laid the city under interdict ;
and it was not until 1287 that the matter was finally
cleared up and the Dominicans returned to their interrupted task.   Such reverses were exceedingly rare.   For
the most part the war against heresy went forward steadily
and inexorably.   In 1304 Fra Giordano da Rivalto
declared that heresy had been virtually stamped out in
Tuscany ; and Villani asserts that, by the middle of the
century, there were no heretics left in Florence.   " This,"
remarked Lea, " is doubtless too absolute an assertion."
It is certain that the Waldensian Church was still flourishing like a green bay tree.   In 1332 Pope John XXII
called attention to the huge number of Waldenses in
Turin, declaring that these heretics held their assemblies
in public and made no pretence of concealment.   But
even at this time the Waldenses were practically unmo-
lested.   The real heretics *par excellence* were the Cathari,
or, as they were usually called in Italy, the Patarins.
And it would seem that, as in Languedoc, the sect was
to all intents and purposes extinct by the middle of the
fourteenth century.   Lea has noted that " in the collected
statutes of the Dukes of Milan from 1343 to 1495 there
is no allusion of any kind to the Inquisition, or to the
punishment of heretics." [1]

IV. *The Inquisition in Germany*

The Inquisition—or rather the Inquisitorial methods—
made a brief but spectacular incursion into Germany
under the ægis of the redoubtable and notorious Conrad

[1] Lea, Vol. II. p. 270.   Concerning this section see Villani's *Florentine
Chronicle*, Book VII. ; Lea, Vol. II. pp. 191–289; T. Okey, *Venice*,
passim ; Turberville, pp. 166–71, etc.

of Marburg. A most eloquent preacher and a very ardent evangelist, this Dominican Friar had risen to a position of great prominence in the Church, having been honoured in 1214 with a special commission to preach the Crusade in Germany; whilst in 1220 he had been entrusted with the delicate task of persuading Frederick II to carry out his long-delayed promise to lead an expedition to the Holy Land. In 1227 Gregory IX, as a further sign of the high esteem in which his talents were regarded, charged him with the special duty of combating heresy throughout the German kingdoms, and, for that purpose, armed him with particular powers which made him the foremost German ecclesiastic of his time.

We have no record of his activities against the heretics during these first years of his mission; and it seems likely that he devoted himself chiefly to vigorous reforms of the monastic houses throughout the country. He was a prominent figure at the court of Thuringia, being the spiritual adviser of St. Elizabeth of Hungary and a trusted counsellor of the reigning prince, who once went so far as to declare that Conrad shone like a star throughout all Germany. In 1231 the gentle St. Elizabeth died at the age of twenty-four; and during the succeeding months the earnest Dominican threw himself strenuously into the task of obtaining her immediate canonization.

Meanwhile Gregory IX had issued a variety of fresh instructions concerning the suppression of heresy, coupled with the most earnest exhortations to greater energy in this most vital matter. Conrad responded immediately. Late in 1232 he abandoned four heretics to the stake at Erfurt; and during the next few months a number of further convictions were obtained. Loud complaints were raised against the arbitrary fashion in which his so-called trials were conducted. The Archbishops of Treves and Cologne felt called upon to utter remonstrances of his conduct and to urge the necessity of moderation and discretion. But the austere Friar was unmoved. In July 1233, evidently stimulated by his reverses to even greater efforts, he was summoning the faithful at Mainz to go crusading against certain heretical noblemen who had failed, after summons, to appear before his tribunal. The plan met with considerable opposition and Conrad, refusing the offer of an armed escort, decided to return to his home town of Marburg.   An ambush was laid for him upon the road; and, like St. Peter of Verona and Guillem Arnaud, he met his death from the knife of an assassin.   His body was carried subsequently to Marburg and buried beside that of St. Elizabeth.   It is, perhaps, significant that the Church has never set the seal of canonization upon his martyrdom.   Many hard things have been said of him, and perhaps with justice.   He was one whose zeal often outran his discretion, whose inflexible sternness often degenerated into the most undisciplined fanaticism.

The Inquisition had not, however, been established in Germany; and it was not destined to be established there until some years after the catastrophe of the Black Death.

" In the codes which embody the customs current in mediæval Germany," writes Lea, " there is no recognition whatever of the existence of such a body as the Inquisition. The Sachsenspiegel, which contains the municipal law of the northern provinces, provides, it is true, the punishment of burning for those convicted of unbelief, poisoning or sorcery, but says nothing as to the manner of trial. . . . The Schwabenspiegel, or code in force in Southern Germany, is much more complaisant to the Church, but it knows of no jurisdiction over heretics save that of the bishops. . . . It provides death by fire for the heretics. It directs that when heretics are known to exist, the ecclesiastical courts shall inquire about them and proceed against them. . . . (It) shows ample readiness to accept the received ecclesiastical law of the period as to heresy; but utter ignorance of the Inquisitorial process is revealed in the provision which inflicts the *talio* on whoever accuses another of certain crimes, including heresy, without being able to convict him." [1]

During the latter half of the thirteenth and the first half of the fourteenth centuries the bishops were the sole

[1] Lea, Vol. II. pp. 349, 350.

instigators of the infrequent and leisurely proceedings that were conducted against heresy. Catharism was practically unknown. The heresies which flourished furtively throughout this period were for the most part quaint pseudo-mystical cults which often comprised the wildest extravagances. Thus there were the Brethren of the Free Spirit, who said that everybody should go about naked; and the Friends of God, who claimed to have reached such a state of sanctity as to be incapable of sin. Then there were several mendicant communities, of whom the most important were the heretical Beguins and the Beghards. They maintained a fanatical hatred of the idea of property and an unbalanced enthusiasm for the life of complete poverty. But all these curious sects, between whom it is difficult to make any exact distinction, were distinguished by exaggerated and rather unwholesome mystical tendencies. They all taught, with slight variations, a kind of vague pantheism. They said, for instance, that man is so completely animated by the Divine essence as to be himself divine. After a probationary period of austerity and contemplation man can so fully unite himself with God as to be God. In this desirable state he is sinless and may therefore gratify every passion and whim that possesses him in the firm confidence that, since he is God, he cannot commit a sinful act.

Of course this kind of thing was little removed from insanity. And unless these wild sectaries openly violated the public peace or set themselves aggressively in opposition to the Church, they were, as a general rule, left pretty much to themselves. We hear of occasional acts of suppression. In 1317 the Bishop of Strasburg proscribed their meetings and ordered the burning of all their books of devotion and instruction. There were a few executions and those who recanted were ordered to wear crosses—the first record of the imposition of this penance in Germany. In 1323 a priest, convicted of heresy, was degraded and burnt. In 1336 at Angermunde fourteen heretics were sent to the stake. In 1339 three aged heresiarchs of the Brethren of the Free

Spirit were captured at Constance and made full abjuration. Such anti-heretical actions were local and infrequent. There was no attempt at organized persecution and in many districts there seems to have been complete toleration. At any rate heresy was not regarded as being sufficiently widespread or sufficiently powerful to justify the introduction of the Monastic Inquisition. The sole judges in the matter were the bishops.

The fearful scourge of the Black Death, widely regarded as the just vengeance of God upon a sinful world, produced throughout Europe an immediate outburst of ultra-ascetical and penitential movements. In 1349, 200 Flagellants entered Strasburg, where they received the warmest welcome. They announced that they had taken upon their shoulders the sins of the people, that by their prayers and mortifications the wrath of God might be turned away and the pestilence averted. Their example spread with even greater rapidity than had the plague itself. Bands of Flagellants sprang up all over Europe ; and everywhere the shining eyes of those who witnessed their penances told of the gratitude, admiration and approval of the people. Houses were placed at their disposal ; women embroidered banners for them ; the ringing of church bells announced the glad tidings of their arrival in a town.

" Penance was performed twice a day. In the morning and the evening they went abroad in pairs, singing psalms, amid the ringing of bells ; and when they arrived at the place of flagellation, they stripped the upper part of their bodies and put off their shoes, keeping on only a linen dress reaching from the waist to the ankles. They then lay down in a large circle in different positions according to the nature of their crime—the adulterer with his face to the ground, the perjurer on one side holding up three of his fingers, etc.—and were then castigated, some more and some less, by the master, who ordered them to rise in words of a prescribed form. Upon this they scourged themselves, amid the singing of psalms and loud supplications for the aversion of the plague, with genuflexions and other ceremonies, of which the contemporary writers give different accounts; and at the same time constantly boasted of their penance, that the blood of their wounds was mingled with that of the Saviour." [1]

But the enormous enthusiasm with which the movement had at first been greeted soon turned to indifference and then to dismay.   In the earlier months they had behind them the public opinion of the vast majority, and any interference with their activities was warmly resented.   Two Dominican priests, who attempted to interrupt one of their meetings and to reason with the ringleaders, were set upon with stones; one managed to escape, but the other was stoned to death.   The total lack of directing authority in the movement led speedily to abuses and corruptions.   Cases of housebreaking occurred.   In Strasburg the Flagellants undertook to raise a dead child to life; their failure to do so did a great deal to destroy the prestige that they had enjoyed in that city.   In some cases the wandering bands degenerated into mere gangs of hooligans, who displayed no regard for the rights of person or property.

On October 20, 1349 Clement VI issued a Bull in which he pointed out that the Brotherhood of the Cross— as the Flagellants styled themselves—had the sanction of no ecclesiastical authority for their actions.   The bishops were to use every means in their power to suppress and discourage them; and in cases of disorder and disturbance of the peace the aid of the secular arm was to be sought.

In Germany, at any rate, the effects of the Papal pronouncement seem to have been negligible.   Excommunications were fulminated against all who should join the Flagellants or take part in their ceremonies.   The chief result of the formal condemnation of the sect by authority was to promote a general joining-up of heretical forces.   United by their hostility to the Church and by the general tenor of their doctrines, the Flagellants, the Friends of God, the Free Spirit people and the various other sectaries soon formed a virtually homogeneous

[1] J. F. C. Hecker, *Epidemics of the Middle Ages*, pp. 37, 38.

body, whose strength and obvious danger to the social order occasioned immediate alarm. In 1367 the Monastic Inquisition was at last established in Germany, when Urban V appointed two Dominicans, Louis of Willenberg and Walter Kerlinger, as Papal Inquisitors with full powers. Two years later the Emperor Charles IV issued edicts in their favour and ordered the full enforcement of the established laws against heresy.

A brief but vigorous campaign followed. We hear of a Beghard being burnt at Erfurt in 1368. At Nordhausen in 1369 Kerlinger secured the arrest of forty heretics, of whom seven were abandoned to the stake, whilst the rest abjured and were penanced. In the same year the Inquisitors were entrusted by the Emperor with the important task of censorship; and great masses of heretical propaganda were suppressed. On February 16, 1370 four " Beguinages " at Mulhausen—that is, the communal houses in which the heretics lived—were consigned to the secular magistrates by Kerlinger and apparently converted into public buildings. These are the chief acts of suppression of which we have record; and in 1372 Gregory XI declared that the Inquisitors had exterminated heresy from the central provinces of Germany. Six years later both the Pope and the Emperor Charles IV died. The Great Schism followed immediately, and in Germany, as in France and Italy, had the effect of greatly weakening the power of the Holy Office. From 1377 onwards until nearly the end of the century we have no record of the presence of Inquisitors in Germany.[1]

V. *The Waldenses*

Round about the beginning of the thirteenth century the Waldenses seem to have been energetically harried in more than one European country. By the angry legislation of Pedro they were exiled under pain of death

[1] Lea, Vol. II. pp. 316–95; Hecker, *Epidemics of the Middle Ages*, pp. 32–49; Turberville and Vacandard, *passim ;* Montalembert, *St. Elizabeth of Hungary*, pp. 176 ff., 307 ff., etc.

from Aragon ; and amongst the eighty heretics who were burnt at Strasburg in 1212, a large proportion were Waldenses. With the establishment of the Inquisition, however, the attitude of the authorities towards them relaxed considerably. Only seldom were they systematically persecuted ; and in France they were often not only tolerated but even protected by the Church. Possibly the reason for this was that the Inquisitors, with their eyes upon the main issue against the Cathari, had little time to bother themselves with comparatively innocuous heresies like that of the Waldensians. At any rate during the thirteenth century the Holy Office took little official cognizance of their existence.

In 1248 the Count of Burgundy complained to Pope Innocent IV that the heresy was rampant throughout his dominions ; and Innocent replied by ordering the Dominican prior at Besançon to despatch two of his brethren to combat the heresy in Burgundy. Unfortunately we have no record of subsequent events in the matter. But from two bits of evidence in Bernard Gui's register we gather that during the 1260's the Burgundian Inquisitors were exceedingly active. One witness said that he had seen two Waldensians burnt in Burgundy, whilst another had heard that " about forty-five years ago "—he was speaking in 1320—" the Inquisitors in Burgundy had pursued the Waldenses, who were captured and burnt when they could be found."

In 1251 several Waldensian heretics were condemned to perpetual imprisonment by the Archbishop of Narbonne. Some twenty years later we come across a few odd sentences against them in the Inquisitorial records ; and after that there is silence for nearly half a century.

During the first eight years of his office Bernard Gui passed no judgments against Waldensians. But they appear in the *autos-da-fé* of 1316, 1319, 1321 and 1322, and it seems that during this period he abandoned six of them to the secular arm, five as impenitents and one as a relapsed. In 1321 a fairly large number, arrested and examined in the diocese of Valence, were penanced to wear crosses.   Under the Inquisitor Henry de Chamay, successor to Bernard Gui, there were a few condemnations in the diocese of Toulouse.   But by this time the Waldensian heresy seems to have been almost completely extinct in France; and from then onwards it is found almost exclusively in the hilly and mountainous districts of Provence, Piedmont and Savoy.

Occasional repressive measures are recorded during the pontificates of Benedict XII, Clement VI and Urban V.   In 1338 and 1339 the bodies of several dead heretics were exhumed in the valley of La Vallouise; and the usual confiscations of property followed.   In 1348 twelve Waldenses were burnt in front of the cathedral at Embrun.   Between 1352 and 1363 we hear of the vigorous missionary enterprises of Guillaume des Bordes, Archbishop of Embrun.   He travelled in person through the mountain valley of his diocese, preaching the Faith and seeking to turn the heretics from their errors.   He became known as the Apostle of the Waldenses, and by his sympathy and eloquence he seems to have made many converts.   But after his death in 1363 the attempt to continue the good work by such peaceful methods was abandoned.   During the next twenty years and more the stage is held by the redoubtable Franciscan Inquisitor, François Borelli.

A small armed expedition was despatched in 1366 against the heretics of the hills, resulting in numerous arrests and in several burnings and exhumations.   Of the miserable rapacity which characterized the proceedings one may judge by the minute thoroughness with which the subsequent confiscations of property were conducted. Thus:

" Guillaume Pelat, burnt alive, had a cow and a calf which were sold.   Guillaume Long and his wife, burnt alive, possessed a cow which was sold. . . . Martin Chabret, burnt alive; two florins were found in his purse." [1]

This raid upon the heretical stronghold, which one

[1] De Cauzons, Vol II. p. 326, note.

can only regard as a mere marauding expedition, was not
repeated or followed up.   We have no record of further
activity against   the   Waldenses   until   1375,   when
Gregory XI appointed Borelli as Inquisitor for the dioceses
of Arles, Aix and Embrun.   The bishops were reprimanded for their laxity in the pursuit of heresy and for
their failure to provide payments for the expenses incurred
by   the   Inquisitors.   The   effect   was   immediate.   A
vigorous prosecution of the heresy was commenced under
the direction of Borelli.   Within a few months all the
available   prisons   were   packed   with   victims ;   and   on
August 15, 1376, Gregory was forced to issue an urgent
appeal to the faithful to contribute towards the enormous
cost of upkeep.

Borelli's mission in the Embrun district lasted, with
several interruptions, until 1393.   Throughout his whole
active term of office he maintained the utmost severity ;
he was unquestionably one of the most ferocious and
fanatical Inquisitors of whom we have record.

"During   this   long   period," said M. Tanon, " he
delivered over to the secular arm a very great number of
inhabitants   of   these   luckless   valleys ;   although   it   is
difficult in the absence of   source   evidence   to   accept
without reserve the figures given by the historians—for
instance, of 150 at La Vallouise and of eighty for
Freyssiniere and Largentiere. . . . It is still more permissible   to   doubt   Chorier   when   he   relates   that   150
inhabitants of La Vallouise were burnt at Grenoble on
the same day.   Leger, in his *Histoire des Églises vaudoises*,
agrees with Perrin in giving eighty as the number condemned at Freyssiniere and Largentiere ; but he reduces
to fifty the number of those burnt at Grenoble, and he
gives us to understand that that was the total number of
executions during the thirteen years of Borelli's term of
office.   We have no authentic documents to enable us to
decide   between   these   contradictory   estimates   and   to
arrive at the exact number of victims.   But it must have
been considerable.   The information which is given us
in Gregory XI's Bull of 1375 concerning the multitude

of prisoners . . . is sufficient to demonstrate the fact." [1]

When Borelli was relieved of his Inquisitorial duties, the repressive activities against the Waldenses collapsed completely. During the next forty years we have no record of their being in any way molested or constrained.

VI. *The Spiritual Franciscans*

The heresy of the Spiritual Franciscans was certainly the most revolutionary and for that reason, perhaps, the most interesting of the mediæval heresies. In 1254 the schools of Europe were thrown into a state of excitement and alarm by the sudden publication of a book called the *Everlasting Gospel*. It was stated to be the work of Joachim of Flora, a Cistercian abbot, who had died in 1200, famous alike for his deep sanctity and for remarkable prophetic gifts. There is reason to believe, however, that Joachim was not actually the author. The *Everlasting Gospel*, as it appeared in 1254, consisted of a long collection of apocalyptic effusions, probably culled from Joachim's writings, together with very voluminous commentaries and a most daring introduction, neither of which could possibly have been his work. Indeed the authorship of the notes and introduction was never discovered for certain; the Franciscan chronicler Salimbene says that they were composed by Gerard da Borgo san Donnino, whilst Eymeric, writing more than a century later, names John of Parma, Master-General of the Franciscans, as the author. Only one thing is beyond dispute—that the author was a Franciscan, who belonged to the section of the Order which was at that time led by John of Parma.

From the very days of its establishment the Franciscan Order had embraced two very distinct tendencies. On the one hand were the Conventuals who interpreted the Rule in a practical and rather broad-minded fashion, claiming that a strict compliance with the principles laid down by St. Francis was not only impracticable but

---

[1] Tanon, pp. 105, 106 (author's trans.).

undesirable. It was essential, they urged, to the success of their mission that the Mendicant ideal of absolute poverty should be tempered in some degree by a due regard for the circumstances under which they were called upon to work. It was essential that they should be allowed to possess, not as individuals but as a community, the necessities of life. Moreover, in spite of the suspicion with which St. Francis had contemplated learning and scholarship, they recognized clearly that to cut themselves off from the teeming intellectual life of the schools and universities was quite out of the question.

The Spirituals, on the other hand, stood for the full letter of the Franciscan Rule. They urged that no compromise of any kind should be tolerated. The central principle of their Rule was absolute poverty. Neither our Lord nor the Apostles had possessed property. Like the Master, they were to go forth into the world stripped of all their possessions. All attempts to tamper with the literal strictness of their vows were weak-minded quibbles, constituting a betrayal of their founder and a repudiation of the special characteristics of the Order.

It may well be imagined that to such men the mystical outpourings of Joachim made a strong appeal. They were eager and devoted students of his work, and they found in his prophecies many striking confirmations of their own theories concerning the special message of St. Francis to the world. Under their auspices the *Everlasting Gospel* was launched upon the world in 1254. Herein it was boldly stated that human history was divided into three great periods, the Age of the Father, the Age of the Son and the Age of the Holy Ghost. The Age of the Father had lasted from the Creation to the Incarnation; the Age of the Son from the Incarnation to the present time; the third Age, the Age of the Holy Ghost, inaugurating a new reign of universal peace and love, was shortly to commence. Various mystical computations fixed the exact date of this interesting ceremony as 1260; and the Spiritual Franciscans were to be its founders and its prophets. The passing of the Age of the Son was to be accompanied by great tribulations and travailings.   But these would form the prelude of the great millennium, ushering in an age of perfect concord and prosperity in which all men would be filled with the love of God and in which the Church and her Sacraments would be needless superfluities.

The sensation was terrific.   A commission of cardinals condemned the book in 1255.   The University of Paris ˉ was convulsed.   In 1256 John of Parma, accused of adherence to the opinions of Joachim and of strongly supporting the Spirituals, was invited to resign the Master-Generalship and was replaced in that office by St. Bonaventura.   As to the ferment which the publication of the book occasioned and the horrified surprise with which it was received, we have an interesting declamation on the part of Jean de Meun :

> " Twelve hundred years and fifty-five
> Had fled since Christ stood forth alive
> On earth for men, when first was seen
> (None will gainsay my words, I ween)
> The prime exemplar of a book
> So vile that by the devil's crook
> It well were written, and about
> 'Twas set for clerks to copy out
> And circulate when duly dight.
> The *Everlasting Gospel* hight
> This trash, and Friars avowed its merit
> As writ by God's most Holy Spirit.
> Right worthy was it to be burned.
>   *   *   *   *   *
> The University till then
> Had been asleep, but roused it when
> This blasphemy assailed its ears,
> Wakened at once by wrath and fears.
> Straightway, its arms and armour dight,
> It sallied forth with will to fight
> This hydra and delivered o'er
> The book to judgment.
>   *   *   *   *   *
> And many a wicked devilry
> Straightly commanded one may see
> Within this book of froth and foam
> Against the holy law of Rome,
> For Antichrist doth dwell within
> The covers of this book of Sin." [1]

---

[1] *Romance of the Rose*, 12449–12536.

The initial excitement seems to have died down fairly quickly. Jean de Meun, who wrote in 1273, says that the book had been hidden by its authors and that nobody knew what had become of it. But some years later a certain Pierre Jean d'Olive, a Franciscan of Beziers, revived the line of thought suggested by the *Everlasting Gospel*, declaring in a book called the *Postilla* that human history was divided into three eras and that of the Church into seven. It was, like the *Everlasting Gospel*, a sort of Adventist scare; and, although its author died in 1297 without having been reprimanded by authority, his works were condemned by John XXII in 1336. In the meantime two clearly-defined groups appeared, basing their beliefs specifically upon his teaching. The first was the Spiritual Franciscans; the second consisted of laymen belonging to the Third Order of St. Francis, who came to be known as Beguins.

During the years following the appearance of Pierre Jean's book the movement seems to have steadily gained ground. There was as yet no question of heresy involved. The thing was merely a regrettable cleavage within the Franciscan Order. Indeed the Council of Vienne, adjudicating upon certain disputed points, decided in favour of the Spirituals. Still it was clear that matters were approaching a head. In 1311 a number of Italian Spirituals cut themselves away from the Order and declared themselves a separate community. Six years later Pope John XXII, at the urgent request of the Master-General, pronounced formally in the matter, ordering the Inquisitors of Languedoc to consider as heretics and to treat as such all who styled themselves " Fraticelli," " Brothers of Poverty " or " Beguins." This Bull was issued on February 17, 1323; on April 13 of the same year the Papal constitution *Quorumdam* condemned the special habit which the Spirituals had adopted and ruled explicitly in the matter of personal property. Henceforward the wearing of the distinctive dress was forbidden and the possession by the Franciscan communities of cellars, granaries and necessary provisions was authorized. Poverty, remarked the Pope, is praiseworthy; but more praiseworthy is obedience.

The Inquisitors in Languedoc got to work at once. Sixty-four Spirituals of the Convents of Beziers and Narbonne were promptly summoned to appear before the tribunal; and the order was contemptuously disregarded. On April 23 the sixty-four defaulters, led by Bernard Delicieux, who had re-emerged from obscurity to cross swords once more with the Holy Office, set out for Avignon and presented themselves before the Pope. After a long conference forty of them abjured their errors; but the other twenty-four and Bernard Delicieux were obdurate. The Pope accordingly handed them over to the Inquisitor of Provence, instructing him to proceed against them as suspected heretics. At the subsequent trial twenty repented and received penances. But four of them steadfastly refused to abjure. They were condemned as impenitents and burnt alive on May 7, 1318.

Bernard Delicieux was tried by a special tribunal in which apparently the Inquisition played only an auxiliary part. He was, of course, a notorious agitator and an inveterate enemy alike of the ecclesiastical and civil authorities. Besides the specific accusation of heresy, the old charges were revived against him—that he had been plotting against the French King and had opposed the Dominican Inquisitors. He was treated with horrible brutality. Refusing to make full acknowledgment, he was twice put to the torture. The final sentence was that he should be degraded from his office and imprisoned for the rest of his life. The ceremony of degradation took place on December 8, 1318; less than two years later he died.

During the next ten years the Spirituals and Beguins were energetically harried by the Inquisitors of Southern France. We hear of executions at Carcassonne, Toulouse, Agde, Lodeva, Narbonne and Lunel. The first mention of them in Bernard Gui's sentences occurs in 1322, when he presided over an *auto-da-fé* at Pamiers. Several Beguins were condemned to imprisonment and one of them was abandoned to the stake. In the same year Bernard held an *auto-da-fé* at Toulouse, in which three more were handed over to the secular arm. Even by this time the movement seems to have lost all the fineness and deep sincerity which had inspired its founders. Its history from about 1320 onwards becomes merged with that of such disreputable sects as the Beghards and the Brethren of the Free Spirit.

This fact is strikingly demonstrated by a study of Bernard Gui's later sentences. Here we find arrested Beguins giving details, under interrogation, of the most revolting debaucheries in which, as members of the sect, they had participated. Perhaps it is unjust to the Spiritual Franciscans to trace any connection at all between these degenerate extremists and the Franciscan Order. Certainly it is a far cry from the deeply mystical thought and the rather unwholesome asceticism of the *Everlasting Gospel* to the neurotic fancies of the Beguins and Beghards. Both movements were unbalanced and undisciplined. They sprang from a common root, in that both looked forward to a reign of the Holy Ghost upon earth and the immediate advent of the millennium. But it is one thing to look forward to so desirable a consummation and another to say that the age of peace and love has already commenced and that you are one of its first-fruits. That way lies madness and the perversion of all right thinking. To say that the soul is so completely filled with the Spirit of God as to be incapable of sin can lead nowhere but to the exaltation of all the cravings of the flesh into divine inspirations. There is, perhaps, no more sublime, as there is certainly no more insidious aphorism than that which says that " to the pure all things are pure."

These crackbrained pseudo-mystical heresies, which are found cropping up in most of the European countries during the fourteenth century, are of little interest to the historian. Indeed they can scarcely be dignified by the name of heresies; for none of them professed to uphold any coherent system of doctrine or belief. As to the

Spiritual Franciscans proper, we have record of a few trials and subsequent abjurations between 1328 and 1330. From then onwards references to them became more and more scarce. That they continued to exist, however, is shown by the complaints of Clement VI, who wrote to the Franciscan Provincials in 1346, urging them to apprehend and punish the guilty. In 1354 a priest and a lay brother, accused of resuscitating heretical theories concerning the poverty of Christ, were tried by the Inquisition at Carcassonne. They refused to abjure and declared that, since John XXII, all the Popes had been heretics. The Inquisitors abandoned both to the secular arm. This is the last capital sentence of which we have any knowledge.[1]

[1] Vidal, *Bullaire*, pp. li–lvii, 35–40, 48–51, 161–4, 330–32, etc.; Tanon, pp. 71–87; Turberville, pp. 34–54; Douais, *Documents*, Vol. I. pp. 117–27, etc.; *Liber Sententiarum* (ed. Limborch), pp. 268–73.

CHAPTER X

CONCLUSION

WE have insisted repeatedly that the mediæval heresies with which in the present study we have been concerned were not based upon intellectual protest against the claims and doctrines of the Church. They necessarily involved such protest, but they did not spring from it. They were not the product of the great revival of thought and learning which began in the eleventh century and reached its climax in the thirteenth. They added nothing of value to the culture and knowledge of their time; in realms of theology and philosophy they have bequeathed nothing of serious interest to posterity. In the history of opinions their significance is almost negligible.

It is, indeed, a complete mistake to look upon the Middle Ages as ages of intellectual intolerance. It argues a complete misunderstanding of mediæval achievement in general and of scholastic philosophy in particular to do so. One is inclined to doubt whether inquiry and debate have ever been conducted with greater freedom and with a greater regard for the dignity and capabilities of the human intellect than in the schools of Paris, Bologna, Oxford and a score of other mediæval universities. One wonders whether any synthesis of human activities has ever been worked out upon so broad and comprehensive a foundation, whether controversy has ever been so sympathetic and so single-minded; so that the most ardent adversaries were united by their determination rather to arrive at the truth than to score debating points against one another. Everything could and must be proved; nothing should be taken on trust. I will not say that it was an age of rationalism; for rationalism nowadays is usually taken to mean something that is necessarily anti-Christian—the tacit assumption being that anyone who uses his reason will inevitably reject Christianity as a childish superstition. Rather I will say that it was an age of reason; and that the syllogistic method of the Schoolmen was, perhaps, the most daring attempt that has ever been made to extend the light of reason over the whole province of human experience.

It was not the Dominican Schoolmen who said that philosophy and theology were separate and distinct subjects, which must be approached by different methods. That was the suggestion of the Averrhoists, and in particular of the famous Siger of Brabant. And it was upon that particular point that St. Thomas and Albert Magnus most vigorously joined issue with them. "Reason," declared St. Thomas boldly, "is the dominating factor in all human activity." It was St. Thomas who urged that there must be an overlapping between the propositions discoverable by reason and the articles of the Christian revelation; and that certain truths, such as the existence of God, were demonstrable by the light of pure reason. It was Averrhoes who said that truth was not discoverable by reason; that a statement which was true as an article of the Faith might be false as a philosophical conclusion; in other words, that there is no such thing as absolute truth, and that no synthesis based jointly upon faith and reason can ever be arrived at.

Now, although the Averrhoist position led necessarily to heretical statement, it is highly important to note that there was never any question of persecuting its upholders or suppressing their freedom of speech. We are continually amazed by the enormous intellectual sympathy of the mediæval Church, and the ready encouragement which she gave to scholarship and inquiry. It may not be quite unfair to say that " philosophers were at liberty to debate the problem, but were only allowed to arrive at one conclusion." But there is something very splendid in the Church's dual confidence both in the unshakable truth of her own message and in the power of human reason to appreciate that truth. It was no part of her policy to stifle discussion and debate. Rather she was convinced that the sober and balanced use of the reason must necessarily lead to enlightenment, and that the scholar, piling syllogism upon syllogism until the very summit of truth seemed to have been reached, would find that the ladder which he had been ascending was actually the ladder of Jacob.

Consequently we find controversy and debate conducted, as a rule, upon an extraordinarily lofty plane. Let us dismiss once and for all the idea that the age of Dante was an age of intellectual arrogance. Actually it was an age of enormous intellectual charity, of reconciliation rather than schism, of synthesis rather than analysis. In all controversial writings of the time there is a note of studied tolerance and courtesy. St. Thomas' *Summa contra Gentiles*, for instance, is consistently dignified and persuasive; and there is no trace of mere denunciation or of impatient emphasis. If we turn to Dante—" the poet of St. Thomas," as he is so often called —we find the same thing. Dante's attitude to heresy is astonishingly liberal. It is often ignorantly asserted that he places Averrhoes and his disciple Avicenna in the flames of hell. The whole point is that he does nothing of the kind. Averrhoes is found in Limbo in the company of the great pagan figures of antiquity—Socrates and Plato, Cicero and Seneca, Euclid, Ptolemy and Galen. " I wish thee to know," says Virgil, " before thou goest further, that they sinned not; and though they have merit, it suffices not; for they had not Baptism, which is the portal of the faith that thou believest. And seeing they were before Christianity, they worshipped not God aright; and of these am I myself. For such defects and for no other fault are we lost; and only in so far afflicted that without hope we live in desire." [1]

Averrhoes himself is described, not in terms of contempt or denunciation, but as " he who made the great

[1] *I.e.* of the Vision of God. " Inferno," Canto IV. 32–42.

commentary "—a reference to his labours in the field of Aristotelian philosophy.

As to the great Averrhoist teacher, Siger of Brabant, he is placed by Dante in the full glory of Paradise. Siger was one of the stoutest and most eloquent champions of Averrhoist principles in the schools of Paris. In 1277 the Bishop of Paris, acting under the instructions of Pope John XXII, drew up a list of his errors under 219 headings. It is worth noting, however, that, although this imposing document was aimed primarily at the Averrhoists, it sought by a number of studied vaguenesses to confuse them with the Thomists and to discredit the Scholastic methods in general. At any rate, Siger and his friend, Boethius of Dacia, were cited to appear before the French Inquisition on the charge of heresy. They appealed to Rome, protesting their firm adherence to the Church and the Faith. What happened to them subsequently is not clear; there is no evidence to suggest that they were constrained or punished in any way. The interesting thing is that in the " Paradiso " Siger appears in the illustrious company of St. Isidore of Seville, of the Venerable Bede and of Richard of St. Victor, the great mystic; whilst St. Thomas Aquinas is made to refer to " the light eternal of Siger, who syllogized truths that brought him into envy." [1]

It has been suggested that Dante was ignorant of Siger's reputation and knew nothing of his formal condemnation by authority. That idea has recently been exploded by Mr. W. H. V. Reade in the *Journal of Theological Studies*.[2] It has been urged that Dante was at heart an Averrhoist himself; and that theory is, perhaps, too childish to be discussed. Mr. Turberville thinks it possible that " he wanted to place in Paradise someone who should represent the philosopher *par excellence*, as distinct from the theologian. It was not

---

[1] " Paradiso," Canto X. 136–8.
[2] *J.T.S.*, October 1925. See also *Islam and the Divine Comedy*, by Miguel Asin (Eng. trans. by H. Sunderland), pp. 262, 263.

easy to find such a one ; and of the possible candidates Siger of Brabant was the most distinguished." [1]

The truth, we fancy, was simpler than that. In a high degree Dante possessed a real respect and admiration, very characteristic of his time, for scholarship and learning and creative thought. St. Augustine is echoed by all the greatest mediæval canonists in his dictum that " we should by no means accuse of heresy those who, however false and perverse their opinions may be, defend them without obstinate fervour and seek the truth with careful anxiety, ready to mend their opinion when they have found the truth." Truth is indivisible, absolute and central. It may be approached by an infinitude of paths. The sifting of evidence and the consequent throwing-out of opinions conclusively disproved in debate cannot be other than beneficial. Or we may say that all forms of discussion and inquiry represented a deepening of the foundations upon which the structure of truth reposed. Indeed the real issue underlying the disputes of the schools was the fundamental question as to whether reason is the ally or the enemy of religion. Emphatically, declared St. Thomas, reason is the ally of religion ; and by the act of canonization the Church set the seal of her approval upon his verdict. Boiled down to its essence, the Averrhoist teaching implied a denial of the validity of reason.

One other point in the *Divine Comedy* may be briefly noted. Joachim of Flora was a saintly man and one whose prophetic gifts made him, during his lifetime, famous throughout Europe. It is difficult to decide how much of the *Everlasting Gospel* was actually the work of his hand. But it is undeniable that he was regarded during the thirteenth century as the founder of the Religion of the Holy Ghost, of which the Spiritual Franciscans considered themselves the prophets and expounders. Moreover the *Everlasting Gospel* was visited by all the most imposing thunders of ecclesiastical censure. The orthodoxy of Joachim himself seems never

[1] *Op. cit.*, p. 69.

to have been questioned. Yet anyone who does not understand the real meaning of mediæval heresy must find it rather surprising that Joachim is placed in Paradise in the company of such illustrious persons as St. John Chrysostom, St. Anselm, Hugh of St. Victor and Rabanus Maurus. "And at my side," says St. Bonaventure—

> " and at my side there shines
> Calabria's abbot, Joachim, endowed
> With soul prophetic." [1]

So much, then, for a lot of current misapprehension about the Middle Ages, which finds expression in such phrases as " intellectual bondage," " cringing superstition " and so forth. We turn now to a cognate point —the particular relation of the Papacy to the suppression of heresy. And it may be remarked at once that in the twelfth and thirteenth centuries the Papal authority bore no resemblance to the grinding, stifling despotism which many have represented it to have been. Indeed, as Henry Adams aptly remarks—

" A Church which embraced with equal sympathy and within a hundred years the Virgin, St. Bernard, William of Champeaux and the school of St. Victor, Peter the Venerable, St. Francis of Assisi, St. Dominic, St. Thomas Aquinas and St. Bonaventure was more liberal than any modern State can afford to be. . . . Such elasticity long ago vanished from human thought."

Now it is unquestionably true that the heretics, with whom the Inquisition was concerned, came into direct conflict with the Papal power and were united in their vigorous hostility to its claims ; and it is true that the Popes laboured strenuously to secure the fullest cooperation of the ecclesiastical and lay authorities in the task of suppression. For this very reason a number of modern writers have been disposed to sympathize with these heretics and to regard them as pioneers in the struggle against what is usually termed the " over-

[1] " Paradiso," Canto XII. 130-2.

weening power " of the Church. In the present study we have attempted to show that this position involves a serious narrowing-down of the real points at issue. These heretics came into conflict with the Popes, not because the Popes were universally loathed and feared, but because the Papacy was the visible, tangible centre of European Christendom. Any secret society, any anarchistic or anti-social movement necessarily regarded the Pope as an enemy. And to sympathize with an heretical sect simply because they did so is virtually to make a hero of any mad anarchist because one of his bombs happens to be aimed at the Pope.

This is a fundamental point. The Inquisitors, with all their failings and shortcomings, with all their curious obliquities of vision and with all their startling equivocations, were yet striving for the cause of civilization and progress against the heretical forces of disruption and decay. Whatever may be one's private opinions concerning the Papacy, one must see clearly, if one has any historical vision, that in the thirteenth century the Papal office stood for law, order and social stability. It is true that the position of the Pope was by no means a bed of roses and that he was in frequent conflict with the secular princes upon matters of discipline, administration and private conduct. But such disputes implied no repudiation of the Papal office as such; still less did a quarrel with the Pope mean that the particular ruler had pledged himself to a campaign against the Church and the Faith. A man may have a row with the local vicar without feeling bound to become a militant atheist. And, with a difference of degree, the same is true of the relations between the Popes and sovereigns of the Middle Ages. The quarrel might be a trivial or a grave one; but that the natural duty of the ruler was to uphold the Faith was a thing so obvious as to demand no discussion.

The suppression of heresy, then—and we have already repeated the point *ad nauseam*—was not a mere manifestation of Papal aggression, but a measure which was supported by the most ample secular legislation. No mediæval heresy, however wild its theories and however purely political its aims, could fail to be anti-Papal. For the Papacy simply represented the unity of the Church, and hence of society. Even an infidel like Frederick II clearly recognized this. He may have been, and undoubtedly was, a thorn in the side of the Papacy; but there were few more fervent champions of the Faith as far as the belabouring of heresy was concerned. It is, indeed, impossible to ignore the purely political aspect of the struggle. In Languedoc the Holy Office tended —I do not think one may use any stronger term—to represent the interests of the French Crown against the Languedocian nobility. In Northern Italy its identification with the Guelph faction was at times most marked; and in Spain it became, during the later period, almost swamped in politics. Throughout the Middle Ages the interests of Church and State in this matter were identical; and in estimating the work of the Inquisition it is impossible to forget this. We have to remember that it was concerned in the dual enterprise of suppressing crime and combating sin; and if we concentrate upon either aspect of its mission to the exclusion of the other we miss the whole point.

For we have to admit the dual aspect of those mediæval heresies which came in for serious persecution. They threatened not only the integrity of the Faith but the security of the social order. The mere act of belonging to an heretical sect was a crime for which death was the legal punishment. It is essential to note that when we speak, for instance, of the Albigensian heresy, we are speaking of a society and not of a mere school of thought —a visible, concrete society, whose members were bound by a definite discipline, by their adherence to certain doctrines and by their participation in certain ceremonies. They regarded themselves and were regarded by others primarily as members of that society rather than as adherents of such-and-such particular beliefs. This fact is demonstrated by innumerable examples in the Inquisitorial registers. The question is rather whether the accused belongs to the heretical society than whether he believes, as an individual, certain heretical doctrines. " He saw the heretics,—received them into his house,—had been present at their ceremonies,—had taken part in this-that-or-the-other heretical service,—had adored the ' Perfect,"—had received their benediction,—had employed the heretical form of greeting,"—such phrases as these constantly recur in the records of the Holy Office. And it is only seldom, when the accused is a ringleader or prominent person of some kind, that any detailed statement of doctrine is either demanded or proffered.

Here, then, is the fundamental difference between the heresies that were persecuted and those that were not persecuted—between, say, the Albigenses and the Averrhoists. The former constituted a society, separate and distinct from the Church and violently antagonistic to it. The latter were simply a school of thought within the Christian commonwealth. It was the difference between the mob, marching through the streets with cries of " Down with the King," and the aged University Don who, over his glass of port, speculates mildly concerning the disadvantages of government by monarchy. The Albigensian was a member of a subversive secret society, which the State could not tolerate nor assimilate. The Averrhoist, like the orthodox Scholastic, was a philosopher whose task was the co-ordination of knowledge and the advancement of learning.

Turning to the details of Inquisitorial methods and procedure, we shall confine ourselves to one or two general remarks. Clearly there can be no two opinions concerning the measures taken to suppress heresy. Such judicial forms as the secrecy of the trial, the prosecution carried on independently of the prisoner, the use of torture, the denial of proper facilities for defence were, as Vacandard points out, " despotic and barbarous." In our own time the idea that any criminal, however atrocious, should be burnt alive in public is horrible and repulsive. Yet we do well to remember that the humanitarian feeling of the present day is a thing of very recent growth. We must completely dismiss the idea that there was anything abnormal or peculiar in the ferocity with which the mediæval heretics were punished. As late as 1788 a woman named Phœbe Harris was burnt alive in front of Newgate for false coining; and we are told that " a great concourse of people attended on this melancholy occasion." It is rather striking to consider that persons who are alive to-day may well have had this ceremony described to them by eye-witnesses. During 1837, 437 people were executed in England for various crimes; and until the passage of the Reform Bill death was the recognized penalty for forgery, coining, horse-thieving, rick-burning, burglary, arson, robbery, inter-ference with the postal service and sacrilege.

The exposition of the dead bodies of executed crimi-nals was quite a regular thing until well into the nine-teenth century. In 1811 a murderer called Williams committed suicide in prison; and it was decided that a public exhibition of his body should be made in the neighbourhood of the crime which he had committed.

" A long procession was formed, headed by constables who cleared the way with their staves. Then came the newly-formed horse-patrol with drawn cutlasses, parish officers, peace officers, the high constable of the county of Middlesex on horseback, and then the body of Wil-liams, ' extended at full length on an inclined platform erected on the cart . . . giving a full view of the body, which was dressed in blue trousers and a blue-and-white striped waistcoat. . . . The countenance of Williams was ghastly in the extreme and the whole had an appear-ance too horrible for description.' The procession . . . halting for a quarter of an hour in front of the victims' dwelling, was accompanied by an immense concourse of persons, eager to get a sight of the murderer's remains." [1]

The exploits of this man Williams, by the way, inspired De Quincey's famous essay on *Murder Con-sidered as One of the Fine Arts*.

Pepys has a few remarks upon the public execution of a certain Colonel John Turner in 1662; he describes how he " got to stand upon the wheel of a cart for a

[1] Arthur Griffiths, *The Chronicles of Newgate*, pp. 437, 438.

shilling in great pain above an hour before the execution was done." In 1784 the official place of execution was changed from Tyburn to " the great arena that has lately been opened before Newgate." The sheriffs of London, in a formal notification of the change, declared that in future, " instead of carting the criminals through the streets to Tyburn, the sentence of death is executed in front of Newgate, where upwards of five thousand persons may easily assemble." [1] It was not until 1868 that public executions were abolished by Act of Parliament.

It is clear, then, that in indicting the Inquisition upon specific charges of physical cruelty and callous brutality, we must proceed with some circumspection. Lord Acton's exhortation—

" never to debase the moral currency or to lower the standard of rectitude, but to try others by the final maxims that govern your own life, and to suffer no man and no cause to escape the undying penalty which history has the power to inflict on wrong,"—

—this exhortation, I say, fine and inspiring though it is, is a counsel of perfection which few historians would have the temerity to apply in its literal fullness. We cannot indict a whole civilization, a whole continent, a whole era of human activity. Perhaps we have become more kindly, more sensitive to cruelty, more ready to make allowances, more charitable in our outlook upon such matters. It may be legitimate to hope that, after two thousand years of Christianity, some sort of corporate moral advance would be apparent. Yet the present age has its crudities, its absurdities, its obliquities and its abominations—things at which our ancestors would have shuddered in horror. We can make no claim to pass absolute and final judgment upon the actions, manners and thoughts of the past. We have not a scrap of justification for supposing that our standard of values in such matters is any more final than were those of the Middle Ages. Some of us, indeed, may be disposed to think that the men of the Middle Ages were

[1] Arthur Griffiths, *The Chronicles of Newgate*, p. 177.

building upon the surer foundation. They strove mightily and they failed; we of the so-called " modern era " have not so much failed as given up the attempt altogether. We have neither attempted nor achieved any such synthesis as that which inspired the minds of the Schoolmen. We have lost the very conception of unity; so that mediæval society, endlessly diverse, yet based first and foremost upon a unity of culture, seems to us a strange and exotic thing, with its fierce enthusiasms, its great hatreds and its even greater loves. We are at home in the spacious days of Imperial Rome. For every good book on the Middle Ages we have twenty on the Roman Empire. Cicero, we feel, would naturally take his place on the front bench of the House of Commons. But in the presence of a great character like St. Bernard, are we not sometimes bewildered and awed ? Are we not conscious that some great driving-force has gone from our world—a force which has something of the fierce heat of the mid-day sun and something of the keen freshness of the wind upon the moors ?

The irregularities and palpable injustices of Inquisitorial procedure have already been discussed at sufficient length. A more serious matter—" possibly the worst aspect in the whole story of the Inquisition,"—was the fact that—

" its pernicious methods of procedure were borrowed by the admiring secular princes for their own courts, which did not pretend to have the double nature which was the explanation, if not the excuse, for the Inquisition's adoption of its system. Thus civil courts in Europe came to be tarnished by the system of *inquisitio*, the secret inquiry, the heaping-up of disabilities for the defence, the application of torture—all these having the august sanction of ecclesiastical use." [1]

It is a little curious to find that M. de Cauzons regards this fact—the adoption of Inquisitorial methods by the secular courts—as being anything but deplorable. He even thinks that " the criminal and penal codes of our

[1] Turberville, p. 242.

modern civilization are approaching more and more
closely, both in their spirit and in their practice, to those
of the Inquisition of heretics." [1] We find it difficult to
agree with either judgment. The Inquisition was a
special tribunal, called into being by special circumstances
for the performance of a special task. It cannot be
treated, as we have seen, either as a purely penitential
office or as a criminal tribunal. Essentially, of course,
it was the former; but, as a consequence of the special
circumstances under which it was formed, it became
actually a combination of the two things. I submit that
the attempt to organize secular legal forms upon the
Inquisitorial model would be productive of as many
anomalies and injustices as would be the attempt to
introduce interrogatories and denunciations by third
parties into the routine of the confessional.

For the methods adopted in combating the more
subversive mediæval heresies the historian can hold no
brief. The Inquisitorial registers record some of the
worst acts of oppression and stupidity of which we have
knowledge. But it may safely be asserted that such
acts seldom escaped the heaviest censures of authority.
The ruffianly Robert the Bougre was suspended from
office and condemned to perpetual imprisonment. The
Papal commissioners in Languedoc in 1305 ordered the
dismissal of a number of officials who had abused the
authority entrusted to them. After the first trials of the
Knights Templars Clement V suspended all the French
Inquisitors from the exercise of their duties. Abuses
were recognized as such and condemned; and to ignore
their condemnation is not less one-sided than to ignore
their existence. Finally, it must be remembered that
the first Inquisitors were very far from being the aggressive champions of an already triumphant cause. For
many years in Languedoc they were fighting with their
backs to the wall; and the heretics made it very clear
that it was to be a fight to a finish. It may be doubted
whether any anti-social conspiracy at once so venomous
and so powerful as the Albigensian heresy has ever

[1] *Op. cit.*, Vol. II. p. xliv.

appeared in Europe. It may be doubted, further, whether the stamping-out of so formidable a menace to society could have been accomplished by any purely secular tribunal with such complete success and with, comparatively speaking, so little bloodshed and violence. For it is certain that no policy of toleration would have been either possible or desirable.

Moreover, even if we look at the problem in its most abstract form, we must be prepared to qualify the contradiction between Inquisitorial methods and the " spirit of the Gospel." As Mr. Nickerson puts it:

" The logical conclusion is irresistible, that if (as all Christians must) we assume our Lord's doctrine and example to be of inestimable value to mankind, we must admit that any attempt to pervert that doctrine and example so as to make our Blessed Lord say and do as He did not is a more serious matter than any crime recognized by law. Furthermore, this argument from reason is, in a measure, supported by authority in the person of our Lord Himself, because of the extreme bitterness with which He denounced the Pharisees for perverting religion." [1]

All of which leads us to the important consideration that the Holy Office is still in existence to-day, although it is no longer staffed exclusively by members of the monastic Orders. The Monastic Inquisition, as we have seen, was simply an extension of the Episcopal Inquisition which Lucius III had established in 1184; and at the present time the Holy Office is concerned with the same work of inquiry, or inquisition, as in the time of Innocent III and Clement V. It is superfluous to point out that its methods have changed; the elaborate organization of bygone days is no longer necessary; and the stake and the *strappado*, in the use of which it had no monopoly, have disappeared from all penal procedure. But its purpose and functions have remained unaltered. It is concerned with the general task of supervision and the guardianship of the Faith; and at the present time it is chiefly occupied

[1] *Op. cit.*, pp. 251, 252.

in the important work of censorship—or rather, with the formal condemnation, when necessary, of books or propositions contained in them.

There has, therefore, been no breach of continuity and no change in the teaching of the Church concerning liberties of conscience. The principles are the same, although the methods of the Monastic Inquisition are happily obsolete. We cannot conclude better than by quoting once more from Vacandard :

" The Inquisition established to judge heretics is, therefore, an institution whose severity and cruelty are explained by the ideas and manners of the age. We shall never understand it unless we consider it in its environment and from the view-point of men like St. Thomas Aquinas and St. Louis, who dominated the age by their genius. Critics who are ignorant of the Middle Ages may feel at liberty to shower insult and contempt upon a political system whose severity is naturally repugnant to them. But contempt does not always imply a reasonable judgment, and to abuse an institution is not necessarily a proof of intelligence. If we would judge an epoch intelligently, we must be able to grasp the view-point of other men, even if they lived in an age long past.

" But although we grant the good faith and the goodwill of the founders and judges of the Inquisition —we speak only, be it understood, of those who acted conscientiously—we must still maintain that their idea of justice was far inferior to ours. Whether taken in itself or compared with other criminal procedures, the Inquisition was, so far as guarantees of equity are concerned, undoubtedly unjust and unfair." [1]

We cannot isolate the mediæval Inquisition from its setting and pass judgment upon it as though the humanitarian feeling of the present day had been prevalent in the Middle Ages. At the present time the Holy Office still performs, with wise and generous use of its authority, that same task of inquiry and supervision which in more turbulent times involved the employment of more vigorous and more terrible methods.

[1] Vacandard, *op. cit.*, pp. 185, 186.

APPENDIX

THE organized stamping-out of the Albigensian heresy
by the co-operation of Church and State was undertaken
about the beginning of the thirteenth century and was
completed by about the end of the first quarter of the
fourteenth. It involved the deaths of a number of the
ringleaders, as well as the punishment of comparatively
large numbers by imprisonment, exile, loss of citizenship
and enforced military service. It involved also the
destruction of great quantities of heretical literature—
text-books of doctrine and ceremonial, unauthorized
translations of the Scriptures and so forth. So far as I
am aware, no single book of this kind has survived to the
present day. We possess no contemporary account of
the Albigensian heresy which was written by a member
of the sect. All our records are, strictly speaking, the
work of men who were bitterly hostile to it; and, in many
cases, of men who gave their whole lives to its extirpation.

The consequence of this exceedingly regrettable fact
is that the real character of the Albigensian heresy has
been a matter of warm dispute amongst historians. For
it is clearly uncritical to accept without examination the
statements of contemporary writers who admittedly
loathed the heresy and everything connected with it, and
who naturally tended to exaggerate every fact that could
tell against it. Before we pass judgment we must in
fairness hear the other side. But unfortunately, thanks
to the energetic labours of the Inquisitors, there is, in this
case, no other side to be heard.

Justly reacting, therefore, from the extreme position
taken up by the mediæval propagandists, a number of
historians have proceeded clean to the opposite extreme.

It has been maintained that the only reason for the persecution of the Albigensian heretics was that they came into conflict with the Papal power. So far from proposing any anti-social or immoral doctrines, these heretics, we are told, were simple Bible Christians who stood against the meddling bigotry of the Popes and the mercenary worldliness of the clergy for a return to the pristine purity of the early Church. They were hated with a hatred that was based upon fear and consciousness of guilt. The Church had, if one may use the term, an inferiority complex. And this, combined with her hatred of anything that might threaten her hold upon the souls, bodies and pockets of the people, decided her course of action and led to the wiping-out of the Albigensian heresy.

This view we have been quite unable to accept. In our second chapter we have given some account of the heresy and, throughout our study, have consistently maintained the thesis that it was a wholly corrupt system of ethics and beliefs, whose triumph would have threatened the civilization of Europe. We have recognized that it would be absurd to believe all the scandalous tales that were related about the conduct of the heretics— about their orgies of promiscuity in darkened rooms and so on. Stories of this kind have been told about almost every secret society in history. But we have claimed that, in the main, the orthodox mediæval writers on the subject were not far wrong in their descriptions. And it may be well here to urge one or two points in support of that claim.

In the first place, on all the more important points of heretical practice and belief, the mediæval writers from the eleventh century onwards to the fourteenth are in absolute agreement both with one another and with the apologists of the Patristic age. In the autobiography of the famous Abbot Guibert of Nogent we have a spirited account of the punishment of heretics at Soissons in 1114. And the author goes on to describe these new Manichee beliefs in terms that might have come straight from

Bernard Gui's *Practica*.   In 1177 Count Raymond V of
Toulouse writes despairingly of the way in which family
life is being wrecked by the spread of the heresy; and it
seems like an echo of St. Athanasius and Pope Leo I.
All the writers on the subject, from the Popes down-
wards, concur in ascribing to the Albigenses the beliefs
of the Manichees of the old Empire.   There is no disagreement on the point.   They are always referred to
as modern Manichees.

The next point is more important.   It is only partially
true to say that our information is derived from men
who, without exception, hated the heresy.   Or rather
it is only true in a sense.   For we have very voluminous
information concerning the Albigensian heresy in the
archives and records of the Holy Office.   These records
were, it is true, transcribed by the officials of the Inquisition.   But no one has ever suggested that the records
were faked or subsequently tampered with.   They record
the verbal statements of heretics.   We find concurrent
testimony of half a dozen witnesses concerning the speech
or actions of an accused person.   We find a man defending himself by declaring that " I am not a heretic; for I
have a wife and I live with her, and we have sons."   The
Inquisitorial registers, in fact, provide ample material for
the compilation of a complete text-book of Albigensian
beliefs and ceremonies, derived from the words of those
who regularly practised them.   Let us take one or two
specific examples.

We possess the full account of the proceedings conducted by Bernard of Caux and Jean de St. Pierre between
August 22 and December 10, 1247, against the celebrated heretic Peter Garsias.[1]   Witnesses on oath, whose
statements in most cases overlap and corroborate one
another, asserted that Garsias had frequently and publicly
maintained the following doctrines :

That Christ and the Blessed Virgin and Blessed John
the Evangelist had descended from Heaven and were not
of this flesh.

[1] Reproduced in Douais, *Documents*, Vol. II. pp. 90–114.

That St. John the Baptist was one of the greatest devils who had ever lived.

That under no circumstances may justice condemn anyone to death.

That marriage was mere harlotry (*purum meretricium*), and that no one who had a wife could be saved.

That the preachers of the Crusades were murderers.

These propositions are taken at random from a mass of evidence that occupies some twenty-five pages. In the register of the Inquisitor Geoffrey d'Ablis an accused heretic is reported as saying that " the only marriage was between God and the soul; and that it was a greater sin to lie with one's wife than with some other woman, since the thing was done more openly and without shame." In the presence of Bernard Gui the heretic, Pierre Autier, asserted that " the marriage-act is always sinful and cannot be performed without sin " and that " the sacrament of marriage was not ordained by God." The same opinions were expressed, in slightly different words, by Peter Raymond who was sentenced on April 30th, 1312.[1]

It is, of course, arguable that such extravagant views as these were held and taught only by a few extremists. A number of heretics who were examined by the Council of Lombers in 1176 protested vigorously against the assertion that they condemned marriage. According to the judgment of the Council, " they had been accustomed to teach that a man and woman could not be saved if they had been carnally united." To this charge they replied by a specific denial, declaring that the marriage-act was not in itself sinful; and the presiding bishop inquired drily whether they were speaking under fear of God or under fear of the people. At any rate they refused to ratify their profession of faith by taking the oath of purgation; and the Council did not amend its judgment.[2] The great schoolman, Alan of Lille, says

[1] *Liber Sententiarum* (ed. Limborch), pp. 92, 178.

[2] *Chronica Rogeri de Hoveden*, anno 1176 (Rolls Series 51, ii, pp. 105–117).

explicitly that the Albigenses condemned marriage.
They maintained, he tells us, that if there were no such
thing as marriage, there could be no such thing as
adultery.[1] At all events it is undeniable that the condemnation of marriage was a perfectly logical deduction
from the dualistic principle. It would seem that in
districts where the heresy was most powerful and widespread the insistence upon such ethical points was
boldest and most uncompromising. The heresy was
innocuous only so long as it was not taken seriously.

Then there was the " Endura "—" a barbarous practice," as M. Tanon observes, " which we could scarcely
believe unless we had such frequent allusions to it." [2]
It consisted simply in the practice of suicide as a religious
rite. Sometimes, of course, the thing took the form
of going on hunger-strike after arrest by the Inquisitors. But it was regularly undertaken as a separate and
wholly voluntary exercise and was encouraged by the
" Perfect " as being highly meritorious. We have
already discussed the ceremony at sufficient length (see
Chapter II) and we need not repeat ourselves here.
Suffice it to say that the " Endura " was frequently
entered upon by persons in perfect health. In one
of Bernard Gui's trials we hear of the " Consolamentum "
being administered to a " certain little girl." The
mother was strictly forbidden by the " Perfect " to
nourish her child ; and a few days later it died.[3]

Thirdly, we have to note the hatred with which the
heresy was universally regarded. The Albigensian
heretics were detested by everybody. Their most implacable enemy was the infidel Emperor Frederick II.
Even the Waldensian heretics had little use for them ;
and during the early years of the thirteenth century
occasionally manifested the greatest zeal in securing their
arrest.[4] From the time of their first appearance in Europe

[1] Alanus de Insulis, *Contra hereticos* iv, 62 in Migne, P.L. 210,
cols. 365-7.
[2] Tanon, p. 224.
[3] *Liber Sententiarum* (ed. Limborch), p. 104.
[4] See Douais, *Documents*, Vol. II. p. 110, note.

we find the Albigensian heretics everywhere looked upon and treated as enemies of society.

It may be admitted that there was much in their teachings that was fine and inspiring. No philosophy that is wholly anti-social, wholly wrong-headed, has ever engaged the serious attention of any large number of people. Dualism solves many problems that have vexed the mind of man throughout the ages. Yet it is a tenuous, fragile thing which can flourish only in the hot-house atmosphere of sentiment, pious emotion and lazy irrationalism. When it is brought out into the light of day, when the searchlight of logic and reason is turned upon it, it is hideously metamorphosized. It is seen to be a thing of hard, jagged edges. It is like some great mountain which, when seen from the distance in its soft shadows and easy, unbroken ascents, invites one to scale its heights. Yet, when the attempt is made, the traveller finds grim precipices, great boulders which may fall upon him and crush him, precarious footholds and, withal, an atmosphere of desolation and fear.

The Albigensian heresy, then, was a perfectly logical dualistic philosophy—no more and no less. It was one of the most reasonable religions that have ever appeared amongst men. Matter, it declared, was evil, the creation of the evil God. Therefore the destruction of matter was the destruction of evil. The human body is material; therefore suicide is virtuous and the procreation of children is sinful. It was all as reasonable as it could be. And it was one of the most virulent poisons that has ever entered the veins of society.

INDEX

Abelard, 6, 27–9
Accusatio, 106–11
Acquittal, seldom granted by Holy Office, 153; reasons for this, 153–4
Acton, Lord, *quoted*, 260
Adams, Henry, *quoted or referred to*, 10, 27, 50, 61, 255
Ad Extirpanda, Papal Bull, 158, 213
Alaman de Roaix, condemned by Inquisition, 178–9
Alan of Lille, 10, 29, 268
Alaric I, 55, 56
Alberic, Inquisitor in Lombardy, 94, 229
Albert Magnus, 9, 23, 251
Albi, Council of, 212; riots and street-fighting at, 221, 224
Albigensian Heresy, regarded as a revival of Manichæism, 37–8, 267; theology of, 39–40, 265; ethical and social teachings of, 41–2, 267–9; reasons for its spread, 47–51; its comprehensive organization in Languedoc, 67–71; a society rather than a school of thought, 257
Albigensian Heretics in England, 52
Alexander III, Pope, 33, 71
Alexander IV, Pope, 131, 143, 147, 158, 209; allows Inquisitors to assist at examinations under torture, 159
All Fools' Day, 6
Alphonse, Count of Poitiers, 175, 213, 216–17; his revenues from confiscated heretical property, 215; his expenses in maintaining the Holy Office, 215
Alphonso the Wise, king of Castile, founds University of Seville, 57
Amaury de Bènes, 86, 204
Angermunde, executions of heretics at, 236
Anselm of Lucca, 86
Aragon, heretics banished from, 36, 78; Inquisition established in, 227; anti-Jewish disturbances in, 228
Arles, Council of, 206
Arnold Dominici, murdered by heretics, 151
Arnold of Brescia, 20, 205

Arras, employment of torture at, 160; diverting incident during *auto-da-fé* at, 167
Asin, Don Miguel, *quoted or referred to*, 58, 62, 253
Assizes of Clarendon, 52, 208
Aucassin and Nicolette, 62, 66
Autier, Pierre, 41, 268
Auto-da-fé or *Sermo Generalis*, 170, 171, 207, 225; nature of the ceremony, 166, 168–9; when and where held, 167
Averrhoes, 252
Avignon, Council of, 65, 83, 113
Avignonnet, massacre of Inquisitors at, 118, 222
Aymon de Caumont, Inquisitor, 210

Beghards and Beguins, 236, 248
Benevento, battle of, 229, 232
Berengar II, Archbishop of Narbonne, 65, 75
Berengar Frédol, Cardinal, 188, 224
Berengar of Tours, 26
Berlaiges, executions at, 175
Bernard de Castanet, 188, 217
Bernard de Ventadour, 60
Bernard Delicieux, comments on the subtlety of Inquisitors, 155; tortured during his trial, 160; his successful agitations against the Inquisitors, 170, 223; his political schemes, 224; arrested by order of Clement V, 224; assumes leadership of Spiritual Franciscans, 247; final arrest and condemnation, 247
Bernard Gui, Inquisitor of Toulouse, 34, 108, 118, 160, 167, 179, 184, 195, 200; summary of his sentences, 171; on the necessity for simple procedure in heresy trials, 108; his exhortation to Inquisitors, 126; his views concerning sorcerers, 142; orders destruction of Jewish literature, 145; on the "time of grace," 145; on the suppression of the names of witnesses, 149; on the cleverness of Waldenses under cross-examination, 155; his eighteen *autos-da-fé*, 166, 170; his complaints of the Clementine reforms, 189; on

271

the wearing of crosses, 195; orders demolition of houses, 210; his posthumous sentences, 206–7; correspondence with Bishop of Compostella, 227; his sentences against Waldenses, 240; dealings with Beghards, 247–8

Bernard Versavin, 210

Bernard of Caux, Inquisitor, 83, 160, 182, 183, 184, 196, 200, 211, 267; appointed Inquisitor of Toulouse, 118, 222; his treatment of relapsed heretics, 173, 178; commutes a sentence of imprisonment, 183

Bertrand de Born, 60

Beziers, 69; captured by crusading army, 77; Council of, 178, 194, 196, 201, 212

Black Death, 237–8

Bœthius of Dacia, 253

Boniface VIII, 150

Borelli, François, his activities in Piedmont, 241–3

Brethren of the Free Spirit, 236, 238, 248

Burgundy, Inquisitorial activity in, 240

Cambrai, mob violence at, 43, 45; anti-heretical activity at, 128

Carcassonne, captured by crusading army, 77; Inquisitorial records destroyed at, 223

Carcassonne tribunal of the Inquisition, 148, 157, 160, 178, 182, 185, 187, 193, 195–6, 199, 201, 202, 205, 210

Castel Faure, 205

Cat, Arnald, 130

Charlemagne, 4

Charles Martel, 4

Children's Crusade, 10

Clement IV, Pope, 158

Clement V, Pope, 159, 161, 188; appoints commission for reform of Inquisitorial prisons, 188; suspends powers of French Inquisitors, 226, 262

Clement VI, Pope, reproves the Inquisitors for extortion, 218; permits re-building on anathematized land, 210; his formal condemnation of Flagellants, 238; letter to Franciscan Provincials, 249

Confiscation of Property, 211–17

Conrad of Marburg, 20, 94–5, 233–5

Consolamentum, Albigensian sacrament, 40–2, 49, 268

Constance, anti-heretical action at, 236

Constantinople, riches of, 55

Cordes, heretical demonstrations at, 220; removal of interdict upon, 166, 171

Coulton, Dr. G. G., 2

" Courtly " Love, 60–2

Cram, Dr. R. A., quoted, 5, 11

Crosses, wearing of, introduced by St. Dominic, 192; imposed as a penance by Inquisitors, 183, 194–6

Crusade, Albigensian, 77

Curés, duties of, in furthering work of the Inquisition, 120, 199

Dante Alighieri, 11, 14, 15, 99, 252–4

David of Augsburg, Inquisitor, 156

De Castelnau, Pierre, 75–6, 95

De Cauzons, Th., quoted or referred to, 16 note, 94 note, 103, 139, 153 note, 157 note, 158, 168, 175 note, 202, 213, 261

De Maistre, Comte Joseph, 116, 173

De Montfort, Simon, 15, 34, 84; killed in action at Toulouse, 77

De Quincey, Thomas, 259

Dead Persons, procedure of Inquisition against, 203–7; reasons for ditto, 177, 207

Death Penalty for Heresy, how introduced, 102–4

Denunciatio, under Roman Law, 111

Denunciatio cum promovente, 112–14

Divine Comedy, 15, 16, 21, 252, 255

Dominicans as Inquisitors, 93, 219; ask to be relieved of Inquisitorial duties, 118, 222; expelled from Toulouse and subsequently recalled, 221

Elipandus, Archbishop of Toledo, 3

Embrun, executions at, 241

Endura, Albigensian suicidal rite, 42, 50, 268

Eon de l'Étoile, 30, 31, 46

Erfurt, four heretics executed at, 234

Ermessinde de Foix, condemned for heresy thirty years after death, 205, 227

Everlasting Gospel, 243–6, 248, 254

Excommunication, alarming effects of, 12, 124

Expenses of Inquisition, 130, 217–8

Eymeric, Nicolas, Inquisitor, 108, 155, 228; objects to heresy trials by accusatio, 109; his views concerning sorcerers, 142; on the minimum number of witnesses, 147; on the treatment of obstinate suspects, 157; on the futility of examinations under torture,

161; on liberties permissible to prisoners, 185; on the poverty of the Aragonese Inquisition, 216, 228
Ezzelin da Romano, 231

False Witnesses, severity of Holy Office towards, 147–8
Fautors or Favourers of Heresy, their culpability in the eyes of Inquisitors, 141
Felix, Bishop of Urgel, 3
Ferrier, François, Inquisitor at Narbonne, 219, 221
Flagellants, 194; at Strasburg, 237; condemned by Clement VI, 238
Flogging as a penance, 200
Florence, street-fighting between Guelphs and Ghibellines at, 230
Fra Landulpho, Inquisitor, 108
Franciscans, as Inquisitors, 93, 219
Frederick Barbarossa, Emperor, 87, 208
Frederick II, Emperor, 103, 147, 229, 231, 269; compares heresy with treason, 88; his vigorous legislation against heretics, 89–91, 269; Moslem sympathies, 91–2; refers to Inquisitors delegated by the Pope, 93
" Friends of God," 236, 238
Fulk of Marseilles, Bishop of Toulouse, 15, 60, 80
Fulk of St. Georges, Inquisitor, 223

Galand, Jean, Inquisitor of Carcassonne, 185
Geoffrey d'Ablis, Inquisitor, 161, 268
Gilles de Rais, 20
Godescalcus, 3, 26
Goslar, condemnation of heretics at, 40, 43, 45
Gregory VII, Pope, 45
Gregory IX, Pope, 90, 104, 113, 128, 212, 229, 234; inscribes Frederick's law for Lombardy on Papal register, 88; letter to the bishops of Languedoc, 94; letter to Conrad of Marburg, 95
Gregory XI, Pope, 104, 117, 141 *note*, 177, 210, 239, 242
Guibert of Nogent, 39, 266
Guillaume des Bordes, Archbishop of Embrun, 241
Guillaume du Pont, commutation of his sentence, 133
Guillem Arnaud, 132 *note*, 235; appointed first Inquisitor of Toulouse, 219; expelled from Toulouse, 220; assassinated by heretics, 118, 222

Guillem Arnaud Bornh, notary, 130
Guillem Pelhisse, Inquisitor, 139
Guiraud, Jean, *quoted or referred to*, 64, 83
Guy Foulques, Inquisitor, on the minimum number of witnesses, 147

Harris, Phœbe, burnt at Newgate, 259
Havet, Julien, *quoted or referred to*, 44, 67
Hecker, J. F. C., *quoted*, 237
Henri de Chamay, Inquisitor, 241
Henry of Clairvaux, 73
Henry III, Emperor, 45
Henry II of England, 52, 64
Henry VIII of England, 19, 211
Henry of Lausanne, 31
Heresy, *passim*; distinction between thought and action, 135–8; social significance of mediæval, 97–8; negative character of ditto, 29–32
Houses, demolition of, 208–11
Hugh, Bishop of Auxerre, 45

Ibn Daud of Ispahan, 62
Ibn Hazm of Cordova, 62
Impenitent Heretics, treatment of by Inquisition, 176; small numbers of, 176
Imprisonment, monastic in origin, 4 *note*, 181; commutation of sentences to, 182–3, 191; the *murus largus*, 172, 185, 186; the *murus strictus*, 186–7; the *murus strictissimus*, 133, 186
Infidels, circumstances under which prosecuted by the Inquisition, 136, 140
Innocent III, Pope, 14, 65, 73–4, 99, 104, 111, 209; his decrees concerning heresy, 87; compares heresy with treason, 88 *note*, 212
Innocent IV, Pope, 103, 118, 201, 213, 240; sanctions use of torture by Inquisition, 158; orders demolition of houses of heretics, 209; rules concerning disposition of property confiscated from heretics, 213; restricts imposition of fines by Inquisitors, 218
Inquisitio, under Roman Law, 114; procedure adopted by the Monastic Inquisition, 114–16
Inquisition, Episcopal, 80, 113, 263
Inquisition, Monastic, *passim*; task of, 99; extent of its activities, 100–1; established in Germany, 239; dual aspect of its work, vii, 115–17, 256

Inquisitors, *passim ;* see Bernard Gui, Eymeric, Guillem Arnaud, Dominicans, Franciscans, Borelli, St. Peter Martyr, Toulouse, Pamiers, Carcassonne, etc.; distribution of, in France, 117; ceremonies attending their arrival in a district, 119–21; rules concerning suspension and deposition of, 126–8; accepted testimony of criminals and minors, 147

Interdict, 8, 12, 141

Interrogations, 150, 154–6

Jean de Meun, 15; on the battle of Benevento, 232; on the *Everlasting Gospel*, 245–6

Jean d'Arcis, complains of leniency of Archbishop of Rodez, 216

Jean de Parthenay, appeals to Rome against accusation of heresy by Holy Office, 152

Jean de St. Pierre, Inquisitor, 118, 222, 267

Jean Langlois, 196

Jews, when prosecuted by Inquisition, 140–1; distinctive badge worn by, 194

Joachim of Flora, 243, 245, 254–5

John XXII, Pope, 12, 233, 246, 249, 253

John, Duke of Burgundy, 130, 240

John of Parma, 243; resigns Master-Generalship of Franciscan Order, 245

John of Vienne, Papal legate, 118

Johnson, Dr. Samuel, on religious toleration, 26 *note*

Kerlinger, Walter, Inquisitor, 239

Koran, 57

Ku-Klux-Klan, 21–2, 195

Langlois, Ch. V., *quoted or referred to*, 2, 172, 174

Languedoc, *passim ;* spread of Albigensian heresy in, 67–73; Inquisitorial action in, 219–225, 247–8

Lateran, Fourth General Council of the, 87, 113

Lea, H. C., *quoted or referred to*, 48, 70, 90, 93, 104, 148, 158, 182, 186, 211, 233, 235

Lecky, W. E. H., *quoted or referred to*, 14, 60

Leo X, Pope, authorizes abandonment of false witnesses to secular arm, 148

Leo XIII, Pope, on religious liberty, 24

Lombers, Council of, 268

Louis of Willenberg, Inquisitor, 239

Luchaire, A., *quoted or referred to*, 32, 65, 69, 87

Lucius III, Pope, 87

Luitprand, Bishop of Cremona, 55

Magistrate, Roman, powers of, 107

Marriage, Albigensian teachings concerning, 41, 139, 268

Marseilles, in Roman times, 54

Mauran, Peter, account of his condemnation for heresy, 72

Milan, first executions of heretics at, 44; executions in 1233, 89; fighting at, 231

Molinier, A., *quoted*, 183

Monk of Montaudon, the troubadour, 60, 71; on feminine vanities, 67

Montferrand, Marquis of, his collection of heretical books burnt by the Dominicans, 144

Montpellier, medical schools at, 58

Montségur, heretical fortress, 175, 222

Montwimer, executions of heretics at, 128

Moranis, Albigensian bishop, 128

Moslem culture in Spain, 56–9

Murus Strictissimus, 133, 186

Multorum Querela, Papal Bull, 188

Naples, University of; founded by Frederick II, 92

Narbonne, 54, 60, 151; held by the Arabs, 56; Council of N, (1227) on synodal witnesses, 113; on imprisonment of heretics, 183; Council of N, (1246) 193, 201, 218; Dominican priory sacked, 221

Newland, William, 198

Nickerson, H., *quoted or referred to*, 9, 13, 31, 68, 72, 76, 100, 110, 263

Nicolas of Abbeville, Inquisitor, 223

Notaries, their duties in connection with the Inquisition, 123–4

Oldrado di Tresseno, 89

Oloron, brigandage and sacrilege at, 69

Ordeals, forbidden by the Popes, 86

Orleans, summary action against heretics at, 43

Oxford, Council at, 52; condemnation for apostasy to Judaism at, 92

Pamiers, Inquisition at, 122, 132, 166, 174, 182, 187, 247; *auto-da-fé* held in cemetery at, 167; Inquisitorial prisons at, 187

Papacy, in its relation to heresy, 255–6

Parma, riots at, 233

Passagium transmarinum, 199, 201

Pedro II of Aragon, 78, 87, 239; his savage legislation against heresy, 33, 36, 78; killed at the battle of Muret, 77

Peire Cardenal, the troubadour, 60, 65

Pegna, on the necessity of secrecy in Inquisitorial trials, 153

Pepys, Samuel, 259

" Perfect," Albigensian priesthood, 40–2, 269

Periti or Experts; their duties in connection with Inquisitorial trials, 131–4

Peter Cella, Inquisitor, 117, 198, 200, 219; his activities at Toulouse and Carcassonne, 220–1

Peter Garsias, 41, 139; his statement of Albigensian beliefs, 267–8

Peter of Bruys, burnt at St. Gilles, 67

Peter of Cadireta, Inquisitor, stoned to death by heretics, 227

Peter of St. Chrysogonus, Cardinal, 71

Peter Pelha, 199

Peter-Roger de Mirepoix, organizes assault on Inquisitors at Avignonnet, 222

Peter the Venerable, 6

Philip-Augustus, 15, 87, 209; his action against heretics, 86, 92

Philip the Fair, 124 *note*, 170, 185, 223, 225

Pierre Fabri, Inquisitor, 131

Pierre Jean d'Olive, condemnation of his works by John XXII, 246

Pilgrimages, imposed as penances by Inquisition, 197–8; distinction between major and minor, 199; method of performing, 199–202

Pœna talionis, 106, 108, 110, 235

Pons d'Espira, Inquisitor, poisoned by heretics, 227

Pons Geoffrey, 215

Pons du Vernet, 68–9

Pons Roger, 82, 192–3

Ponsard de Gisi, 225

Priesthood, corruption of, in Languedoc, 64–6

Priscillian, 3

Prisons, general condition of Inquisitorial, 187–8; horrors of *murus strictus*, 186

Property confiscated from heretics, disposition of, 213–4

Public executions forbidden in England, 260

Quorumdam, Papal constitution, 246

Raimbaud d'Aurenga, the troubadour, 60, 66

Raymond of Miraval, the troubadour, 78

Raymond of Raberstein, Bishop of Toulouse, 65

Raymond V, Count of Toulouse, on the spread of heresy in his domains, 71, 267

Raymond VI, Count of Toulouse, 53, 74, 76–8, 200

Raymond VII, Count of Toulouse, orders execution of heretics at Berlaiges, 175

Raymond Belhot, 42

Raymond Sabbatier, 183

Raymonde Mainfère, 195

Reade, W. H. V., 253

Receipts from confiscation of heretical property, 215, 217

Records, preservation of Inquisitorial, 122, 205

Relapsed Heretics, treatment of, 177–80

Religious persecution, early history of, 2–4

Renaud of Chartres, Inquisitor; complains of conduct of secular magistrates, 175, 217

Richard Cœur-de-Lion, 60

Robert le Bougre, his fanatical persecutions in Champagne, 128–9; his suspension and degradation, 129, 262

Robert the Pious, king of France, 43, 47, 67, 204

Rodriguez de Cintra, first Inquisitor in Portugal, 227

Rolando of Cremona, 229

Roman Law, revival of, 86–8

Ruggiere Calcagni, Inquisitor at Florence, 230

Rule of St. Benedict, 3 *note*, 181

Sabatier, Guillaume; commits suicide by *Endura*, 42

Said of Toledo; his opinion of " northerners," 58

St. Augustine, 3, 254

St. Bernard, 9, 23, 29, 37, 46, 48, 49, 65, 71, 261; his probable disapproval of scholastic methods, 29; visits Languedoc, 65, 69; his description of conditions in Languedoc, 65

St. Bernardino of Siena, 232
St. Bonaventura, 9, 23, 245
St. Dominic, 23, 82–8, 220; early ministry in Languedoc, 75, 79–80; introduces the wearing of crosses as a penance, 192–3
St. Elizabeth of Hungary, 15, 20, 234
St. Francis of Assisi, 32, 35, 36, 49, 244
St. Joan of Arc, 19, 132, 180
St. John Chrysostom, 3
St. Leo I, 3, 267
St. Louis IX, king of France, 15, 20, 92, 209, 215
St. Peter Martyr, Inquisitor, 230–1, 235
St. Raymond of Pennaforte, 23, 227
St. Thomas Aquinas, 9, 10, 23, 29, 99, 179, 181, 251, 253
Schio, Giovanni, 230
Sermo Generalis ; see *Auto-da-fé*
Sicilian Code; prescribes public execution of condemned heretics, 89; recognizes use of torture, 158
Siger of Brabant, 251, 253
Soissons, anti-heretical action at, 45, 266
Sorcerers, treatment of, by Holy Office, 142–3
Sorcery, prosecuted by secular courts, 143
Spiritual Franciscans, 12, 98, 243–9
Sprenger, his *Malleus maleficarum* quoted, 173
Stake, proportion of convicted heretics abandoned to, 171, 174–5, 176
Stephen of St. Tiberi, assassinated at Avignonnet, 118, 222
Strappado, instrument of torture, 159, 162, 263
Strasburg, execution of heretics at, 36, 92; Flagellants at, 237
Suppression of Names of Witnesses, 116–17, 149–51
Suspicion of Heresy, 138–40
Synodal Witnesses, 113–14

Tacitus, *Annals*, 109
Taillefer de la Chapelle, Cardinal, 188, 224
Tankelm, 30
Tanon, L., *quoted or referred to*, 131, 141, 143, 155, 158, 196, 206, 213–14, 242, 268
Tarragona, Council of, 177, 200, 227
Templars, Suppression of, 100, 225–6
Theodosius I, Emperor, 2

Theodouin, Bishop of Liège, 45
" Time of Grace," 95, 121, 145
Torture, its use under Roman Empire, 157; introduced into Inquisitorial practice, 158; its employment by the Inquisition, 158–61; instruments of, 162–3; in the trials of Knights Templars, 225
Toulouse, 43, 56, 60, 67, 69, 72, 80, 124 *note*, 170, 220
Toulouse, Council of, 104, 113, 183, 193
Toulouse, Inquisition at, 117, 166, 168–72, 187, 217, 219–22
Tours, Council of, 51, 69, 85, 87, 124 *note*
Traderii, G., abandoned to the stake for false witness, 133
Trials, Inquisitorial, 151–4
Troubadours, 59–63, 71
" Truce of God," 8
Turberville, A. S., *quoted or referred to*, 35, 36, 46, 50, 104, 146, 180, 228, 253, 261

University of Paris, 73; consulted during trial of St. Joan, 132; condemns *Everlasting Gospel*, 245
Urban IV, Pope, disapproves of advocates in heresy trials, 108; orders co-operation between Inquisitors and committee of experts, 131
Usury, when punishable by Holy Office, 143

Vacandard, E., *quoted or referred to*, 4 *note*, 132, 133, 159, 175, 264
Vaso, Bishop of Liège, 46
Venice, Inquisitorial action at, 100, 232
Verona, Council of, 113
Vienne, Council of, 188, 218

Waldenses, 32–4, 239–43; summary of their beliefs, 34–5; anticipated Franciscan and Dominican reforms, 36–7; their conduct under cross-examination, 155–6; numerous in Florence and Turin, 233; aid in combating the Albigenses, 268
Waldo, Peter, 32
William of Champeaux, 27–9
William IX, Duke of Aquitaine, 60
Williams, the homicide, exposition of his body in London, 259